ONE
MORE

by Matt Trollope

One More, the book, was brought to you by:-
an iMac and the joyous Macbook Air;
BlackBerry Voice Notes;
gallons of Diet Coke, buckets of Haribo...
...and the odd glass of red wine

with unwavering support from:-
Jax, Jean and D Trollope,
Chris Good and Mark Sloper,
Jimmy P and Lindsay Jones...

...and with eternal gratitude to Kate Parker for keeping my
place at journalism college in 1989-90 as I tried to
combine my studies with a degree in acid house

CONTENTS

FOREWORD

So much has been written about the acid house explosion of the late 1980s and the ensuing superclub phenomenon of the '90s, but never before have so many of the key players given such an insight into how it all happened.

In the words of Hacienda resident Graeme Park..."to get us all talking about it now, to document it, in the cold light of day, not off our heads and not all egotistical, is wonderful".

The likes of Park and co were pioneers...lords of the dance, people who took risks, tastemakers who made it all possible for the rest of us - innovators who simply wanted to put on a party for themselves and their mates, often to fuel their own DJ careers, long before clubs became brands.

We reveal what track these trailblazers chose to bring down the curtain on their creation....and the story behind it.

And while our cover strapline reads 1988 - 2008, delving back further than that was vital to discover just what our cast were up to as they approached that stunning acid house revolution.

Photocopied flyers, fanzines and word of mouth largely promoted their parties, years before expensive magazine adverts or the far-reaching internet.

This was an era when the exciting new party drug ecstasy first gripped the nation, when DJs played for a couple of hundred quid, not a few thousand - a time of unrivalled optimism, when waves of clubbers went to the same club or night week-in, week-out.

One More founder Chris Good, by his own admission, is "a guy who had an idea at a barbecue" with pal Andrew Wallace. A conversation with friends at west London film and TV producers 400 Company quickly followed, as did this quest to chronicle the end-of-night anthems that helped put UK clubbing on the international map.

A search that took us all over the country followed, as we tracked down and interviewed the various luminaries involved - the founders, DJs and promoters, who all reveal how their own organic "idea" came about.

Apologies to those we've missed out, but a line needed to be drawn somewhere. Other omissions, alas, were not for the want of trying.

Arguably, the whole scene was made possible when the 'Ibiza three' returned from their ecstasy epiphany in the summer of 1987, and set about revolutionising modern-day clubbing as we knew it.

We talk to Nicky Holloway, who upon his return from the Balearic clubbing mecca with Spectrum's Paul Oakenfold and Shoom's Danny Rampling, quickly launched his own acid house night, The Trip at The Astoria. The trio inadvertently set up a "Balearic network", which promoters outside London were keen to infiltrate.

Holloway point outs: "These nights weren't dreamt up by marketing people at a record label. It wasn't like we thought we were going to change the face of clubbing. It was just a bunch of people who loved what they were doing and it just fell together. It wasn't planned. DJ Alfredo changed all our lives in Ibiza in 1987, but we basically nicked what he was doing and did it better."

While many interviewed here promoted nights at already established venues, some, like the all-conquering James Baillie, persuaded owners to let them take over the whole club, as he did with his groundbreaking Venus project in 1990. We hear from him and how that Nottingham legend inspired almost everyone else interviewed.

'Tall' Paul Newman's case is somewhat unique. As he and brother Danny grew up, their dad owned Turnmills in London. Both collected glasses for pocket money while still at school, before graduating to launch their own Friday-nighter, The Gallery. They developed gay after-hours institution Trade, cleverly ushering in the seminal Heavenly Social sessions too. Danny ran the place, while resident Paul went on to become one of the country's new wave of superstar DJs.

Now a property developer, Paul provides a fascinating insight on inheriting your own iconic nightclub.

Renaissance is one of THE biggest clubbing brands to come out of the UK and was the brainchild of Geoff Oakes, a regular at the much-lauded Shelley's in Stoke in the early '90s. He persuaded resident Sasha, already a darling of the northern underground dance scene, to up sticks and become his marquee signing.

The progressive house heroes-in-waiting bravely plotted in the unfashionable former mining town of Mansfield, and a year later sold 200,000 copies of their debut groundbreaking Renaissance CD. Sasha had been joined at the controls by exciting new co-resident John Digweed, who proved sending mix tapes to promoters did actually work.

The rest, as they say, is clubbing history and Oakes gives us the inside track.

And if Mansfield wasn't in vogue, then the tiny west coast Scottish village of Ayr was no clubbing 'Mecca' either. That didn't stop Ricky McGowan, Jon Mancini and co launching their pioneering Streetrave event on a Sunday afternoon in 1989. The duo explain how that success led to Colours, the biggest club promoters ever seen north of the border, and how the word 'rave' quickly had to be dropped.

But it wasn't all about London, Manchester or the Midlands (or outposts in Scotland!). Dance music, both underground and commercial, was soon literally everywhere.

In particular, we focus on Brighton where former Housemartins star Norman Cook, aka Fatboy Slim, first carved out a DJ career at The Escape Club under the stewardship of John Holland. Years later Cook would host a beach party down the road for 250,000 people. His no-holds-barred exclusive is hilarious, to say the least.

And we also check out Cardiff success stories Lamerica and The Hippo Club, which contrastingly provided the south Wales faithful and beyond with a choice of either leading players in the US soulful house scene, or unashamed big room "bangers".

As underground clubland broke out from the strongholds of London and Manchester in the early '90s, territories soon became important and Russell Davison, of Progress in Derby, explains: "We had our own patches - like Mafia dons would - so we all respected that. But we were also competing against each other."

Progress is the perfect example of how an unfashionable Midlands town became internationally-renowned because of dance music.

Like Stoke-on-Trent, where Jon Hill, also a disciple of Shelley's, launched Golden.

After Sasha's departure to Renaissance, Hill set about filling the void in Stoke (literally, as it would turn out…at a club called The Void) and his clubbing exploits in his home town over the next decade not only saw him "signed" by Liverpool superclub Cream, but also earned him local dignitary status. We find out how.

Jeremy Healy and Jim Shaft Ryan - like Holloway and Park - are veterans whose careers in dance music date back to the '80s, while all clubbed in the '70s too. And like many interviewed here, when the '90s unfolded they were perfectly qualified to lead from the front.

Healy - like Park, influenced by New York clubbing in the '80s - went on to become one of the UK's biggest DJs, and remembers taking pal Boy George to Shoom in the early days, following a tip off from Paul Rutherford, of Frankie Goes To Hollywood fame. Ryan, meanwhile, reflects on his clothes shop in Birmingham, and a clientele which spawned his glam-house Chuff Chuff and Miss Moneypenny's empire. Both add massive weight to this revealing account.

As does Dave Pearce. I, for one, was schooled on hip-hop and house as a teenager in the mid '80s listening to his groundbreaking Fresh Start To The Week and Funk Fantasy shows on Radio London. Pearce typifies a particular DJ set who combined powerful radio jobs with powerful record label roles, and still found time to DJ all over the world too. We welcome his input.

Phil Gifford has also been there, done it and bought the T-shirt. The success of his cult Birmingham Saturday-nighter Wobble, just down the road from Moneypenny's, thwarted a promising hairdressing career, but now 20 years later, the Brummie crimper has his own town centre salon and looks back on his story in between cuts.

The inimitable Brandon Block, meanwhile, probably played more "One Mores" than most...certainly if his Sunday session at Space in Ibiza in the early to mid-'90s is anything to go by. Blocko reminisces about a funk and soul DJ apprenticeship years before that Balearic success - in Wembley pubs when "mixing didn't matter because everyone was so pissed on snakebites" - and describes that notorious residency on the Space terrace as "simply the best club in the world".

Like many, Blocko's crossover to house music was unavoidable - as was a drug habit, in his case so huge he became a harrowing symbol of a superclubbing generation of excess. He is fortunate to have lived to tell the tale.

Back in the '90s anything seemed possible.

Promoters began to city-hop; Renaissance left Mansfield for Derby, while Golden transferred to Manchester briefly.

Big one-offs in neighbouring or nearby towns at stately homes, like Renaissance's Colwick Hall parties in Nottingham and Que Club specials in Birmingham, became the norm for the various kingpins involved as sheer public demand encouraged each club night to spread its wings.

One notoriously nomadic promoter arguably became the biggest success story of the lot.

Gatecrasher began life as a party for a few pals on the outskirts of Birmingham in 1993, but rapid expansion, as trance swept the nation in the second half of the decade, saw Gatecrasher and their mascots the 'Crasher Kids' take the scene by storm, with boss Simon Raine buying clubs in Sheffield, Leeds, Nottingham, and, now once more, back in Birmingham, where his flagship 3,500-capacity city centre venue provides him with a nostalgic HQ and is still going strong to this day.

Pinning down Mr Raine was not easy, but pin him down we did. His thoughts here are fascinating.

Much gratitude goes out to all the club owners, promoters and DJs who gave up their time to contribute to this project in its infancy.

And a big thanks also to the likes of Mark Moore, Danny Rampling, Judge Jules, Allister Whitehead, Eddie Gordon and Sonique whose contributions were also invaluable as the One More documentary and this accompanying book reached their deadlines.

These days you can have your own mini One More moments at home, via YouTube, an invaluable modern day vault of music, courtesy of the millions of people who love music so much they are compelled to share it.

YouTube was my best friend throughout this journey transcribing and writing One More. I suggest you're not too far away from it when reading it either.

But whether it's banging trance, party anthems, soulful garage, acid house or one of those Balearic gems, the list of 'One More' tracks nominated speaks for itself, an emotional soundtrack to this defining era of club culture.

Inevitable financial losses and ensuing personal feuds have left some to lick their wounds, while, in stark contrast, others are still counting their shrewdly-invested cash. Whatever the individual outcomes, the music and memories, of course, will live on forever.

After all, few can turn down one more 'One More'.

JEREMY HEALY

Jeremy Healy has dropped some classic 'One More' anthems in his time, but nothing compared to the names he can drop in one anecdote.

When I caught up with Healy, post-filming, he was enthusing about a £150-a-head party he had just played at a mansion in Oxford where Heston Blumenthal laid on the buffet.

The veteran clubber and former pop star has definitely earned his bragging rights over the years, though, and unlike most here, The Paradise Garage is not on much-travelled Healy's wish (I could of gone) list.

He is one of the lucky ones who made it to Larry Levan's spiritual home in New York and that is, perhaps, a fitting boast for one of the UK's true superstar DJs - and one of the most-loved, at that.

The constant hint of sarcasm in Healy's voice may not always come across in the written form, but here is an infectious guy who has never taken himself or the DJ profession too seriously and whose constant interaction with the crowd always made him a massive hit with the paying public, not to mention promoters and fellow DJs alike.

Born in Woolwich, south London, in the early '60s, Healy began clubbing in his mid-teens, blagging his way into the capital's "cooler" nightclubs. Towards the late '70s he began travelling to the Midlands and beyond too. He had met Boy George on a bus in south east London when they were both 15, and the duo would spend the next 30-odd years playing their own unique game of pop stars and DJs.

You've got to remember that when I first met George everybody in the UK wore flares. There were only about five people in the whole country who didn't wear flares, so we automatically all became friends. Me and George were on this bus in Shooter's Hill, wearing anything but flares, and we got talking. In fact, his mum and my mum were already friends. It was funny, he was already infamous in the area because all the girls loved him and all the boys wanted to beat him up.

Me and George started going to Philip Salon's parties, but the first nightclub I ever went to was probably Global Village in Charing Cross in central London, around '75, when I was about 13 or 14 years old, and that eventually became Heaven. It was like a big discotheque and full of soul boys. Some used to get two pairs of trousers - one of them would be white, one would be black - and then cut them up the middle, sew the alternate legs back up and swap their shoes, wearing one white, one black trouser leg. They had wedge haircuts. It was the end of northern soul, and that was the first mini-cult I came across.

Then through the New Romantic scene, around 1979/80, we used to go up to Birmingham and go to the Rum Runner club, which was owned by the Berrow brothers (Michael and Paul), before they managed Duran Duran, which still feels weird because I've since become good friends with Simon and Yasmin Le Bon.

The Midlands then, and throughout my career, has always seemed like a breath of fresh air. Yeah, we often went up north and had a great time, so I guess quite early on we developed the habit of travelling to go to clubs, whereas most people I knew in London wouldn't even leave Notting Hill Gate…. haha… that would certainly have been a big ask for a lot of them.

Personally, I don't think there's anything that I wish I'd gone to. Studio 54 was probably the only legendary one I didn't get my skinny arse into, but by then we'd done The Paradise Garage, and 54 was probably a bit too grown-up for us.

Healy experienced national chart success in 1982 as a member of the quirky pop act Haysi Fantayzee, with the No 11 hit John Wayne Is Big Leggy, while in September of the same year Boy George and Culture Club hit the tops of the charts with Do You Really Want To Hurt Me.

With Culture Club going on to enjoy global success over the next five years, and Haysi Fantayzee splitting a year later after three further singles, Healy's relationship with George soured.

Me and George had both gone off and done our own thing, in our own bands, but we had got nervous of each other about who was the most successful. But after George was done with Culture Club later in the '80s, we did become good friends again.

With George out of the picture, regular trips to New York in the early '80s with other friends became the norm for Healy. And while

The Paradise Garage is seen by many as the clubbing equivalent of The Holy Grail, back then for Healy it was just another club that he went to.

It wasn't really a big deal at the time. Me and my mates went to New York loads around 1981, to party in great clubs that shut at nine in the morning, because you just didn't have that in London then. We would spend three or four days there partying and sleep on the plane back home. In that respect it was a bit like our version of Ibiza back then.

The Paradise Garage was a club with a really good sound system, but it wasn't like everybody went there. Not like Danceteria, which was on six floors. Madonna was the lift girl there before she made it, and we used to chat to her loads. I've met her a few times since, but haven't been brave enough to bring the lift job up yet.

New York was so exciting then, all the great radio stations playing the dance mixes and Grandmaster Flash doing his thing. I used to buy mixes on reel-to-reels and bring them back to London.

Boy George explained on Dave Pearce's Radio Two dance music in series in the summer of 2011:-

I got taken to the Paradise Garage, quite by accident, in 1986. I was out clubbing (in New York) and someone said "let's go to the Garage". We met Larry Levan and I heard house music for the very first time. One of the tracks played that night, where dance music is concerned, is one of the most influential tracks ever for me. Set It Off by Strafe was so individual, maybe not so much now, but then it was so raw, the vocal was so dry, the beat was kind of off, and it's just this magic. I suddenly thought, "oh my God, what Culture Club is doing, is really over-produced. It's all wrong". House was something that I'd never heard or witnessed before.

Fast forward to November 1987 and Healy was back on good terms with Boy George, who, like Madonna, would emerge from this celebrated decade as a pop music icon. Taking his pal out for the night, however, meant that Healy's introduction to house music almost didn't happen. Frankie Goes To Hollywood star Paul Rutherford had given him the heads-up about an acid house club in their old south east

London stomping ground, but Healy's old mucker was not helping the cause.

The first acid house club I went to was quite a strange experience. Paul had said to me: "You've got to go to this club, it's amazing." And I said: "Why?" He said: "Well, you go in there, and they've got all these strobes and smoke and you can't see anybody and don't know who anybody is and they play this amazing music."

I said: "That's really weird", because, up until then, we had gone to clubs to be seen and to show off. I thought, "God, what's the point of that? If you can't see anybody!" But I was fascinated all the same, just because it sounded like such a weird idea.

So I went down there with Boy George and Boy George at that point was very famous in the UK. We got to the door and if you are very famous you can get in anywhere, right? But the bouncers said: "No, you can't come in." We said: "Why not?" And they said: "We don't know what will happen to you, there's all these people from the East End of London in there and they might beat you up. We won't be able to protect you because we won't be able to see you."

We said: "We really don't care, we'll take the risk." They just seemed so worried that we'd get beaten up and that it would be in the papers and the club would be shut down.

So we didn't get in and we went off home. I told Paul Rutherford what had happened and he said: "Look, I'll fix it with the guys. I know the people who run the place, it'll be cool." So me and George dutifully went down there the next week and it was fine. The doormen apologised and we went in. And that was our first night at Shoom. I also met the promoters Danny Rampling and Jenny - who was his wife at the time - and everybody loved George, of course. There was no chance they were going to beat him up anyway because they were all on ecstasy.

We had a whole new crowd of friends instantly. There were probably 150 people in that club and straight away I knew this new thing was going to be massive. I'd seen it before with hip-hop and the New Romantics, and all that stuff, and it was the same thing. Something very small and very special and the people were very into it. When you witness that, it's actually very easy to recognise.

Shoom would go on to make a life-changing impression on the duo. Healy, then a jobbing hip-hop and funk DJ, had seen first-hand what the likes of Rampling were up to and decided to change tack. Boy George, meanwhile, quickly launched his clubland alter-ego Jesus Loves You, going on to enjoy underground dance hits with tracks like Generations Of Love and Bow Down Mister and performing live in his new Hare Krishna-inspired guise at Shoom within a year. The Culture Club frontman would also cultivate a new vocation as a hugely successful club DJ, following encouragement from Healy, who would also record as E-Zee Possee on George's More Protein label.

Boy George also told Dave Pearce:-

Jeremy Healy was a really good friend of mine. I kind of followed him in dance, because he was a big DJ. He would give me his mix tapes, so through Jeremy I got excited about the whole DJ thing, and then we made that record, Everything Starts With An E. I met MC Kinky, and we formed the E-Zee Possee, and we wanted to put that track out, so I went to Virgin, who I was signed to as an artist, and was raving about dance music, about how it was going to be massive, and, of course, they didn't get it at all, they just thought I was nuts.

But Everything Starts With An E was the beginning of More Protein, because I wanted to put it out on my own label, I wanted to do dance music, because pop music at that time, well, it was all boy bands and girl bands and the start of that formula pop. For me, as a creative person, dance was more exciting, the acid house scene was the most exciting thing to be part of, so I naturally gravitated towards that. I started my band Jesus Loves You, and really immersed myself in dance.

My DJing career started as a real accident. I was at a Puscha party, and there was a chill out room and there was this cassette tape playing and it was playing over and over and I said "you should get people to play 45s in here", and they said "you do it". So the next Puscha, I came along with my records, literally in a cardboard box. I was doing the chill-out room, and I was playing the most random stuff. I remember George Michael dancing to Islands In The Stream. I was playing old reggae, old house, and I started to get other bookings from that. Then I thought I better learn to DJ. And I'm still learning.

Looking back at how his own career as a house DJ unfolded after that fateful first night at Shoom, Healy continues:-

I saw Danny Rampling and Paul Oakenfold and they inspired me, because I'd been a scratch DJ up until then. When I saw what they were doing with house I said: "I can do that." It made me get up off my arse and do it too. It was the first time that the DJ had been elevated to rock star level, and I really liked that. And it was particularly so with Danny, who had this crew who would go around and chant his name and they wouldn't dance to any other DJs until he came on. So it was like a football supporter kind of thing really.

Healy wanted a slice of this action and, of course, the adulation too. It didn't take him long to get it.

The first two club nights in London for me were Shoom and Future, which Oakenfold did. Then all these other nights appeared. Me and my lot already had that culture of travelling so I started to go to Venus, when we were asked up there, and it seemed the clubs in the north were even better than the ones in London.

I was watching some Glastonbury coverage recently on the TV and the presenter was saying how amazing the reaction to Faithless was, everyone with their arms in the air, and I remember thinking it used to be like that every night, certainly every Saturday, at least. It was like the people were mad for this thing.

Suddenly there was one decent club in every major city and you'd just go from one to the next. There was Venus, Renaissance, Golden and Progress, and all those great clubs. And you certainly had to be into it, because it was like 120 degrees in a lot of those places. Everyone was sweating. You had to go through the pain barrier, much like you do at Glastonbury, I guess, with the mud. Later I persuaded (Boy) George to take up the DJing full-time because I knew he would really enjoy it. I even took him out to get all the equipment so he could practise.

I played Renaissance at Mansfield quite a lot when it first started, before the club went on to adopt a more melodic instrumental music policy. It was one of the first clubs that went in for the huge breakdowns, but at the start it still suited my party house style. I remember the wooden floor, and people stomping, this overwhelming noise throughout of people dancing on that dancefloor...stamp, stamp, stamp.

My other overwhelming memory of Renaissance is DJing there during one of those mad Saturdays when I'd be playing three clubs in the Midlands in the same night. It was snowing and really icy and my driver pulled up in the dead end outside Venue 44 in Mansfield, and tried to screech to a halt outside the club, but skidded and crashed into the side of the club. I was due on the decks so I got out of the car and ran in with my records. Fortunately, it had all been sorted out by the time I got outside again.

As the house scene continued to evolve, its success was self-perpetuating. DJs and clubbers alike would be making new friends by the droves – remembering their names and where you had met them before was the tricky bit. Another thing that was adding up for Healy and the other headline DJs on the scene was distance, as demand quickly threatened to outweigh supply.

We got to the point where we were doing 1,500 miles a week on the road, in between all the various clubs in and around the Midlands and up north, which were all 50 miles away from each other. You could fit a lot of them in on a Saturday night and we often had this little convoy of cars following us around.

It was funny, because the more people you had with you the harder it was to get out of one club, and off and in to another. But the more clubs we played at in one night, the more people we picked up along the way. I met a lot of great characters, but as the scene got bigger and bigger you lost touch with as many people as you made friends with. When we had the festivals it was always a good chance to catch up with friends and obviously Ibiza was good for that too, although Ibiza was a lot more hit or miss as to exactly who you'd bump into.

I remember turning up at Progress and the promoter Russell Davison, who is now a good friend, greeted us. I thought he looked a bit worried and I said: "What's up?" He said: "My wife's about to have a baby, and I'm waiting for the call. I've got my phone in the top pocket of my shirt, on vibrate, because I won't be able to hear it in the club otherwise." And, I remember thinking that was hilarious, that instead of being at the hospital he was still at the club. And then a bit later I looked at him and his pocket started vibrating. Let's just say that this was in the early days of the vibrating phone feature because it really took him by surprise and for a moment he thought he was having a heart attack, but it was actually his wife having a baby. Priceless.

But can Healy, a man who has played at most, and been to all the ones he wants to as well, actually pinpoint his favourite club?

The best club I've ever been to? God, there have been so many. I think you could say Shoom, because it was the first time I'd seen that. And later, certainly clubs like Zouk in Singapore. You could talk about all the amazing clubs and the first time you had gone to them when they blew you away. I mean, the first time I walked into Ku in Ibiza I couldn't believe clubs could be that big. Amnesia too, which I still think is amazing.

Back home, Venus was wonderful, so was Golden and Progress - the sweatiest club in the world, haha. There really are just too many to mention. And some of those legendary early nights, well, if everybody who has said they did, actually did go to Shoom, then 50,000 people would have gone in the first few weeks and it only held 150.

I'm always asked what was the best club in the UK at that time? And the answer is, they were all fucking brilliant. At the time, when we were whizzing in between them all, we took them all for granted. I never minded travelling any distance to a club, though. As long as it was good when you got there. Another highlight was Homelands when I DJd in between Leftfield and Public Enemy. That was quite seminal.

The success of UK clubland in the '90s really did creep up on Healy, finally hitting home when he got a call from 10 Downing Street.

I'd been DJing five nights a week for seven years and, being in the middle of it all, I didn't realise just how big it had got. Then Tony Blair won the General Election in 1997 and I got a call from Downing Street asking me to DJ at a reception for the new Prime Minister. They had also asked Carl Cox and I said: "Why the hell are you asking me?" And they said: "Everyone under 25 knows who you are." I remember

*(main picture) * Jeremy Healy at Culture Shock, Hollywood, Romford, 1993 - image: Matt Trollope*
*(clockwise) * DJing behind the bar at Space terrace, 1997*
** At home in West London * Haysi Fantayzee picture disc*

thinking that was mad, because it wasn't like we were on TV loads or on Top Of The Pops... at least I hadn't been on Top Of The Pops for 16 years.

I thought about going to see the PM, but then remembered that when my friend John Galliano won a designer of the year award in the '80s, he had been invited to meet Margaret Thatcher, and because he was thinking about it, I'd called him a wanker, and he decided not to go. So I thought there was no way I could go, and didn't either. For a few years I regretted it, and then the Iraq war happened and I was glad that I didn't go.

I just don't think DJs and politicians mix really. I met David Cameron at a party recently, and he seemed all right, but he did have both his shirt and his jumper tucked in his jeans, which I thought was a bit extreme.

Generally I've mellowed over the years and I have a softer opinion on things like politics. Back in the '90s I was still very punk rock in my outlook. I don't think Carl Cox went to Downing Street either, they got Noel Gallagher in the end. He famously had his photos taken, etc, and has never lived it down since.

When it comes to 'One Mores', Healy has played his fair share and even had his own nickname for the infamous end of the night record.

I used to call it "the police are outside track" because the club owners would be desperately trying to keep their licences as everyone was going mad asking for one more track. The owners or club managers would be saying that the police were outside. I never saw any police, but then I was always still inside, I guess.

But, famously, not always inside the DJ booth.

Yeah, I would often go on to the floor and dance with the crowd, do the odd moonwalk, and people always liked that. The DJ was and is always such a focal point, that if you moved outside of the booth everybody's eyes moved with you. I always felt that the connection with the crowd was so important and have never been self-conscious anyway. Dance music is meant to be about joy anyway, isn't it? And I think at some point later on in the '90s it did all get a bit pretentious, with a lot of DJs starting to take it all very seriously.

Meanwhile, it was always hard to be too pretentious when Jeremy Healy was DJing, playing unashamed anthems all night long, in hot sweaty clubs, with low ceilings, like, in the early to mid-'90s at The Gardening Club in Covent Garden, where he was resident and famously dropped the likes of Nirvana's Smells Like Teen Spirit and Michael Jackson gems in the middle of whatever house tracks were big at the time.

There are always great memories of Club For Life at The Gardening Club. Shelley Boswell, who used to run it, showed me a picture the other day of the queue for one of those nights, and it went all the way around Covent Garden. I was amazed, I never used to see the queue, I was always in and out. They used to have to use the club next door, The Rock Garden, for the overspill. They could have filled that club three times over in those days.

The Gardening Club was one of those clubs in the West End which used to stay open later. It was also one of those clubs where you'd come out feeling like you'd been in a hot shower for four hours. I don't think air conditioning in clubs had been invented back then.

My favourite tracks were stuff like Michael Jackson's Wanna Be Startin' Something, Hamilton Bohannon, Let's Start The Dance and also Two Fat Guitars by Direckt, which was also massive in Manchester. I've still got about four or five thousand records so you can take your pick from most of them. I used to like blending rock and house and was well known for that.

I also remember doing one great party in Leeds at the Corn Exchange, which they'd turned into a shopping mall, but had still managed to put 5,000 people in there. Sasha was headlining and I was meant to be warming up for him, but for some reason Sasha didn't make it so I ended up doing the main spot. U2 had sent me an acetate of this new record they'd done called Lemon. I would normally never play a record if I hadn't heard it, but I'd just literally got it from U2, with this nice note about the Paul Oakenfold remix on it, so I knew it would be good. I put it on as the last track and it was obviously an amazing record, which was handy, and so that was a great moment. I remember dancing around outside the booth when that one came off.

If I had to choose my last record ever, which is an impossible task, it would depend on how you want to leave them – crying or pogoing. I'd probably want to leave them dancing so I'd play Smells Like Teen Spirit, because that would be a good one to die to. I think records do have a finite life and they do burn out if you play them too much. That's why it's great that so much new stuff is coming out all the time.

Healy has cut down on his DJ bookings over the past couple of years, due to his increasing commitments in the fashion world. A regular DJ on the fashion show circuit for some years, he now DJs at more than 25 each year, including for old friend John Galliano, plus Christian Dior and Victoria's Secret.

The travelling involved with the fashion shows can often be as punishing as DJing full-time back in the day, with full seasons in Ibiza, etc, and can mean being in three or four countries in one week. I also work with Gwen Stefani, Tommy Hilfiger and lots of other fashion companies, doing computerised mixes for them, which are used in catwalk shows, so I do a lot in Paris, New York and Milan.

These days, I DJ in clubs for enjoyment, but it also has to be for friends, because I love playing for people who I have worked with over the years. I've also realised over the years that the so-called cooler clubs aren't always that cool really, especially if they are full of people who take themselves far too seriously.

Healy has scaled down his involvement with Ibiza too, shunning the big clubs in favour of smaller, intimate parties, and again for acquaintances he's met along the way. And he chuckles when looking back at his Ibiza heyday.

I don't DJ at the big clubs in Ibiza any more because, to me, they're like DJing at football matches. It's just all got too big and commercial. I'm playing at a really cool new beach bar in San Juan this summer (2011) and then I also play for some Italian friends at a really cool private party they put on for about 500 people at their house. I'd much rather do that sort of thing out there these days.

In the '90s in Ibiza, Clockwork Orange, in particular, was amazing fun. Promoter Danny Gould was larger than life, although his partner Andy Manston was bit more sensible. Danny would be off his head, climbing up the rigs, abusing us all and throwing drinks over everyone. He was king of the nutters, for sure. The promoters out there were making and spending so much money that they just weren't able to put any value on it.

I look back and laugh at some of the end of season parties in Ibiza I played at. For instance, where the DJs had nothing left to give, and neither did the crowd, which were mainly workers by then. We'd played all the records there were to play, and everybody had done everything there was to do. I remember zoning out from the DJ booth at one party, looking out at the crowd, with a load of tired-looking people just staring back at me.

Like his peers, Healy has been forced to keep on top of the advancing technology, but has a word of caution for anyone thinking the progress made will create better DJs.

I've got Serato and use it sometimes, but at the moment, I'm mainly using CDs. I do like the new Pioneer set-up with the USBs too, but I'm fine with CDs, even if they do usually end up in a bit of a state. I'm DJing less and less now, and picking and choosing what I do, so I usually make up CDs for each particular gig, based on exactly what each club wants and needs. There are a million different ways to crack the same egg, so I don't think we should get bogged down too much about the technology used.

At the end of the day, DJs can choose to interact with the crowd or not interact, whatever technology they're using. I remember going to reggae parties in people's houses in the '70s and they would have one deck on top of loads of different amps, and big speakers, and there would be a gap while they put a new record on, and that always worked fine. Then Tony Blackburn and the whole cheesy style of using a microphone came along and suddenly being a DJ was the naffest thing in the world. Then it became the coolest thing in the world to do, and, I guess, eventually it will be the naffest thing again.

MATT TROLLOPE

THE HACIENDA

Aberdeen has a history of providing big clubs in Manchester with long and loyal servants, and when Graeme Park was snapped up by the Hacienda another illustrious career beckoned.

Two years before Park's career-changing move, another precocious talent from north of the border had been tempted by the bright lights of Manchester.

Alex Ferguson pitched up at Old Trafford in 1986, but could not end United's trophy drought until 1990. Park, meanwhile, was offered a transfer to that other Theatre Of Dreams in the town, the Hac', in 1988 and hit the ground running, touring America with New Order only months later.

Park's previous residency at The Garage in Nottingham should not be undervalued, because not only did it earn him his big shot in 'Madchester', but it also paved the way for James Bailee's Venus, and inspired the likes of Russell Davison's Progress too.

The Hacienda story, and that of its owners Factory Records, has been well documented over the years. First came the film (24 Hour Party People), then the book (How Not To Run A Club).

Now former record shop worker turned Hac' legend Park explains how he earned his shot at the big time after plying his trade in the bars and clubs of his adopted hometown.

I got into the club business purely by accident. I used to work in an amazing record shop in Nottingham called Selectadisk, and played in bands in the area too. The guy who owned the shop opened a nightclub and because I worked for him I ended up playing records there, unaware that I would still be doing it a quarter of a century later.

It was absolutely unbelievable. I took to it like a duck to water, mainly, I think, because I'd played in bands and I was used to performing and entertaining people.

I quickly discovered the main difference when you're in band is that with any fee received you have to pay for the PA and the bloke with the van and then split anything left with everyone else in the band so, in our case, we often came home with about a fiver each.

However, when I started to DJ at The Garage in Nottingham, the £25 I got was all mine, three nights a week. Excellent.

It was 1984 when I started at The Garage and I went from one great club to another when I joined the Hacienda four years later. That whole thing started for me when Mike Pickering, then resident at the Hac', was going on holiday for three weeks. He rang me up and asked if I could cover for him and I was like "wow".

I'd met Mike at various things in the past, different clubs' magazine shoots, etc, and he said: "I know we play similar stuff, but come up the week before and have a look, because it's a bit different to The Garage."

I was up there a couple of weeks later having a bit of a boogie and The Party by Kraze came on. That was my first real, but surreal, Hacienda moment, with the guy on the record saying "y'all want this party started, right?".

And the party had started all right for Graeme Park. He would go on to become one of the UK's most popular and successful house DJs.

But he had been no stranger to the Hacienda, even when he was a record shop worker and up-and-coming DJ in Nottingham.

Since 1982 I had been getting the train up to the Hacienda regularly to see bands there, like A Certain Ratio, Orange Juice, Aztec Camera, Joy Division, New Order and, if you really want me to be obscure, Crispy Ambulance, as well as DJs like Greg Wilson.

As resident, Mike Pickering used to play such an eclectic mix at that time, but then I stopped going for a while as my own DJ career took off in Nottingham. And then when I started DJing at the Hacienda on a Friday night with Mike in 1988, that was just at the point house was really taking off, and literally anything went.

The four years from 1984 were all a bit of a whirlwind. I had only started DJing in 1984, three nights a week in Nottingham and around the east Midlands, and by 1988 I had joined the Hacienda, and before long I had been on a tour of north America with New Order, who really were a massive band at the time.

Apart from the sheer size of the place, the notoriety of the club and the people who ran it, there was one other massive difference between The Garage and the Hacienda.

I had been DJing to 400 people regularly at The Garage, but Mike had been playing each week to 2,000 people. And where I was playing to people who liked a drink, he was playing to people who were completely off their nuts. The music out at the time just matched the euphoric feeling that everyone was experiencing.

I mean, nowadays, well, I haven't had a pill for ages, but they're obviously not a patch on what you could get back then. They were just pure MDMA with a little bit of casing agent to keep them together.

There was little casing agent keeping the Hacienda together, however, and how it actually survived so long is bewildering. The trials and tribulations of its existence are well detailed in How Not To Run A Club, as author Peter Hook, his New Order bandmates and the pioneering likes of Hacienda and Factory Records founder Tony Wilson, muddled their way through. With the help of Park and Pickering, if anything, they showed everyone just how to run a cultural and musical revolution.

And it would be a braver man than me that attempted to explain the finances of the Hacienda or why it eventually closed. That's why Hook needed 337 pages to do so.

Park feels honoured to have been involved in the unique Hacienda set-up.

I've obviously met a variety of people over the years who run nightclubs, but I've never met anyone quite like the people who ran the Hacienda and...haha...that's probably why it's not open anymore.

I was a massive fan of Factory Records before I got asked to play at Hacienda, so working for Factory Records and New Order was just amazing. And to have New Order as directors, well, you know, they were just about the coolest directors you could ever have.

Musically, Park was in his element too. The focus was on the 'Madchester' scene, kickstarted by Paul Oakenfold's W.F.L Think About The Future remix of Happy Mondays' Wrote For Luck, and hammered home by Oakey's Madchester Rave On EP for the Mondays. This meant indie dance was massive at the Hacienda when he joined, but, with Park as co-resident on the flagship Friday night Nude party, rave and, more specifically, house would go on to dominate proceedings for the next seven years.

The great thing about the Hacienda was its lack of music policy. The late, great Tony Wilson used to let everyone involved just get on with it, and especially the DJs.

From the time I joined the Hacienda, it was mainly about house music, all that early Chicago and Detroit stuff, but there are also early recordings of me and Mike playing hip-hop and disco. I mean, c'mon, Dan Hartman's Relight My Fire was one of the biggest Hacienda records, but as time went on, house music began to dictate things more and more.

Lots of Hacienda tracks stick out in my mind, but no particular one... Ce Ce Rogers' Someday was a big end of night record. Mike loved that record so much, we all loved that record, all about equality and a better world, and when everyone was off their knackers they loved that. The same with Joe Smooth's Promised Land, DJ Fast Eddie and Kenny Jammin Jason's Can You Dance, as well as The Party from Kraze, of course.

Danny Rampling's first trip to the Hacienda was like Enid Blyton on acid. And the Shoom legend suddenly discovered a rare sharing side to his then hard-edged DJ persona.

I was invited to play at the Hacienda in 1988 by Paul Cons who had an association with Heaven in London, and it really was a great honour. We organised a bus-load of us, and it was like twelve go mad in Manchester. I was amazed by the quality of the club, with the DJ booth high above the dancefloor. I remember I was playing all this funky Italian stuff, this great Italian house, and I had actually gone to Italy, and invested time and money sourcing this music.

At the time, I'll admit, I was covering up the records when I was playing them, because I didn't want other people getting their hands on this music, but looking back on it, music is to be shared, and we had such an amazing night on that visit that I told Mike the names of a couple of the tracks.

After the Hacienda, we were meant to go back to London on the bus, but the driver was a little worse for wear. One minute we were in Manchester, the next we were in the Brecon Beacons. It was like "how have we got here?", but that sort of thing then was a common occurrence. Andrew Weatherall was in that bus too, you know, this group from Shoom, which ended up in the Pennines, staying up there for the night, having a remarkable time, and it really was a fantastic introduction to the northern clubscene, at a time when DJs and people generally didn't travel around the UK.

Graeme Park had first appeared at the Hacienda for a Nude Northern House Review in February 1988, which was essentially him playing alongside Pickering, with the resident's T-Coy production guise and Park's studio alter-ego Groove, both performing live. He was then back in July of that year to cover for Pickering's holiday leave, and by the end of '88 was firmly installed as fellow resident.

But when Park was whisked off to America to tour with his heroes New Order in 1989, he was less than familiar with airports and airplanes.

The New Order tour, dubbed Monsters Of Alternative Rock, was in massive stadiums in places like Detroit, Chicago and Los Angeles, with the Sugarcubes featuring Bjork on stage first, then Public Image Limited with John Lydon, then me DJing for 45 minutes. New Order would come on and three songs into their set each night I would be whisked off to wherever the after-party was to start DJing there. It was crazy, touring with New Order and getting to be around people like John Lydon, who had been with the Sex Pistols and everything, was fascinating.

I was only 24 and I hadn't even left the country or flown anywhere at that stage. I can still remember that first flight like it was yesterday. To go on a plane for the first time and to be checking in your flight case record boxes is a bizarre experience. I still remember the faces of a couple of the flight attendants because I was so in awe of the whole experience and had to ask for some paracetamol to calm me down.

Mike had this thing that either me or him had to be at the Hacienda on a Friday at any one time, and he did some of that tour, but I ended up doing most of it.

Soon New York would become a second home to Park, sharing duties with Pickering for the next three years at a monthly Hacienda residency at The Mars club in the Big Apple, hooked up by New York DJ/producer Mark Kamins. The producer behind an album for Pickering's electronic outfit Quando Quango in 1981, Kamins had also helped launch Madonna's career in 1982 and had worked on Pickering's seminal 1987 T-Coy house anthem, Carino.

Mark had sorted this gig out at The Mars, which was in the meat market area. It had opened on New Year's Eve 1988 in a very rundown part of town. It's much more trendy now, a bit like Shoreditch became in London.

I remember for this trip I'd bought a guide to New York and I had all these plans for sightseeing - the Empire State Building, the Statue of Liberty and, of course, the World Trade Center was there then too. However, I was there for a week and I didn't see daylight for the whole time.

Mark took me out each night to his gigs and to various bars and clubs and it was just a magical time. There were loads of late night bars with great sound systems and DJs in them, which we just didn't have in the UK at that time. You had to go to a club to see a DJ, and most of those shut at 2am.

Then I was DJing on the Friday and when I got to the club I was amazed at the people there. Arthur Baker, who had produced Afrika Bambaataa's Planet Rock and also worked with New Order, was chatting to people by the DJ booth. As was John 'Jellybean' Benitez, who had produced early hits for Whitney Houston, and had remixed just about everyone from Hall & Oates and Talking Heads to George Benson and Michael Jackson. Plus a guy called John Robie, who worked with Baker and Benitez on New Order's Confusion, and who also produced a band called C-Bank, who I really liked at the time.

They were all there in this little room off the DJ booth, and I was like: "What are they all doing here?" Mark said: "They're here to see you, they're here because of the Hacienda." And I just couldn't believe it. The Mars was a great club, on three floors, a capacity of about 1,000 in total, and Robert De Niro's daughter was one of the owners, apparently.

The ante had certainly been upped and regular gigs followed for Park in New York at the Sound Factory bar and club, as he soon entered the colourful world of seminars.

There was a massive seminar in New York at that time, before the Winter Music Conference in Miami had started, called the New Music Seminar. I remember I played at a big Hacienda night there too in 1990, which was an album launch for New York outfit Deee-Lite, who had just released their Groove Is In The Heart hit and debut album. I'll never forget it, the line-up was me, Paul Oakenfold, Norman Cook and Mike Pickering, plus the Happy Mondays and Deee-Lite live. Keith Allen was the compere for the night as well, which looking back, shows you how ridiculous the whole thing had got so quickly.

I also remember a daytime event at one of the seminars with Louie Vega on the decks first, then me, followed by Tony Humphries, who played some of my remixes, which was a special moment indeed.

I was also on a panel with Todd Terry for a debate, which everybody was taking very seriously. I was trying to lighten the mood, cracking jokes, because it seemed so bizarre, but none of the Americans were up for that sort of thing. Looking back you knew at the time something very big was happening, but it's only now you can look back and analyse it, and, in fact, you remember more things now the more you talk about it.

Like when I was touring with New Order and we reached Detroit. Derrick May came down to the venue during one of the sound checks because he wanted to meet New Order. I got talking to him, and he'd heard good things about the Hacienda, so I ended up hanging out with him for the afternoon in the offices of Transmat Records, which was basically the kitchen of his apartment.

He had this four track mixing desk, and he let me mess about with his tracks, Strings Of Life and The Dance, on there. He later taught me how to play baseball in his back yard. It's so bizarre looking back at that now.

Promotion-wise, given the enigma that the Hacienda became in the late '80s and early '90s, and the chaos and sheer anarchy that ensued, it would probably be foolish to delve too deeply into how the club was marketed.

I suppose the Hacienda used to promote itself because it was infamous. You had Tony Wilson, the head of the club, a journalist and TV presenter, who was just the master at getting promotion and saying the right things at the right time, and then Factory Records, New Order's label behind it too, which was just the coolest label around. It was in Manchester, it was an enigma and everyone wanted to go there. It wouldn't happen now, because everyone would know about it immediately and it would be marketed in a very polished way.

I don't know, these days I just find it all a bit more cynical to be honest, but back in the late '80s it was all about your reputation, and we were very lucky at the Hacienda because we lived up to it, and even more so.

Everything you heard about it was true, this hedonism, and mayhem, this bedlam that everyone talks about. That was the best promotion, the word of mouth. You couldn't promote it now, it would be banned. If you tried to do it now and say what was happening as it went along, on Facebook or whatever, you'd be told you can't say that, that didn't happen.

Promoting a club or club night was so much different from how it is today. For instance, for my bookings now, say in 2011, on an average weekend in Aberdeen and Glasgow, or wherever, I will have created a Facebook event or be talking about it on the club's Facebook page, and on Twitter too. In the late '80s and early '90s it was very difficult for a DJ to promote a club or a night - that was really the job of the promoter.

I suppose cassettes were a good way, and I was always one for recording my sets. People would always ask for a recording of my last set, especially at the Hacienda.

When I lived in west London, I was round the corner from a place called Chop Em Out. I'd come back from the Hacienda and drop off my chrome master copy on cassette, and then pick up 50 copies and give all those tapes out. And I suppose that was a great way then of promoting myself and whatever parties I was playing over the next few weeks.

Of course, Manchester in the late '80 and early '90s and beyond was not totally dominated by the Hacienda.

Believe it or not there were other clubs in Manchester at the time. Round the corner from us was The Boardwalk, and Dave Haslam, who had DJd at the Hacienda, was the resident there, at a night called Yellow. And there was Bowlers, which was full-on rave-tastic. Sankeys Soap didn't exist when I started, but towards the end of the Hacienda's time, Sankeys did open. That was probably the first club to take people away from the Hacienda, but then not everyone could get into the Hacienda so there were other clubs that catered for those people and were actually needed for that reason. Then when Canal Street became a centre for the gay community, a lot of people went there, too.

Manchester had always been a great vibrant city and that's what drew me to it in the first place. That's why my association with Manchester is a long-standing one. I love the people there, always have done. It's a great party city. There were other clubs in Manchester, for sure, but at the end of the day, lots of students around that time used to choose the University in Manchester purely because of the Hacienda.

Park mourns the fact that so many guest DJs were later needed to fill clubs. But then, this is coming from a successful resident who went on to make his name with hundreds of guests spots all over the UK, Europe and the world.

We never really had many guest DJs at the Hac', but as the years went on you just couldn't put a party on without any guest DJs. I'd say 99% of clubs now rely on guest DJs and their individual brand, and they certainly do bring in the punters. But I'm concerned now that sometimes the brand is more important than the DJs themselves. I recently did a touring night for the Ministry Of Sound and every single DJ was a guest.

At the Hacienda we relied heavily on residents. Every Friday it was me and Mike Pickering between '88 and '91, and then every Saturday night it was me and Tom Wainwright between '92 and '96. Dave

Haslam was another long-serving resident who played at the club several times a week, between '86 - '90, plus other stints in the '90s.

The residents and the music were the main reasons people came, and, of course, the drugs. We did have guests every now and then, but it would tend to be for the special events like birthdays and New Year's Eve. And when we had guests, it had to be guests that we personally liked, so for me and Mike that was easy, it was people like Todd Terry, David Morales and Frankie Knuckles, who I think is the greatest DJ who ever lived. Also the likes of Tony Humphries...Colin Favor used to do a bit too... and a DJ from Aberdeen called Jackie Morrison came down, because I thought she was fantastic. And, of course, Sasha.

It's funny, looking back now, that we didn't really go for guests. You'd never get away with it these days. If you said "I'm going to open a club now and there are a couple of residents each night and they'll play every week" then it would be busy for the first night and then dead after that. I think that's sad because it means that the art of the resident has gone.

I mean, Tom Wainwright used to warm-up for me on a Saturday night and he would warm the crowd up just enough to the point where I came on and then it went bang. DJs don't know how to warm-up now. People say I've got a great warm-up DJ for you and you turn up and they're playing 130 bpm. The art of the warm-up DJ has gone. Tom was ahead of his time.

Memories-wise, Park claims Pickering has always been better at "that sort of stuff".

I have a lot of great memories, but I've also forgotten a lot. For eight years the Hacienda was a massive part of my life, and it will live with me forever. It was like one big eight-year party, though, so specific nights have stayed with me more, like special occasions...Morales, Knuckles, etc, someone's hair catching fire on NYE because they had fireworks in the Hacienda, again, which you'd never get away with now. We also had a barbecue and a fairground outside for one night. Nobody had a burger, nobody ate any of the food and nobody will be surprised at that.

My mix of Brand New Heavies' Back To Love, naturally, is one big memory. One week I didn't play it, and I nearly got lynched. That was probably my end of night record, not through choice, but because the punters wanted it. That's never a bad thing, I guess, if people demand to hear something you actually crafted yourself. I still play that track now, although after I left the Hac' I didn't play it for three or four years because I was sick to death of it.

Since then, people have been able to go on line and get the mix, no problem, but what you cannot get for love nor money is the dub mix, which was on the b-side of the promo. If I'm correct, on the release proper you couldn't get the dub mix, and it was only on the blue labelled promo. That mix had no vocals and just more of that acid-y breakdown, so back then at the end of the night I would have mixed that into the actual mix, and dragged it out that way.

At the end of other nights I could have quite easily played House Music Anthem by Marshall Jefferson or something by Ten City or Inner City, or some of the Reese and Santonio stuff.

Some clubbers can tell me what I played at exactly what point of what night, and I haven't got a clue what they're talking about. I just need a little bit of help to tease the memories out. I have no bad one, apart from one time this bloke tried to get in the DJ booth, around '95 or '96. He didn't like the music I was playing and tried to come in the booth, which was a stable door. A bouncer appeared and threw him down the stairs. For eight years the Hacienda was the best club in the world so why would there be any bad memories?

The Hacienda shut first time around in January 1991, because of gang violence, and when it opened again three months later Pickering stayed on doing Fridays, but Park was offered Saturdays and was up for trying something different.

It seemed like a different era for the club, and people do now look back at the '88-'91 era and the '91-'96 era as two separate phases of the club, certainly where house music is concerned. Some purists don't even acknowledge the second era at all. Mike only ended up staying a couple of months into the second phase because M-People really took off for him after that, but I feel fortunate to have been there on different nights for both eras. They were all great, great times, not just for me, but for thousands of people, the like of which we will never ever see again.

I actually get all misty-eyed talking about it, but it's wonderful that people are interviewing boring old bastards like me now. To document this is great because in 50 years' time when none of us are here, people like my boys will say, "yep, that was my dad that did that". God, I'm filling up now! To get us all talking about it now, in the cold light of day, not off our heads, not all egotistical, is great.

Allister Whitehead believes there was no comparison between the late '80s Hacienda, and the latter-day version.

I remember it most fondly from the '88, '89 era, when it was complete madness. I'd already wanted to be a DJ and I remember that going to the Hacienda then was like going to Mecca if you're a Muslim. It was almost like a big bang was taking place. What happened in that time is why people are dancing now in all these outposts all over the world, and it was when I realised that DJing, if I could possibly manage to, was what I wanted to do for the next however many years.

However, even though I got to DJ there in 1992 at a foam party, I still actually look back most fondly at the earlier era. At least I got to experience the Hacienda at full pelt. And it is still one of the best gigs of my life, simply because I realised a dream of playing at the Hacienda before it really deteriorated, which really only a handful of DJs actually got to do. I remember when the foam came out it really was madness and added a different element to what was going on. The records picked themselves, and if you can't DJ to that, then you're in the wrong job.

I was really disappointed when the Hacienda closed. It went out with a whimper and, ironically, just as it came in. I went to the Hacienda in 1984 when my sister was at uni, and it was this massive club, but it wasn't busy, and she said "that's how it always is". When it did go, the fact that it was such a style icon, such a template for a nightclub of that kind, made it all the more upsetting.

*(main picture) * Graeme Park at Culture Shock, Hollywood, Romford, 1993 - image: Matt Trollope
(clockwise) * The legendary Hacienda building, with Park outside the entrance to the apartment block it became
* A 1988 Nude flyer featuring Pickering, Park and T-Coy*

The layout is engrained on everyone who went there, and that's what is most disappointing, because the building still had a massive relevance. Whenever I go to Manchester now, I still drive past it, and look at it with so much nostalgia. And it's very frustrating when you talk to people who had a bad experience at the Hacienda, or saw it empty, that they didn't see what you witnessed.

Legendary London DJ Mark Moore doesn't pull any punches when reflecting on the Hacienda. A DJ for Philip Salon's iconic Mud Club from 1983, and the man behind chart-topping S'Express in 1988, Moore is one of the men credited with taking house music to the masses, and also regarded as one of the first pioneers of acid house in the UK.

Park may not thank me for including his comments in our Hacienda chapter. And Russell Davison from Progress, as you will read later, may have a few words to say about UK house music timelines.

Moore explains:-

The first time I went and played the Hacienda it was as part of an ID Magazine tour. I remember going up with Karen Franklin, the style guru, who was one of the editors then, and later a presenter on The Clothes Show. It was early '88, but I had been playing the early acid house stuff for a while - the Martin Luther King speech over Mr Fingers, Fast Eddie's Acid Thunder, etc, and Graeme Park was there saying, "yeah, we have a night where we play this stuff", but you could tell, by the crowd, that some of them knew the music and some of them didn't, that it hadn't quite taken off yet. If I'm being honest, and I love Graeme Park to bits, but the Hacienda, where acid house was concerned, took off a year after the London scene did. C'mon, let's admit it, let's admit it...London did it first.

OUCH! But Moore is adamant...and has 'One Moore' jibe left on the subject.

The thing is, at the start in London it was kept very underground. They didn't want to let in journalists so it wasn't widely reported in 1987 in London and then a year later, all the people who missed it in London could go to Manchester and write about it in the NME. Manchester had all the really great bands to back it up, so they would slap a photo of Stone Roses or Happy Mondays on the piece and call it Madchester...but London did it first.

Intrinsically linked to trance music, Judge Jules is an unlikely Hacienda DJ.

I would never describe myself as one of the core Hacienda Friday night or Saturday night DJs, but I did end up doing a lot of midweek student nights there, during the couple of years before it closed. Due to the gangster element then, those nights were both enthralling and scary at the same time.

I remember I went up to Manchester in the late '80s to visit the Hacienda on a clubbing recce mission, not as a DJ. I just jumped in the back of someone's car who was going up there. And there was this unusual combination of music they were playing, a mixture of early house and indie, like The Smiths and the Psychedelic Furs. It was an amazing venue, and it was the blueprint for a lot of clubs all over the world, but it was a long time before I actually played there.

I've done lots of clubs in Manchester since, and the gang element seems to have been controlled over the years. Unlike a lot of cities in the UK, in Manchester a lot of the rougher areas are very close to the city centre. I've had a couple of occasions in various clubs when I've seen 50 guys fighting, and when you're very young your glass is half-full, so while you are aware of it, you try to not let it affect you.

Adrian Luvdup, of the infamous Manchester-born Luvdup collective, was lucky enough to experience one of the Hacienda's most famous nights. And found himself at the heart of some of the typical extravagance that made it virtually impossible for the Hacienda to ever be in profit.

I first went when I was at school. It was when The Tube was filmed there and when Madonna famously first performed in the UK. I was about 15 and I managed to blag myself in. I next went when I was about 17 and a half. I saw Mike Pickering's night Nude listed in the Manchester Evening News. I just liked the name Nude, and thought there may be some nudity there! I was a testosterone-fuelled 17-year-old and although there was no nudity, there was some great music. I saw The Pogues live there as well around that time.

This was about 1987 and only about 30% of it was house music. Other stuff played included electro funk like Joyce Sim's All In All, but there was no drug culture then, it was about going out and getting drunk and dancing to good music. Then house exploded around '88/'89, that's when the whole atmosphere changed, with the queues around the block and the acid house dancing.

My first link professionally was through the indie scene because my best friend at school, his older brother was the guitarist in The Charlatans, and by then Luvdup had taken off and we did a remix for The Charlatans, and then warmed-up for them at the Hacienda.

In 1993, after the success of our Jolly Roger night at The Paradise Factory in Manchester – which, oddly enough, was the old Factory Records office - we were asked to go across to the Hacienda. We obviously thought "great". When we were at the Paradise we had queues round the block, then we went to Hacienda in August '93.

I remember we had Farley & Heller as guests for the first night and I think Peter Hook quotes in his book that our night was the biggest loss-making night ever in the Hacienda's history. They had constructed the infamous pirate ship in the middle of the dancefloor and put the DJ booth in there, at a claimed cost of £30k. I think Salvador Dali would have had to be involved for it to be that expensive, but even if it did cost that much, we didn't ask for it, unless we said it for a joke, and they just went along with it. Which, with the Hacienda, is quite possible.

Many of Adrian Luvdup's memories revolve around the fashion and trends at that time, and, of course, that emerging drug culture.

Pre-ecstasy, when you went up the stairs people were selling speed and the cloakroom attendant would roll joints for us, and have a couple of puffs on it for his troubles.

Trying to take an iconic bollard from the dancefloor, complete with Hacienda yellow and black trim, out of the club in my big baggy trousers - that is another big memory for me. And fortunately this was way before the gangsters had taken over the door and the so-called 'Gunchester' era, or I would have probably taken a big beating for that stunt. Instead, the doorman looked at me with great pity. The bollard was taken back to the floor and I was allowed to leave. I wish I'd got away with that one, though.

Before the acid house thing, around 1986, I'd be wearing a baker boy hat like Terence Trent D'arby, ridiculously big baggy pants and a polo shirt, and there would be proper dancing down there, before the big box, little box house thing came in.

The Jazz Defectors and Foot Patrol were two regular black jazz dance troupes who used to dance at the Hacienda around 1986. Serious fast footwork, wearing those baggy pants, and quite a different scene to when the acid house thing kicked off.

Fast forward 10 years and a number of factors led to Park's eventual departure from the Hacienda, not least of all the huge offers to DJ elsewhere, frequently turned down to maintain the consistency of his residency.

Meanwhile, the last record at the Hacienda, and who exactly played it, is always up for debate. In the Hook book we're told: *"The last night of the Hacienda was Saturday, 28 June, 1997. Dave Haslam was DJing, and had no idea it was to be the last ever night"*. Various other people have claimed to have played the last record at the Hac' over the years, but not in any doubt, however, is what Park played on his final night at the Hacienda on New Year's in Eve in 1996.

I left the Hacienda five or six months before it closed for the final time in 1997. I don't have many memories of that night, apart from the last record, and, fittingly, it was my own mix of Back To Love. For me, it just seemed like the perfect time for me to leave. The club had lost its spark as far as I was concerned. I'd done this night where I'd done a classics set, playing anthems from the past eight years and everyone went wild, and then the manager wanted me to do a classics set regularly, but I wasn't up for that then. It was very sad to be moving on, but, as it turned out, it was the right thing to do.

I was turning down massive Saturday offers from all over the UK and internationally too. Every now and then one was too good to turn down financially so I would do it, happy on those nights to leave it to Tom Wainwright, because I knew it was in safe hands. But people who only came to the club every three or four weeks would get pissed off if I wasn't there.

Cream, down the M62 in Liverpool, were also on my case for me to play there on Saturdays, but that just didn't seem right, as it was so close to Manchester. And then they started a Friday night called Full On, so I did that regularly and then just decided to leave the Hacienda altogether and take up all these guest offers I had elsewhere on Saturdays.

Ironically, I had lived in Nottingham for all of the first era, and in London for all of the second. Then I left the Hacienda at the end of '96, but in 1997 was asked to present the weekday afternoon show on Kiss FM, which had launched in Manchester the year before. So I moved to Manchester, where I lived for the next two or three years. These days, I've settled in Cheshire, in between Manchester and Liverpool.

That daytime Kiss show was great. It was 50% playlist, 50% records I thought would be on the playlist soon, and there were lots of dance tracks in the charts and on the playlist at that time. You just wouldn't be able to do that on an FM station now.

When Kiss was bought by Chrysalis Records, and renamed Galaxy, Park was retained for a new show which was syndicated across various other Galaxy stations, including Bristol, Leeds, Newcastle and Birmingham.

I did the Saturday night show for six years, various two and three hour slots between 6pm – 10pm. It was called Graeme Park – Across The Galaxy, and you could drive from the north east of England to Bristol in the south west and listen to the same show. I also had shows at that time on Juice FM in Liverpool and Brighton and Forth One in Edinburgh.

I still do a weekly show, which I syndicate to many regional stations all over the UK, some internet ones too, and in various corners of the world. There is no money in it anymore, but I use it as a promotional tool and it helps advertise my website. I recently got to tour South Africa because of the show and 27 years later it's great because it helps me carry on what I've been doing all these years.

I'm very lucky I've still got a great reputation through the heritage of things like the Hacienda. I was in the 24 Hour Party People film. Me and Mike are in the DJ box in one scene, and people say, "well, you can just about see you", but I tell them to look at the credits at the end of the film, because my name flashes up nice and big in the "thank yous" because I was an adviser too, and that made my day.

Danny Rampling believes it took Manchester a long time to get over the Hacienda's closure.

When the Hacienda shut it was a very sad time for the club scene in the UK. Such a pivotal club, such a beacon of light in Manchester that created so many good times, and platformed so many artists and DJs who, even pre-house, came through that club. It was a sad day in particular for Manchester, a great city, with a great music scene. The city continues to have a healthy music scene, but the Hacienda was really the jewel in its crown.

When the club did close the landscape had changed, the crime element had come into clubbing, not just in Manchester, but everywhere, I guess, and that undesirable element had contributed to the demise of the club. Unwittingly, I think, people got that club closed down without really realising the huge impact it would have on the city. After that, nightlife-wise, it took a long time for Manchester to get back on its feet again.

Today Graeme Park is one of a constantly shrinking group of DJs who still get regular work across the weekend. And he's happy to take the work while it's still there. He boasts 14,000 followers on his Facebook fan page, is active on Twitter, and keeps his thisisgraemepark.com website fully uploaded with video blogs.

A quick look at that website at the time of going to press showed Park would be playing in Leicester, Amsterdam, Stoke, Leeds, Nottingham, Hemel Hempstead, Southampton and Edinburgh over the following two and a half weeks.

I'm still DJing, been doing it almost 30 years now. It was 1984 when I started at The Garage, and the move to the Hacienda couldn't have gone better. But I was also resident at the Ministry Of Sound when it opened in 1991, and later on at Cream in Liverpool. I've travelled the world and I'm glad to say that, in my 40s, in the second decade of this century, I'm still doing it.

In the late '80s, early '90s, if Park wanted to, he could work on both Wednesday and Thursday, take two gigs on a Friday, two on a Saturday and maybe one on a Sunday too. These days there are a couple of gigs a week, with the odd weekend off a chance to spend quality time with his wife and kids. And he tends not to use an agent anymore, because the clubs prefer dealing with him direct and so he avoids *"stupid rows about commission"*.

I continue partly because you cannot beat the buzz of putting on a tune and people reacting to it, and partly because people still want me to do it. As long as those two things run in tandem, I see no reason not to continue.

I play a lot of eclectic stuff, all types of house… I play vocal house, funky house, soulful house, deep house, tech house, gay house and some other types of house as well. However, it always annoys me when people ask what specific type of house I play.

These days, a lot of clubbers want to know the exact sub-genre… I just play house, and I also love to play some classic funk and soul because I think it's important that we don't forget some of the great music that inspired house music in the first place. At one point house music took over and lots of stuff got forgotten.

Some people who go out clubbing today, they might ask for a club mix of the latest Black Eyed Peas record, or ask for the original mix of a track, when I'm actually playing the original. They say stuff like "call yourself a DJ?" and I know they just want to have a good night, but if their idea of a good night is asking for a shit record, then that's their problem.

Park also keeps himself busy with various stints of daytime radio presenting, when called upon, and enjoys his role as a part-time university lecturer.

I'm involved in some music-based modules in Wrexham, which I absolutely love. I've been doing it for three years now, at the Glymbrwr University. There are a couple of courses I take part in, which means I do one day a week between October and May, maybe more if you count prep and marking.

Most of the students are 19, 20 years old and haven't got a clue who I am. But at the start of each course, I tell them what I've done over the years. They don't say much and then a couple of weeks later, after they've Googled me or maybe spoken to their parents, they come up and talk to me about it and are intrigued about the whole thing.

Park has always tried to keep up with technology, but wishes he had taken one geek he met more than 20 years ago rather more seriously.

I still make music and do the odd remix. But at the end of the day I'm a DJ, not a DJ / producer. I'm a DJ and that's an art that needs to be kept alive. I embraced DJing with CDs quite early on, but I got fed up with spending all week downloading and burning stuff on to CDs. Then I went to Canada and every club had Serato hard-wired in. For me, Serato is like going back to vinyl again, you just need your laptop and two Serato discs.

Sure, some clubs don't have vinyl decks any more, and that's very sad, but most do. Serato means you have access to 20,000 tracks and you're ready for anything, whatever the crowd wants and whatever random thoughts come into my head. Then there's the Pioneer set-up where you could effectively turn up at a club which had that system, with all your records on one USB stick. Meanwhile, Ableton, is a fantastic piece of kit, and I'm now using that more and more.

I'll never forget, in the late '80s, when I was making music for Submission Records, under the name Groove, and this sound engineer said to me: "You realise, in 25 years' time you won't be lugging all those records around in boxes, all your music will be on something the size of a credit card." And I remember thinking this guy was mad. But why didn't I listen to him? Why didn't I say: "Let's work on this now?"

MATT TROLLOPE

THE ESCAPE CLUB

Brighton has not always been marauding mods painting the town red, white and blue, or free beach parties attended by hundreds of thousands of people.

It's hard to imagine, but there was an early-'80s lull down on the south coast in desperate need of a storm.

Like many interviewed for One More, John Holland dreamed of opening the sort of venue he would like to go to, attracting the sort of people he would like to club with.

The result was The Escape Club, still going strong today under Holland's leadership, albeit more recently as Audio, and undoubtedly the longest-running operation featured in One More.

The Escape started because I'd been in Brighton a couple of years, I liked clubbing and there was this huge empty void in the town, where clubs were concerned, for the kind of things I wanted to go to and for the people that I wanted to attract.

There were a couple of one-nighters here and there - good nights - and Norman was playing at one, but other than that nothing much was going on. So I found the venue and the rest is a bit of clubbing history.

Holland makes it sounds all so easy, but keeping a club or promotion going for nigh on three decades is virtually impossible, as everyone interviewed here will testify.

Meanwhile, Norman is, of course, Norman Cook, aka the irrepressible Fatboy Slim, who, since he made Brighton his home shortly after The Escape opened in 1984, has become synonymous with the creative coastal hub.

Cook (born Quentin Leo Cook in 1963) is the star of those massive Big Beach Boutique events and the club's influence on his career is not lost on him.

I did a lot of my formative years growing up at The Escape. It was our clubhouse, where we got up to all our shenanigans.

Holland had been keen to give Brighton clubbers somewhere different to hear decent alternative music, a dedicated purpose-built venue.

Our aim was to provide somewhere to go for a certain crowd of people, because that's what was wrong with Brighton, this huge void. There was nothing really else going on at the time so there was an open book for us.

The few good nights that there were around were shoved into horrible little back rooms in local hotels. They were still good nights, but the décor was pretty awful, the sound systems were poor and we wanted to offer more to people. We managed to do that and it was a great success.

I have to say that, in the beginning, promotion was not really my forte. Some of the flyers were made on pretty poor paper and stuff like that. It took a year or so to get it all together and back in those days, to be honest, it didn't always take a lot of promotion. If the club was right and you got the word of mouth, you were OK. You'd get the right crowd in.

A couple of years before The Escape opened, Cook had seized on an older sister's relocation to Brighton and quickly spent as much time hanging out there as he could.

The first nightclub that I ever went to was Sherry's (Dance Hall) in Brighton around 1982, when I was around 17 or 18. I had grown up in Reigate and a group of us used to drive down on Wednesday nights, which was the Futurist night. It was great because they were playing anything from James Brown to hip-hop to New Romantic. But it was very much a New Romantic night in terms of fashion and so my early clubbing days involved wearing high-waisted trousers, and having watch chains, even though I didn't have a watch.

I really got into hip-hop at Sherry's, which was basically when I was old enough to go to a nightclub. The first record I heard there was Planet Rock by Afrika Bambaataa, which was one of THE first seminal hip-hop records. So I think I kinda lucked out there, going to nightclubs when electro, as it was called then, had just started…the golden years.

When I first started DJing and going to clubs all those years ago house hadn't been invented yet. We had "alternative dance", which in those days was non-high street music. Back then that could be anything from the Clash to Siouxsie & The Banshees, to kinds of New Romantic electro stuff like Heaven 17, and early electro records. It was all just called "alternative dance" in those days.

Mentions must go out to a DJ called Dave Clark, who used to play at Sherry's on a Wednesday, and a bloke called Rory, who used to play at a gay club called Coasters on a Tuesday.

Rory would play a major part in Cook's musical schooling in those early days.

I got a job in a record shop in Brighton Square called Rounder Records, which was the only place then where you could get underground dance music, and which, in 2011, is still around to this day. Rory would be playing all these gay disco records at Coasters, which in those days were essentially underground dance tracks for white British clubbers. Tracks by people like Bobby Orlando and Giorgio Moroder - music which was, I guess, prototype house music.

In fact, Giorgio Moroder dubbing out Donna Summer on I Feel Love is the record that turned me from punk rock to dance music. The record that absolutely captivated me. The Patrick Cowley Megamix of I Feel Love is 15 minutes long, but you had to play the middle four minutes, the dub out section, which was basically acid house ten years before anyone else invented it.

People would come into the shop and ask for stuff that Rory had played, and that meant I had to research exactly what he had been playing, and I started getting good at that.

One thing Rory taught me then was that if you're going to make music, make sure it is instantly recognisable if people try to hum or sing it in a record shop. So that means a great vocal hook or loop or sample, and I've always tried to do that since, when making music.

Back then dance music was very word of mouth. This was long before the internet or Shazam. And in those days, and we're talking 1983, '84, we only had one column about underground dance music to go on each week - in the Record Mirror by the legendary James Hamilton.

So by 1984, as far as Brighton was concerned, Norman Cook was in place, and Holland had opened The Escape. Meanwhile, local aspiring DJs like Gordon Kaye were grateful the area now had a much-needed and decent platform for dance music.

I started DJing in 1985, probably before I should have been allowed into a club, at a bar called Electric Grape, up by the railway station in Brighton. Within a year of that I had started up my own midweek night at The Escape called Sunshine Playroom, which became very, very popular and ran for six years.

At The Escape, because it was still pre-acid house, the music was a real mish mash, so lots of funk and Motown as well as the latest indie records, stuff like The Jesus and Mary Chain. The club quickly became the coolest place to go in Brighton. It just had the right atmosphere and, importantly, no dress code. The doormen at a lot of other places were very intimidating. The Escape, meanwhile, was full of like-minded people with a really nice sound system.

From Norman Cook's family home in Surrey, Brighton was 30 miles one way, and held a massive pull for any aspiring DJ or musician. The West End of London, meanwhile, was 25 miles in the other direction, and home to Soho and hugely influential venues like The Wag Club.

Brighton has been, apart from punk rock, the biggest influence on my life. Where I grew up, you either went up to central London or you came down to Brighton. My sister was at university in Brighton so I started coming to Brighton. There were nightclubs and Uncle Sam burgers and girls. So the lure of Brighton has always been there for me and as soon as I could, I went to college here, moved down and have lived here ever since.

There is just something about the spirit of Brighton. There is always a lot going on, it's quite hedonistic and quite artistic as well. I dunno, I just sort of fit in with the whole kind of Brighton vibe, doing things a little bit wrong. There's a big gay population and also loads of anarchists and squatters. Brighton has always tolerated different lifestyles, so in terms of DJing, nightclubs and general hedonism, I'm right at home.

DJs that inspired me included Carl Cox. He was big down here, very much the don of Brighton. Carl had just experimented with three-deck mixing and just the fact that he could mix was impressive, because not everybody could in the early days.

It always seemed that me and Carl were going to be making a track together, but we never did. Over the years, I have bumped into him loads at the same events, and, more recently, I've always played for him at his parties at Space in Ibiza. We could be performing in front of thousands of people and there's always a point where we look at each other, as if to say "still getting away with it". Yeah, Carl was a very big influence on me back then and I also got in with his crowd, which was a big thing for me.

The Escape Club had come along just at the right time for Gordon Kaye and he had welcomed the chance to turn his hand to promoting. His Sunshine Playroom night naturally provides him with his fondest Escape memories.

We built up a huge following for that night over the next five or six years. People like Alan McGee and Bobby Gillespie were living in Brighton and we used to see these kinds of faces coming in every week. You know, the most exciting times were those pre-acid house times. We were still playing a lot of the funk records and a lot of the indie stuff too, but you could already see that a lot of people were turning around to acid house. Then suddenly, one week you'd have Bobby Gillespie coming in and asking for an acid house record. Those sorts of things are great memories.

And soon in Brighton there were other things going on too. Carl Cox had just moved into the area and was making it really big with various nights he was putting on. He was doing a pub in Hove on a Sunday night and he'd end up leaving that and setting up, almost what you'd call a guerrilla party, I guess. He'd leave the pub and move into an empty house somewhere and set up a system. So there were lots of late night afters activities going on.

Tonka were huge down here, too. They'd do a monthly party at The Zap and again, when that wrapped up, Harvey, Rev and Choci would all go over to Ovingdean, just along the undercliff and set up by the sea. They wouldn't be annoying any local residents because the sound wouldn't carry, so these parties would go on all night, outside with the sea on your doorstep.

Back inside at The Escape, word was spreading. Its ambitious owner's masterplan was panning out nicely. As the '90s edged ever closer, a musical revolution was beginning to take place. Holland remembers the transition and what had been on offer beforehand.

The music policy had to be something different on different nights. If you went into the High Street clubs it was Top 40 music, you know, chart music, every single night of the week. The same old rubbish and we wanted to cater for different audiences. The other clubs I admired were The Mud Club in London, the Hacienda in Manchester and, a little bit later on, going up to Heaven in Charing Cross. I used to love that. Early days, great atmospheres and weird and wonderful people, and, for me, that's what clubs are all about. Raw, also - all those places were really great nights.

A year after The Escape debuted in Brighton, another club that would go on to have a long history in the town opened its doors, after previously running as a promotion at The Escape.

We always had a friendly rivalry when The Zap opened as a venue in its own right. One year we were on top and the next year they were. It's always been that way. I've got fond memories of The Zap and I'm sure they have of The Escape, but there were very few other clubs when we first opened... two or three years after that, a plethora of them had popped up.

For us, Saturday was the biggest dance night, while Fridays were always a little bit alternative. We had jazz on another night - people like Paul Murphy played - so really good acts and always busy nights. There was even a good midweek indie night with all the Factory Records stuff being played.

My favourite memories of The Escape are too numerous to mention, but they include some of the silly little things that used to happen, some

*(clockwise) * Gordon Kaye chats to One More, Brighton beach 2010*
* Early press shot of one of Brighton's famous 'sons', Carl Cox
* John Holland outside Audio (previously The Escape), 2010
* Norman Cook is interviewed for One More, 2010

deep
AND DIRTY

**EscapeClub
Brighton**

Deep and Dirty
Shades of House Music

Saturday Nights

of the scary things too. One that stands out is when we had a party at my house out in the countryside in 1987. We had a couple, in fact. They were called House Of Holland. The first was on a summer Sunday, the day after a busy Saturday night, and a lot of my regulars, who had become really good friends, were all hand invited. All good people, and most hadn't had any sleep from the night before.

We had an absolute ball, drank a great deal of booze, and everything else, put a marquee up, and had a really, really good time. Carl Cox came over and DJd for £35, and we had a pool there. Everyone jumped in, but we did have a scary moment at one point - the local dealer had pigged out on his own product and was found face down in the pool. Me and another guy got him out, just in time, apparently.

Carl Cox, though, what a lovely guy and thanks to him for playing. There were hundreds of people there, in a big, big garden in the middle of summer. Those parties became legendary and I will live on those memories. A couple of years after we opened, I realised The Escape was a success when I took a big holiday, a holiday that I could never have afforded before. It took off pretty quick, I guess. It was already quite a success after six months and I'm really proud of that.

The big house in the country and Carl Cox playing poolside might just have given Holland a few clues as to his success, too. Next up was a trip to Ibiza for all the DJs and some of those befriended locals.

In the late '80s I organised the Ibiza trip and we went out with a lot of our own DJs and punters. All the Escape DJs had taken record boxes full of Run DMC and Beastie Boys records, stuff like that. But we met Paul Oakenfold and Trevor Fung, and all those guys, on the beach one day, and all my DJs came back to Brighton playing house music. And that's when it all changed, that was the pivotal moment for us really.

Rewind to 1985 and Cook had left Brighton to join friend Paul Heaton's band, The Housemartins. Despite little experience on bass – he had, in fact, recently played drums in a cleverly-titled new wave band called Disque Attack – aspiring DJ Cook answered Reigate college pal Heaton's SOS after the group's bass player left suddenly. He famously went on to enjoy his first taste of chart success in the process as The Housemartins quickly earned a No 3 hit with Happy Hour in 1986 and topped the Christmas UK charts at the end of that year with their cover of Caravan Of Love.

By 1988, however, the band had split and with Heaton about to form The Beautiful South, the wandering Cook prepared to return to Brighton to reacquaint himself with his first love - dance music - and uses an interesting analogy to describe his first incarnation at the "top of the pops".

I look at it a bit like sex. Like your first shag, it was fairly successful, but it wasn't particularly good. I actually left the band because I'd started to make some music, and one track had appeared in the Record Mirror under the name Norman Housemartin. The band were saying: "We can't be associated with dance music." So I left. I had always been the only member of the band interested in the production side of things, the only one who went to the mix-down of the records and the only band member who had been intrigued by all the studio equipment involved.

Once back on the south coast the change that greeted him at The Escape was impossible to miss. But, importantly, around the same time, Cook had embarked on a studio project with producer of the moment Dancing Danny D, who would go on to have a massive hit as D Mob with We Call It Acieed.

An A & R friend had asked Cook if he had any ideas how to remix US rap duo Erik B & Rakim's I Know You've Got Soul, and with his early Fatboy Slim hat on, Cook had quickly suggested using sections of The Jackson 5 classic I Want You Back.

Promptly thrown in the studio with Danny D, the duo's quick and impressive collaboration became the now legendary Double Trouble Remix.

After DJing regularly at The Escape in 1984 and 1985 I moved up to Hull to be in The Housemartins. When I came back in '88, the acid house thing had literally happened while I was in Hull.

I remember going down to The Escape, my old stomping ground, and everybody was dancing on the bar, like it was New Year's Eve. I didn't realise that ecstasy had just been invented. All my friends were wearing bandanas and that's when I did my first pill.

I think the track that sums up The Escape the most for me is Finally by Ce Ce Penniston, which came out later. Looking back the "finally it's happening to me" chorus line was relevant to me.

But I didn't make a house record until 1995, when I did the Pizzaman track. I was more interested in using rare groove and old disco or soul tracks to make stuff, and so the Erik B & Rakim mix was great for me. Up until that point I didn't have a sampler, I would mess about at home with two copies of one record over a drum machine, and that's how I originally came up with the I Know You Got Soul idea. That mix was the start of my solo production career.

More than 20 years later and The Escape Club is still going strong as Audio, its most recent guise. John Holland took the sensible step of bringing down the curtain on The Escape on its 20th anniversary in 2004, with Cook and Cox fittingly playing the last night.

As well as Norman and Carl, my favourite other DJ had to be Derrick Carter, but it's really hard to say, they all impressed me to be honest. I'm not sure I can name one track that sums up The Escape for me. Early on, I'd say something like Beastie Boys' Fight For Your Right, but after that, I don't know. There are so many tunes that, when you heard them, you would say "ah, I love that".

The last track that was ever played at The Escape? Well, I think Carl Cox was DJing, but I couldn't tell you its name. I can't remember, my head was so filled by everything at that point. The Escape finished because it had seen 20 years of great clubbing and had a lot of respect in the town. Everybody loved it, but I felt it had kind of run its course.

I felt that it couldn't really do any more in the form that it was in. I wanted to add some different bits and pieces so that was a signal for me and I thought, you know what, "we'll have a refit, a proper refit, and we'll turn the upstairs into a cocktail bar and relaunch it". We reopened as Audio a few months after The Escape shut and it has been a great success ever since.

I still think I've got a couple of years left in me. As old as I am, I still enjoy it. I don't come down as much as I used to, but I'm still running the show. Most things don't happen without me knowing about them. I never have been a 'muso' and I've lost a lot of what music knowledge I did have, but I know there's still a great scene out there. There are so many different types of music now, dubstep, and whatever, so as well as the likes of Tiefschwarz representing the house side of things, we've also had leading dubstep DJs like Skream in more recent times. So, hopefully, that shows we still know what we're doing 27 years later.

Cook, meanwhile, has gone on to achieve so much since the late '80s, but it wasn't until 1996 that he became Fatboy Slim, with The Heavenly Social night at Turnmills - which Cook enthuses about elsewhere in this book - a catalyst for that particular guise.

In 1990, he enjoyed his first No 1 hit, as Beats International featuring Lindy Layton on vocals, with Dub Be Good To Me - a cover of Just Be Good To Me by The S.O.S Band. He also enjoyed more UK chart success in the early to mid-'90s as Freak Power and Pizzaman, before Fatboy Slim became his most successful and career-defining alter-ego.

As well as a whole host of chart-topping hits (The Rockafeller Skank, Gangster Trippin', Praise You and Right Here, Right Now reached Nos 6, 3, 1 and 2 respectively in the space of 12 months) as Fatboy Slim, he would also headline his now infamous beach party in Brighton in 2002, the second in his Big Beach Boutique series.

It was originally planned for 60,000 people, but attended by 250,000, and, despite police banning him from holding such events in Brighton for several years because of the ensuing chaos, Cook describes it as the highlight of his career.

Other memorable moments include receiving the Ivor Novello Award in 2007 for his outstanding contribution to British music.

For Cook, narrowing down his favourite memories is surely an unenviable task.

I've got so many fantastic memories of The Escape Club, because if you think about it, I started going down there when I was 18 when I moved down to Brighton. I first played The Escape, I think, on the opening night, but it was about a quarter of a century ago, so if I didn't play the opening night it was the second night. And the last time I played there was the 20th birthday, when it shut.

So I've spent a lot of my formative years there. I definitely took my first pill in there, leaning against one of the pillars. And the first time I ever had sex in a club toilet was down there. Yeah, I did a lot of growing up at that club… I was resident there on Saturday nights for three years, so a lot of great memories.

The best club I've ever been to is probably Manumission in its heyday at Privilege in Ibiza - in terms of a wall-to-wall club experience hitting you. The music, the lunacy, the spectacle and being semi-outdoors in a hot country, completely off your nut.

I think, for every DJ, definitely of my generation, The Paradise Garage in New York, is the one club we all wanted to go to. But it closed down just before DJs started to really travel. I played at the Sound Factory, which is kind of a close second, but I think everything you've read and heard about The Paradise Garage sounds like perfection in a nightclub.

My last track, if I was playing my last set? Well, as soon as I think of that, I've got We'll Meet Again or My Way in my head, but I suppose the ego in me would mean it would probably be one of mine, in which case it would be Praise You. Generally at festivals I finish with a version of Praise You, and, yeah, I guess that would be a fitting end to my career.

My favourite record to finish a night with down at The Escape, though, would have been Frankie Knuckles' Your Love… perfect for the end of a night, not a screamer, more of a hugger.

BRANDON BLOCK

Brandon Block has probably played more 'One Mores' than most...but on one occasion on the Space terrace in Ibiza, circa 1993, he was unable to carry out such obligatory duties because, as another epic afternoon drew to a close, he was so excited he had thrown all his records into the crowd.

And as Blocko volleyed back with his own cry of "no more, no more", he was only saved by a handful of charitable clubbers who returned him the odd piece of trampled-on vinyl. Anything was possible at Space in those days and party prince Block needed little encouragement in adding to the madness.

At the end of that set everyone was shouting "one more, one more" but I didn't have any records left. It wasn't until a couple of people gave me some back that I was able to put another tune on.

Space was very different then to how it is now, and even how it was at the end of the '90s. There were no teams of security guards in uniforms walking around the place. It was basically Chicko and Tony managing the venue, and Ariel running the door. Although their English wasn't fluent, we seldom had to use anything more than sign language to communicate. I think the reason they tolerated our tomfoolery was because we not only brought good business to the club, but also a sense of fun.

It was quite common, at the end of another epic day at Space, to find me laying on the bar as the shutters came down, wedged between the bar and the shutter, protesting at not being allowed to play another record. More often than not the security would relent and allow us to play another three or four records, behind closed shutters, so to speak.

Block's humble roots DJing for a tenner in his local pub in Wembley were a far cry from the glamour and downright hedonism of Ibiza. Soon there was always one more party to go to, nobody sober enough to say no more, while later his dramatic appearance at The Brits, when he went head to head with Rolling Stone Ronnie Wood, was a classic case of one too many.

I got into clubbing and DJing in the mid-'80s, and I started down at my local, playing soul and funk and disco. I couldn't mix as such, but everybody was so pissed on snakebites that it didn't matter. After the pub closed we'd go to clubs in the West End of London with special offers meaning drinks could be as cheap as 25p, including a place called Hombres. But there were also a lot of other clubs on the so-called trendier scene, like Crackers in Dean Street, Gullivers in Mayfair and also Cheeky Pete's.

Me and my mates had been collecting hip-hop, funk and jazz 12 inches for a few years. We spent fortunes and our record collections were building nicely. We'd started going to other clubs like the Goldmine in Canvey, Zero 6 in Southend, also to south London and over towards Ascot, to The Belvedere. DJs who were an influence back then were Robbie Vincent, Tony Blackburn in his day at The Lyceum, Norman Jay, Chris Hill and, of course, Froggy and Steve Walsh, God rest their souls.

To be honest, we were happy getting pissed on cheap drinks, then 1988 came along and lots of other things came along too. It was the birth of a new era and suddenly everything changed.

Consumed by acid house, Block quickly made a name for himself in and around the London area, and launched his own night on a Tuesday at Queen's in Slough at the start of 1989 with Dean Thatcher (later of The Aloof) and Charlie Chester. It was named Flying, because they were all "flying" on new party drug ecstasy. Chester would take the night forward and host a seminal weekly Saturday-nighter of the same name at The Soho Theatre Club in the early '90s, where Block would often guest.

However, he would branch out on his own more around that time with his weekly Sunday promotion, Thirst, at Haven Stables in Ealing, and then with another weekly Sunday session, FUBAR with Lisa Loud, at Nicky Holloway's Milk Bar, across the road from The Soho Theatre Club.

Sunday would prove to be a massive day for Block once more when he gambled on a six-week trip to Ibiza in 1991, and landed a residency on the Space terrace, courtesy of Alex P, who had guested the previous year for him at Haven Stables.

Space terrace would become the defining residency of his career and over the next five years would provide the backdrop to an era he regards as his most significant.

The first few years that myself and Alex were doing it, Space was without doubt the best club we'd ever played. It's been said by so many people that it was the best club that they went to. In the open air, the after-hours, the wide selection of people, the whole vibe. It used to go on all day and we could get away with playing anything we wanted, which we certainly always tried to do.

A few of the tracks we used to end up with at Space were La Passionara by the Blow Monkeys, a relatively slowish one and also a Balearic anthem, Soup Dragons' I'm Free and the Ashbrooke Allstars' Dubbin' Up The Pieces, a hip-hop come breakbeat track which sampled an old Steeleye Span track, and also included the "woo woo" bits from Sympathy For The Devil by The Rolling Stones. All of those would provide a fantastic end to the day at Space. Well, if you could ever play a last record at Space, that is, because everybody would be shouting and screaming "one more", and I always wanted to play another one.

Musically, Blocko and Peasy, as the Space terrace heroes were quickly dubbed, became known for dropping tunes that you just would not expect to hear during a standard house set, in true Balearic spirit, and just like Alfredo had been doing during the late '80s at Amnesia, when he wowed messrs Oakenfold, Holloway, Rampling and Walker.

I remember Block playing Phil Collins' In The Air Tonight one Sunday afternoon in 1993 on Space terrace to dramatic effect…with the whole crowd 'air-drumming' to the famous middle section. The trick, though, was not playing too many tracks like that back in Blighty, because few of them worked as well on a winter's night in the West End.

They were brilliant times. We used to play all sorts - Depeche Mode's Just Can't Get Enough (live mix), Chris Rea's Josephine, Dire Straits' Money For Nothing, New Order's Blue Monday, Tears For Fears' Shout, Magnificent Seven by The Clash and Sympathy For The Devil.

At that time Liverpool DJ Steve Proctor used to play some really way out there records, and was a bit of a pioneer where the Balearic influence was concerned.

Obviously the beginning of the Balearic thing has been attributed to Alfredo, and quite rightly so, but a few people had the balls to play non-house records at clubs in the UK after that. I remember him playing Lucy In The Sky With Diamonds by the Beatles at a Sunrise rave in the morning when everyone was tripping off their nuts, for instance. Seeing people being brave and doing that when house or acid house was fully expected was a big influence and something that I took with me when I started on Space terrace.

It was ideal for me as I've always liked all types of music, and it's strange, because before acid house came along, if you went to a decent nightclub or a so-called discotheque you expected to hear disco and funk and a fair amount of pop music, but suddenly house had taken over. The fact that you could drop Jesus On The Payroll by The Thrashing Doves or some of the Belgian stuff like Code 61's surreal Drop The Deal track, opened up so many things again. Suddenly those tracks weren't out of place and all came under the acid house umbrella, as such.

But Block was dropping more than just records. Like most of his generation, in the late '80s and early '90s ecstasy had been the revolutionary, yet largely recreational, drug of choice. And while he took his fair share of party pills over the years, like many, Block's poison of choice quickly became cocaine. He went on to develop a formidable habit, one which led his consultant psychiatrist to exclaim: *"I've never come across someone who was taking so much cocaine and was still able to stand up."*

Somehow Block managed to drag himself out of the mire, and reveals the full extent, snorts and all, in his fascinating biography, The Life & Lines Of Brandon Block.

Ibiza would continue to dominate each year well into the Millennium for an (eventually) drug-free Block, and throughout the '90s he was a privileged member of an elite band of British DJs who could play up to seven gigs a week, with the Midlands and the north of England almost becoming a second home.

The Midlands around 1992, '93, '94, with Progress in Derby and Wobble and Moneypenny's in Birmingham, Renaissance in Mansfield and Golden in Stoke literally were golden years. And then there were so many others that sprang up, many more further up north, like Up Yer Ronson, which was my little baby with Tony Hannan and Adam Wood and, of course, Cream in Liverpool and Gatecrasher in Sheffield. Later there were the likes of Godskitchen and Passion in Coalville. All these nights were massive, and many led to huge festivals like Creamfields, Homelands and the big 'Crasher and Godskitchen events. Suddenly the bookings were coming in thick and fast and it would stay that way right up to the Millennium, and for some of us several years after that.

In the early '90s Moneypenny's was at the top of the tree and its spin-off, Chuff Chuff, was legendary in itself. I remember doing some very silly things at Chuff Chuff, climbing up lighting rigs, and I've also ended up naked there several times - you know, the normal sorts of shenanigans. I always loved those and to be part of the Chuff Chuff parties, well, they were just fantastic. Like Space terrace in the early days, they were on a Sunday and because of that they were an event that loads of DJs headed to, even if they weren't on the line-up.

Tracks that sum up that era for me, and it's hard to remember as such, were always happy tracks and you could always get away with an early '90s classic throughout the '90s. Tunes like Fog's Been A Long Time; Victor Simonelli's Feel So Right as Solution and the various versions of George Morel's superb Grooves track. They were always big, big tracks and have been for many years, while the longevity of many tracks around that time was very short.

When Kelvin Andrews was resident at Golden, around 1994, '95, and went under the remix guise of Sure Is Pure, the sound he had was just perfect for that era. He remixed these huge records which just became massive hits again - Sister Sledge's Thinking Of You; Doobie Brothers' Long Train Running and South Street Players' Who Keeps Changing Your Mind, plus various bootleg mixes of Alison Limerick.

As a headline guest, Block would rarely play the last record at any one night, but the crowd would always anticipate the conclusion of a guest's set, intrigued by what track they would finish with.

As guest DJs we would usually have an hour and a half set and wouldn't always play at the end. You would, more often than not, be doing the middle bit at a club that finished around 3am or 4am, like Moneypenny's, and then go off to another club somewhere which shut around 6 or 7am and do a middle to late set there, so not the last one at that place either.

I would never play the last set at Moneypenny's, for instance, because the resident would do the last bit. But Up Yer Ronson in Leeds was my residency, where I often ended up, and we had a couple of tracks we toyed about with each week. These days, the erection section hasn't happened for a long time. I always thought that was a shame, because at the end of the day it was for blagging birds, wasn't it?

By the '90s the whole Move Closer/Rock Me Tonight era had gone, but at Up Yer Ronson, we used to play this record, which was quite slow, and it was on Dave Dorrell's label, called I Believe by Nikki Nicole. It had a mix on there, which was just perfect. It was ecstatic, even, and it had every sound on there that you needed for that "oh I love you" thing at the end of the night. And we played that every week for ages, and then moved on to another slow, breaks type record, Scoobs In Columbia by Plaid, and it was very apt for what we were all up to at the time. It was a bootleg I used to play, and it was a record that Sasha loved when we used to play up there together. So those were two of the records that stick in my mind, for sure.

And when it comes to 'One Mores', for Block, they don't come much bigger than seminal hip-hop anthem Rapper's Delight by The Sugarhill Gang, a track which was, more often than not, the last record each week at his own beloved FUBAR night at The Milk Bar in the early '90s.

Lisa Loud remembers:-

FUBAR was all Brandon's idea, a brilliant idea, and famously standing for 'fucked up beyond all recognition', the best name in the world for a club, fantastic. Amazingly, among our little group we had basically decided that over the last few years, after being out on a

*(clockwise) * With Alex P at Aqualandia water park party, 1994*
* Blocko's very own Viz comic strip * At home in Ruislip
* Causing havoc at The Brits, 2000 * With Claire Manumission
* Armed and not very dangerous at Space Terrace, Ibiza

ravey davey gravy

HE'S LIKE BRANDON BLOCK ON ACID...

ON ACID!

Monday at Spectrum, Tuesday at Loud Noise, Wednesday at Future, Fridays and Saturdays playing out wherever and Sunday daytime at Full Circle, that we still needed to do a Sunday evening party. Bonkers.

I was working daytime at a major record company too, and you couldn't really get more high profile than that back then. All the record executives and people from the media would be trying to get in, journalists from ID, MixMag, DJ Mag, MixMag Update, the lot. There would be 500 people queuing down the road, unable to get in to a club that held 200, loads of people who wanted to go in the Astoria, also queuing for FUBAR by mistake because our queue was so big and, with everything going on, there were police every where. Total carnage, all night, every Sunday.

Block remembers:-

Wherever I had played out that weekend I'd make sure I'd get back to London by Sunday night for FUBAR... it ended at midnight, but that was just the start for us, and we'd keep partying until at least Tuesday and sometimes Wednesday, by which time the weekend was almost about to start again.

We used to play some wicked records down at FUBAR, some great funk, tunes like Tina Marie's I Need Your Loving, Fat Larry's Band's Act Like You Know, Space Base by Slick and Francine McGee's Delirium... loads of stuff we couldn't play in the house clubs at the weekend, loads of 'One Mores', and, of course, our sing-a-long anthem, the 14-minute mix of Rapper's Delight.

Sometimes when FUBAR had finished we'd go to Fish on Oxford Street, with our records, and try and see if they'd let us play some more tunes. I'd be saying "c'mon, let's get round there and play Rapper's Delight again, do it from the start, the whole way through". Silly arse.

And "silly arse" pretty much sums up Block and his unscheduled appearance on stage at The Brits in 2000.

This was the latest instalment of Brits-gate, which had previously seen Samantha Fox and Mick Fleetwood 'die' on stage, Jarvis Cocker moon at Michael Jackson and Chumbawumba drench MP John Prescott. It was an interesting cast already, but now Block, Ronnie

Wood, Big Brother presenter Davina McCall and American movie star Thora Birch were entering stage left or, in Brandon's case, stage front!

No stranger to awards ceremonies after winning various other dubious clubbing awards, Block's association with The Brits started the year before when he had secured the coveted after-party DJ gig. In 2000 he was booked to be back behind the decks there once more, and was up for an award as well, in the Best Dance Act category for his No 3 hit You Should Be Dancing, a remake of the Bee Gees anthem.

The full details of how events at The Brits unfolded play out in The Life & Lines Of Brandon Block, as a blottoed Blocko attempted to accept the award for Best Film Soundtrack, called Ronnie Wood "an old bastard" in front of millions of TV viewers, and was then escorted off stage by security guards wearing the Rolling Stone legend's drink for good measure.

Block's DJ cheque for the night was ripped up in front of him, as he was relieved of his DJing duties and sent on his merry way, slap bang on to the front of the morning's tabloids and with Richard & Judy appealing for his whereabouts on TV later that evening. It was, it has to be said, classic Brandon Block.

Norman Cook remembers:-

I remember Brandon had a particularly glazed expression on his face that night, but we hadn't been listening to what was happening on stage any more than he hadn't. In fact, I thought he'd won the award too. I'll never forget his face on his way up to the stage. And poor sod, he really didn't mean to cause anyone any harm. I felt quite sorry for him that night, but I guess he did earn a certain notoriety from it.

His then agent Karen Dunn confirms:-

When the Brits thing happened the phone just didn't stop...we got loads of work off the back of that...and it was typical naughty Brandon...you just couldn't pay for that kind of publicity.

Block has thrived on publicity ever since he took the British club scene by storm in the early '90s. Always a firm favourite with the punters for his hands-in-the-air, total interaction style, this is the DJ who single-handedly invented the 'Caner Of Year' category, romping home in the Caner stakes at Muzik Magazine's inaugural SAS Awards

1996. The dubious award was the result of a punishing decade of partying, in which he wore his heart on his sleeve wherever he played.

In the mid-'90s, a year of so before an inevitable stint of rehab saved his life, rumours had actually circulated that Block had died of a cocaine overdose. MixMag even arranged to interview him as he left his west London clinic and ran a four page feature on his plight.

Over the next four years, as the Millennium edged ever closer, Block's star continued to rise, and when he teamed with M & S production duo Ricky Morrison and Fran Sidoli in late 1998 to record that cover of the The Bee Gees track You Should Be, as Blockster, the trio signed a lucrative album deal with Ministry Of Sound. A top three national chart place followed, as did an appearance on Top Of The Pops.

In the mid-to-late '90s, Block's Space terrace residency had given way to the sheer demand of British promoters setting up shop in Ibiza, so summer residencies on the island for Clockwork Orange, Godskitchen and Up Yer Ronson dominated the later half of that decade, and now clean, at least from drugs, his DJ star was still rising.

When MixMag celebrated their 200th issue in September 1999 an inside front cover pull out was a bizarre 'photoshopped' version of an official Royal Family-style wedding photo, which had Block as the King and Alex P as the Queen. Other notable inclusions were Judge Jules as the Queen Mum and Keith Flint, the Prodigy frontman, as a pageboy.

Like many DJs of his standing then, Millennium Eve was hit and miss for Block.

I was initially booked to play at three events….Millennium Village at Three Mills Studios in Bow, east London, which was a complete disaster; Godskitchen in Birmingham which was reduced to just residents in the run-up and Golden at Manchester Academy, which I was penciled in for, but that never happened either.

At one point in 1999 I was offered an unbelievable £50,000 to play exclusively at the Godskitchen gig or £20,000 for a non-exclusive set. I opted for the non-exclusive one, which meant I could do Millennium Village and Golden, and meant that I would earn more than £50k in total. It also meant that I was spreading my options across three parties, so if there were any problems I stood a better chance of getting paid.

Once the big events were announced after the summer of that year, and it was confirmed that most of them would be charging £100, people had quickly started talking about whether the whole thing would be an anti-climax, so I always tried to remember that when negotiating.

I accepted a decent cancellation fee from Godskitchen a couple of weeks before the event, as it was fast becoming clear that the whole thing was going tits up! Generally, the promoters thought they would have two or three thousand people paying £100 each, and so if that netted them two or three hundred thousand pounds they could afford to give four of us DJs £20,000 each, and still have loads left.

At the time I got offered the £50k I thought this was going to be the big one, the big pay day, and that I could pay my mortgage off with that. But about a month before we knew it wasn't going to be as amazing as everyone thought because all the hype had been ruined by the ticket prices. I guess a number of things were responsible. Everyone was trying to earn a quick buck, from the people hiring out all the equipment, staging and kit to the promoters to the security. But I don't think most of the DJs ever expected to earn as much as we were being offered. We were on good money anyway, but when we were offered it, we were hardly going to say no, and at least we had the cancellation fee clauses in our contracts.

You couldn't blame the punters at all. I still had enough of a punter in me to appreciate what was going on wasn't right. They were saying "why should we pay £100 to listen to the same old DJs in the same old club that we usually pay fifteen or twenty quid to see". And they were right.

Golden head honcho Jon Hill can shed some light on how he avoided paying Block thousands of pounds on Millennium Eve.

Brandon wasn't the most reliable of DJs, but let's just say when he did turn up, he never let me down. I actually put on two parties on Millennium Eve, one at the Manchester Academy, which broke even, and one at The Void in our hometown of Stoke, which ended up just residents, and which I made five grand on. Both parties were basically just residents in the end, and the odd guest. I did bid for Brandon at one point, but like all the DJs for Millennium it was silly money, and I'm glad I got outbid, thank God I did get outbid. In the end we saw sense and basically charged what we did every other New Year's Eve. I think I was one of the few people who did make any money that year.

I always thought Brandon was unique in that he was probably the only DJ from the Balearic network in London, who had a foot in both camps and then crossed over to the big-room bookings. I bet he made more money than all of the so-called cooler DJs who started out with him at Flying or wherever.

Karen Dunn adds:-

The Millennium was a big disaster for a lot of people. Everyone got greedy and the bottom really fell out of the market. Where a lot of the top guys used to earn a couple of thousand pounds a gig their fees now went down to a grand and under. Brandon was one of the DJs who stayed at the higher level for a while longer yet and is still working to this day, and three or four times a week as well, when many of the other DJs have thrown in the towel. That's because of Brandon's personality and notoriety and because he interacts with the crowd.

And Brandon had the perfect antidote to any Millennium blues – a trip on a Lear jet to Ibiza on the morning of New Year's Day for a Manumission party later that day on his beloved Space terrace with Alex P and Judge Jules.

Covered by MixMag, the editorial exclaimed: *"Outside the Kings Of The Terrace are warming up. There's no doubt that the Carl Coxes and Basement Jaxxes of this world rock the Space terrace, but no one does it with the spirit of Blocko and Peasey. Brandon's brought his "box of old chestnuts" and Alex, goes one step further, putting on Wham's Club Tropicana. Jules joins the duo for a one-in-three session, but gets booted off."*

Block adds:-

After the disaster that was…we had the perfect tonic with the New Year's Day trip to Space. We had to get to Luton Airport for 7am and although I was a bit drunk, I was clean and looking forward to the new Millennium. Space was packed and they didn't seem to have charged over the odds or anything like that. It was expensive enough out there anyway, of course. It was brilliant to be back at our spiritual home and causing havoc on the terrace once more.

Block continued to kick on into the new Millennium, continuing to DJ all over the UK and the world, and also individually building on the success of his celebrated Kiss FM show with Alex P and MTV slots like the aptly-titled Off Yer Med, with his own 'binge-drinking' TV series Brandon Block's Brits, followed by a handful of reality TV appearance including Extreme Celebrity Detox, Celebrity Scissorhands and Trust Me I'm A Holiday Rep. His celebrity, particularly fuelled by that appearance at the Brits, also saw him guest on mainstream TV quiz shows like Fifteen To One and Never Mind The Buzzcocks. He had even managed to win further Caner awards, despite being clean from cocaine since 1996!

That overall notoriety means his bookings diary is still healthy to this day. After an eleven year absence he was booked to play the closing party at Space in Ibiza in 2011.

Given what we know, then, Block's favourite club is probably either the next one he's going to or the last one left open. Once again an unenviable question to answer, when you have literally performed at hundreds, but, for him, not so difficult when you have been fortunate enough to be resident at a certain club in Ibiza for the best part of a decade, and a truly glorious decade at that.

The best club I've ever been to? No disrespect to any others, but it has to be Space terrace. Those first few years, well I guess they made me as well. Of course, I had FUBAR, my own night, but you can't compare the Milk Bar with Space terrace. One was an open-air heaven in Ibiza, the other one was basement heaven in Soho, London. There have been so many clubs that I have had such great nights in, but I can say, unequivocally, Space is the best club I've played. Other highlights include Up Yer Ronson, the Hacienda, Back To Basics, Cream, The Honey Club, The Zap Club, The Hippo Club in Cardiff, in its time, and also parties on Hastings Pier. In fact, every area of the UK had a great club at one time and I'm just so happy to have had the chance to play them all. We had a great era of music, we really did.

Block chooses from two eras at either end of the dance music spectrum when quizzed about clubs or events he wishes he had gone to, while he digs out two gems from his jazz funk and soul crates when given that difficult task of choosing the last record at his hypothetical last ever gig.

If I was old enough at the time, I would have loved to have gone to Studio 54 in New York, for the impact it had on disco in general. In modern day times I would have liked to have been at Norman Cook's infamous beach festival in Brighton. I've been to every festival, all over the world, but the fact that this was a one-man show, to 250,000 people, and that I love the man and his music, well, that would have been epic and I'm gutted I missed that huge one.

If tonight I was going to play my last gig ever then, well, I'd have to pick two 'One More' tracks, because I'd like to have the option. The first one would be Glow Of Love by Change, featuring Luther Vandross, just because it says everything, and is one of my favourite tracks ever. The other, another crooner, or a funkmaster, would be George Benson's Love Ballard. Both those tracks hold so many memories for me, both sound so fantastic and they are both so apt for last records.

TRIP & SIN

Like a lot of great clubs, Nicky Holloway's seminal Saturday-nighter Trip (within months renamed Sin) was an accident waiting to happen.

Holloway had stumbled across The Astoria Theatre in Shaftesbury Avenue after the venue he had booked for a sell-out 700-capacity party fell through at the last minute. Despite his doubts he would fill a legendary West End venue at least twice that size, the Special Branch promoter took a huge gamble that quickly paid off.

But back then, in the late '80s, Holloway typified all that was wonderfully optimistic about club culture. Soon enough he was stumbling out of The Astoria every Sunday morning with thousands of pounds in his pockets.

I realised Trip was going to be a groundbreaking club on the first night. My main worry was whether we would get 700 people to fill the ground floor of The Astoria, because, if we did, that would cover all my exes, and the place would look all right. We weren't even planning to open the top bit, but on the first night we had 2,000 people there, queues round the block and for the next two years you just couldn't fail with it.

After that first night we were asked to go weekly with Trip, but initially we could only do a 12-week run because The Astoria had this play booked, The Black Heroes In The Hall Of Fame. The production was meant to last for six months, but folded after six weeks, and then we were asked to go back. I changed the name to Sin, because during that summer period there was so much negative stuff in the national papers about ecstasy and acid house that I thought we were going to get into trouble. So we carried on as Sin, and carried on from where we left off, no problem… and we were there every Saturday for another couple of years.

I guess I knew at the start we were going to be part of something that would define our generation, just like anyone who went to Woodstock, or who saw the Stones in Hyde Park, knew. In the late '80s we all knew that this was going to be our movement, we all knew then that this was our time. It was great for me, because I wasn't just the resident DJ, and most nights it was just me and Pete Tong playing, but I was also promoting the place so I was walking out each night with a big pot of cash. I was going to warehouse parties with five grand in cash, off my nut. I wouldn't do it now, but then the chance would be a fine thing!

The One More film crew took Holloway back to his old stomping ground in London's legendary Soho, which was not only home to The Astoria, but also two other sites that further helped shape his career.

And he explained:-

This building site in the West End of London, for more than 10 years, was the site of three iconic clubs. Over there was The Astoria Theatre, where I ran Trip and Sin, from 1988 to 1990, and a little basement over there was where The Milk Bar stood, which I had from 1990 to 1993. Right here is where my club Velvet Underground was, from 1993 to 1998. It's all been knocked down to a pile of rubble now, but that's progress.

And that progress Holloway sarcastically refers to is the massive Crossrail project, which will link the east and west of London like never before. Twenty years earlier it was Holloway and co who were linking and uniting all parts of London.

But even before that, throughout the mid-'80s, Holloway had made his name as part of the infamous Special Branch club at London Bridge, where for four years, the so-called 'trendy' London set would converge for nights of hip-hop, rare groove, soul and jazz, and even a hint of early house music.

The likes of Pete Tong and Gilles Peterson plied their early DJ trades at Special Branch and Holloway went on to promote a series of one-off events called Do At The…at unusual venues, like The Natural History Museum, Lords Cricket Ground, Jubilee Gardens, and most famously, London Zoo, while he also ventured outside of the capital with Thorpe Park, Chislehurst Caves and, famously, Rockley Sands Caravan Park in Dorset all the settings for seminal events.

And it was with this following that early trips to Ibiza were arranged, in 1985, '86 and most notably in 1987.

I'd been doing these Do At The Zoo parties for a few years. I had done about 17 in total, and then we started the Trip club at The Astoria in the last week of May, 1988. The Astoria was only supposed to be for one night, but the management there liked the bar takings and the crowd and said come and do it every week and we started like that. Pure luck really. The Trip never had a mission statement as such, but on the back of T-shirts we had made it said "turn on, tune in and drop out" so I suppose if we had one, that was it.

We were just a load of kids having fun. It wasn't dreamt up by a load of marketing people at a record label so there was no ethos, as such. It wasn't like we thought we were going to change the face of clubbing, it was just a load of people who loved what they were doing, and it just fell together. It wasn't planned.

Holloway is convinced the success of Trip and then Sin, was built on the diverse music policy that was hard to avoid during the two-year period in which those nights thrived - the years before the 'genre' itself really became genre-defining.

The thing about Trip and Sin which was different then, was that there wasn't one flat line. In more recent times DJs have played the same music all night, whether it be minimal, tech-house, garage or whatever. Back in 1988 and '89 when Trip and Sin was thriving we were playing NWA and Soul II Soul alongside acid house, plus some funk and then some good garage and vocal house too. It was like a little journey that would go up and back down again three or four times a night so, looking back, I guess it was quite adventurous. They called it Balearic because we were playing Carly Simon's Why and Donna Summer's State Of Independence, but half an hour later we were playing banging acid house in the same room. It worked then and it's a shame more people don't do that now.

And if the music policy was different back in the late-'80s, then so was the way you promoted the clubs.

What we were doing when we started Trip, well, you wouldn't be able to get away with it now. Westminster Council was heavy anyway then, but now it fines the venue as well. For Sin, I got some stickers made to fit perfectly on the side of parking meters, and we went around

71

and put one on every meter in Soho. It just said "Sin", the venue's address and "Saturday nights". If you did that now you would get nicked and fined heavily for every one.

When we had the Milk Bar I actually hired a milk float, dressed up as a milkman and went round to every single shop in Soho, delivering them a pint of milk and dropping off flyers at the same time. We tried loads of different things like that, you know, to get people talking.

Eddie Gordon, the former club boss, promoter, journalist, DJ agent, Radio 1 producer and, these days, a Los Angeles-based Grammys-panelist, goes way back with Holloway.

In the mid-'80s Nicky ruled London with Special Branch and my club, The Slammer, had Kent locked down. The magic recipe? Take over an unpopular venue, preferably with two rooms to dance in. Put in big, loud soundsystems, deck out the room with cool banners and book the best young DJs to play in each room - so Paul Oakenfold, Norman Jay, Gilles Peterson, Mark Moore, Tim Westwood, CJ Macintosh, Dave Dorrell and Jay Strongman.

The Slammer in Kent would book Oakey, Tong, Holloway, Peterson and Jay to all play on the same night for £500 in total.

Nicky's Special Branch, meanwhile, was resident at The Royal Oak in Tooley Street, London, SE1, and Nicky would put on big events anywhere else he could create a wow factor, including The Astoria in London's West End, until he found a home a stone's throw away at The Milk Bar. Both Nicky and I even became young licensees for our clubs. Whatever it took!

Mark Moore was lucky enough to witness the first night at Trip and to also be one of the few guests used by Holloway.

Nicky told me he was going to open a new club at The Astoria, and it was called Trip. At this stage of the game it was really early days, before acid house took over, before all the raves started happening. You had clubs like Shoom, The Phuture and Spectrum and they were the main clubs doing the acid house thing in London, and suddenly Nicky Holloway wanted to take it to this huge club in the West End on a Saturday night, and it was like, 'hang on a minute', but he did it, and the first one was completely roadblocked.

I went there that first night and I thought, 'this is it, this whole scene is going to go overground now'. I think that really was the turning point. I remember everyone going mental in there, and when it closed, everyone coming out, dancing in the street, in the fountains at Trafalgar Square. The police put on their sirens, but everyone was dancing around the police cars, shouting 'acieeed, acieeed'. It was simply amazing.

I got to play at The Trip and it was an acid house set, everything from Marshall Jefferson's Phuture - Acid Tracks, Joe Smooth's Promised Land to Fast Eddie's Acid Thunder, and then I'd also play some of the poppy house mixes, Natalie Cole even...Strings Of Life, of course, and Frankie Knuckles' Your Love, so you could slow things down a bit, and before they slapped Candi Staton's vocal over it.

I remember I was at Trip once and Paul Oakenfold dropped the Fluffy Bagel Mix of my S'Express track Super Fly Guy. And it put me in a position, thinking, "should I stop dancing now?", but I thought "what the hell', and then loads of people came and had a pop at me for dancing to my own record. Typical!

Trip was mental, all these people on podiums, loads of bodybuilders, mad lights, and football hooligans in one corner with their sworn enemies, saying how much they loved each other. It was utter madness, kind of carnival meets a Fellini movie.

And while few, if any, were using analogies with cult Italian film director Federico Fellini at this point, as Trip and Sin evolved, London's new breed of clubbers were talking. The word was definitely out and the sheer demand was still outweighing the supply of the various acid house-inspired nights that were popping up everywhere. And '88/'89 London was a very different London to the one the '90s would witness, let alone the noughties.

Holloway continues:-

In London at that time there weren't all these China Whites-type places or style bars that you see in the press now, where all the footballers go. There was nothing like that. Rikki Tiks opened in Greek Street later in 1993 at the same time as Velvet Underground did in

Charing Cross Road, but when the Trip started in 1988 there were only a few bars in the area - The Soho Brasserie in Old Compton Street, long before it became Old 'Campton' Street, and then the Spice Of Life was a good pub people went to as well, plus Mitchel O'Briens and Fred's. But other than that there wasn't a pub, bar or club on every corner like there is now.

In those early days me, Paul Oakenfold and Danny Rampling had come back from Ibiza in 1987 with this 'thing'. So Danny started doing the Shoom for 400 people, Paul started doing Spectrum on a Monday night, which started with 300 the first week, 500 the second week, 800 the third week, then thousands. Soon they were getting 1,500 people on a Monday night at Spectrum, which was amazing, but then I went and started the first big Saturday night with Trip, so I suppose Spectrum was our nearest rival, but it was on a Monday, so it wasn't really a rival.

It was a strange transitional period. There was Discoteque downstairs at Busbys, which was like a pre-Carwash Carwash, playing disco, and the Raw club going on with Ben and Andy and Dave Dorrell. That was still all Dr Martens and flying jackets and rare groove and funk and hip-hop. House came along, crept under the radar between 1986 and '87 and just went mega. Suddenly it was off the radar.

The other club that I admired, as well as Spectrum, was Delirium at Heaven, on a Thursday night, before Spectrum came along. That was great and like a little breeding ground for what would happen later.

So the various scenes, bars and clubs in and around Soho and the West End were breeding clubbers that the acid house scene needed to prosper, but various DJs and producers were also plugging away at their craft, waiting for their chance to impress clubbers and record buyers alike, who were increasingly becoming the same people.

In 1988, we were the first to have Todd Terry, Kevin Saunderson and Derrick May play in the UK. Nobody had heard of them. They did become big mega stars, but back then nobody knew them. I remember

*(clockwise) * Mark Moore 'dancing to his own track' at The Trip*
* Nicky Holloway (right) with his fellow Trip resident Pete Tong
* Holloway being interviewed for the One More documentary
* Trademark bandanas, dungarees and waistcoats at The Trip

MEMBERSHIP

Pete Tong had the FFRR label at London Records and he rang me up one week and asked if this American guy who was doing a remix for him could play on the Saturday night, and I said "fine". At the end of his set I gave him £100 and he was more than happy with it. His name? David Morales. These guys went on to become huge players in the scene, earning thousands of pounds, and you look back and laugh at those moments now.

My favourite DJs? Well, I've always liked Alfredo, but he's one of these DJs that could either be really, really good or really, really bad. If he was happy, then you would get a good night out of him, so he was a bit hit and miss. But when he was good, he was great. And there's a lot of respect there between me, Paul and Danny for Alfredo because he was the DJ who changed our lives when we heard him in Ibiza in that summer of 1987. Some people don't take him as seriously as they should, because at the end of day we basically nicked what he was doing and did it better.

I remember spending the night at one Sin event, in 1989, perched up the top at The Astoria, at the back, with a group of mates, looking down, literally in amazement, at the sheer size and madness of the whole thing, with the sound of Debbie Malone's rave anthem Rescue Me ringing in my ears for the rest of the week. Unsurprisingly, there are a mixed-bag of records that typify the Trip and Sin sound for Holloway, and they are well-remembered, given the circumstances.

I've got so many favourite memories of Trip. It's worth noting that this was 2,000 people off their heads on Es every night, but this was before the police even knew what Es were. You've got to remember we used to finish at 3am and there was a whole generation of people who were doing Es for the first time and who didn't want the party to end. So everybody would be dancing in the streets, dancing to car stereos, the roads would be blocked off, and the police were scratching their heads. They didn't know what to do because this was the late '80s and they were used to dealing with loads of football hooligans fighting, not seeing people dancing in the streets, hugging each other - complete strangers saying they loved each other - large group hugs, all that stuff.

So many records summed up Trip, stuff like Royal House, Can You Feel It; A Day In The Life, Black Riot, early Todd Terry stuff, but also tracks like Sympathy For The Devil by Rolling Stones, which was huge at the end of the night. I mean, how did that come about? The Balearic influence, I guess. Things like Tyree Cooper, Acid Over; Lil Louis, French Kiss; Ce Ce Rogers, Someday, all those tracks that are now known as club classics were being played as new import records. Patti Day, Right Before My Eyes; Karriah, Let Me Love You For The Night, all brand new records at the time.

I honestly can't remember for the life of me what the last record at Trip was, but I can remember that nobody would leave, so much so that I came up with this cock and bull story that we'd hired a van and put a sound system in it and we were having a party in the car park of the YMCA building opposite.

However, I went out and carried on partying somewhere else. Over the years, I have had muppets come up to me, though, and say "remember the time we all went over the road to the car park and partied all night?". It didn't happen, but it got written about. It was in Time Out, it's been in about three books, but it didn't happen.

But what did happen was that Holloway went on to be one of London's club kings for the best part of the next decade, opening The Milk Bar in 1990, and then Velvet Underground in 1993, both with business partner Leon Lenik, and DJing all over the world in the process. The Milk Bar would go on to become particularly iconic, with the juxtaposition of swapping the huge capacity of The Astoria with a couple of hundred at The Milk Bar just down the way, an inadvertent attempt to make the scene more exclusive again. Flying Records would occupy the equally compact Soho Theatre Club opposite, as Soho and the West End became a one-stop shop for house music for the next few years.

In 1990 we took house back underground with the opening of the Milk Bar. At one stage the club's residents list read like a who's who of 20th century dance music. Darren Emerson and Paul Harris held court on Mondays with Recession Session, Danny Rampling's Pure Sexy took over Wednesdays, Paul Oakenfold and myself ruled Fridays, Pete Tong and Dave Dorrell looked after Saturdays with the weekend rounded off by Lisa Loud and Brandon Block's FUBAR on Sunday nights. Even Jamiroquai and the Brand New Heavies played some of their first live gigs there.

After launching Shoom in a south London gym, Rampling was delighted to have a West End base for new club night ideas.

I'd gone through different stages, firstly with Shoom and the whole acid house thing, and then moved to The Milk Bar, and did Pure Sexy midweek, which was about dressing up again after the post-rave scene, and then it was Glam on a Friday, also at The Milk Bar.

Glam was a gay-mixed night, which I promoted with my then wife Jenny, and it was simply about being glam, It was more Jenny's creation and it worked well. We'd gone off to Ibiza for six weeks and we heard Smokin' Jo out there and made her our resident. We put Jon (Pleased Wimmin) in as resident too, which was totally appropriate. He was such a fun character to be around, and all the Pleased Wimmin were perfect for Glam. Alfredo from Amnesia also came over and played quite often.

There was never a bad night in The Milk Bar at that time, and there was a lot of cross-pollination between the various nights there. We would all go and support each other. I have very happy memories of Glam, a lot of social barriers were broken down around that time with the energy of the gay and straight scene mixed together. It was all about having a good time, forgetting about your problems and having as much fun as you possibly could have, and boy did we. The Milk Bar really was a great club, and I don't think I really appreciated how good it was at the time, like a lot of things, I guess.

Alongside the The Milk Bar, which also became Mars for a short period, in the early '90s, Holloway ran twice-yearly Kaos Weekenders at Pontins Holiday Camp in Camber Sands, a take on the popular weekender format championed by the Caister Weekender/Soul Mafia DJs. And his life would continue to be chaotic for the rest of the decade, with his Dance Europe trip to Euro Disney in France particularly notorious.

In 1993 Holloway moved a few hundred yards down Charing Cross Road to open the Velvet Underground, with a certain Chris Good rising through the ranks of warm-up to resident DJ and promotions to general manager over the next four years.

Jon (Pleased Wimmin), so popular at The Milk Bar, was asked if he and his drag act would host a Wednesday session there. With Jon now on the UK guest DJ circuit, travelling up and down the motorway all weekend, it was a chance for a weekly meet up with friends back in London.

At the weekend I'd be doing three gigs on a Friday and three on a Saturday, so when Nicky rang up and asked us to do a Wednesday at the Velvet, we were delighted. At the start, we weren't bothered if people came, as long as we had a good time and saw our friends, but it lasted every week for five years. It only held 200 people, but we always turned another 100 people away each week.

With Pleased, it was the two guys who I'd always done drag with, and so it was always a bit cheeky. We used to stand outside the club at the start of the night, stand on the door and vet people. I remember there was always a pile of bin bags outside one of the shops nearby, and we would take it in turns to run and jump on top of the bin bags. Our friend Peter was lying in the bin bags one night, and this police cortege drove by, with The Queen and Prince Philip staring out of the window of their official car at Peter in some suspenders and some old drag outfit, lying in a big pile of rubbish.

Holloway's reign as a club boss in the West End came to an end in 1997 when he parted company with Velvet Underground, but he continued to party to excessive effect.

I can remember him jumping out of a helicopter with a bevy of 'dolly birds' as I entered a Chuff Chuff party somewhere in the middle of nowhere in the mid-'90s. It was an impressive entrance, to say the least.

Less flamboyant, but certainly more necessary, was his admission in the late '90s to a well-known clinic for a much needed stint of rehab. Holloway revealed in an interview with Muzik Magazine that he had spent around £50,000 on cocaine. A handful of his superstar DJ peers from the early days of acid house are said to have helped fund his expensive treatment.

By then Holloway had DJd in more than 30 different countries, and also for the likes of Madonna, Giorgio Armani and Jean Paul Gaultier. But it's still those pioneering days with Trip and Sin that he can look back at with most innocence and raw affection.

I've lost count of how many times people have come up to me over the years and said, 'we did our first pill in your club', and I think that is probably my legacy - so arrest me, take me away, I am Mr Evil Acid.

These days I've got a little studio, I'm making music, and I'm still DJing more weekends than not, which I'm grateful for. I put on parties called Desert Island Disco, which are for people aged between 35 and 45, who still want to go out, when they can get a baby sitter, and want to party with us. I wouldn't say it's really retro, because they all still think they're cool.

DAVE PEARCE

With his Fresh Start To The Week and Funk Fantasy shows on Radio London in the early to mid-'80s, Dave Pearce was one of the true pioneers of hip-hop and house music in the UK.

He went on to transcend the whole One More era, embracing trance along the way, and later bringing dance anthems to millions via his long-running Sunday night show on BBC Radio 1.

More recently he was handed a tribute series on Radio 2. And it's possibly that decision by bigwigs at 'the Beeb' - to allow Pearce to reminisce about the scene on a station renowned for middle-of-the-road music and staid presenters - that bookends our own fascinating documentary, because dance music surely cannot get much more overground than the likes of Marshall Jefferson's House Music Anthem being played on Radio 2! All a far cry from Pearce's early DJ career, which saw him plying his trade in funk, disco and hip-hop clubs, long before acid house came along.

House music was a really interesting challenge for me, because my whole roots were in black music, not just in hip-hop, but also in funk and soul which is where I started, where a lot of DJs then had started - particularly in jazz funk and disco.

Then when hip-hop first started in America I got really involved in bringing that to the UK. When house music came in it was so raw it just reminded me of all those early hip-hop tracks, and so, as bizarre as it may seem today, you would play hip-hop and early house music in the same set. There wasn't this notion that you could only play one style of music. If it was a good record, you played it.

A lot of those early hip-hop records were quite dancefloor-orientated. Spoony Gee's The Godfather and JVC Force's Strong Island, and those kinds of tracks worked really well with the early Chicago stuff. It was the rawness that I liked.

There was a period then, when hip-hop started getting signed to major labels, and my favourite artists who were on Cold Chillin', or whatever, went in to 24-track studios and suddenly lost that sound.

Whereas house music still had the rawness, so I guess it must have been something to do with the sonics for me.

Pearce presented his first radio show on pioneering pirate station Radio Jackie in the late '70s when he was just 14. He had grown up in Walton-on-Thames close to the station's south west London/Surrey base and pestered a sixth former who had his own show to introduce him to station bosses.

The radio authorities came after Radio Jackie quite a lot, so we used to have three or four different transmission sites, and would rotate where the broadcasts came from to avoid being shut down.

The weird thing about Radio Jackie was that all the broadcasts were from fields. The shows were recorded on cassette and everything was run off car batteries.

To show that you could be trusted you had to prove yourself on transmission duty, which basically meant guarding the transmitter. There would be people hidden in bushes with walkie talkies and whistles, and if the police came they had to unclip the car battery and run away with the transmitter before it could be confiscated.

The younger ones among us were the quicker runners, so I did a fair amount of lying in ditches, waiting.

On his own show, Pearce would play disco and funk and, as the '80s kicked in, championed Brit-funk bands like Light Of The World, Freeez and other acts on the influential Beggar's Banquet label. He got an interesting break in 1980 when, still just 17, he answered an advert in the London Evening Standard "looking for DJs to play abroad".

I turned up for the interview, got the gig, and ended up playing six nights a week at a club called Studio 29 in Bombay. It was state-of-the-art and had been based on Studio 54. It had a jetset clientelle, various Bollywood stars and loads of millionaires. The club even had records flown in each week from New York. I gained great experience at Studio 29, DJing in the same venue every single night. Up until then, I'd just played at the odd party held to raise funds for Radio Jackie and the usual mobile DJ gigs at weddings.

Pearce returned to south west London after a 'season' in Bombay and secured a job as a buyer at his local record shop. He also bagged a role on BBC Radio London as an assistant on a student radio show, before working his way up to answering phones on the Robbie Vincent Soul Show.

Robbie, and Greg Edwards who was on Capital FM, were THE main men in London for dance music on legal radio, and working with Robbie was my first experience of how a professional radio show was made. I got to meet all the great guests he had passing through as well, people like George Clinton and all the other wonderful acts he had on.

I did the odd stand-in show here and there and then in 1982 I was given my own show on a Thursday night called Funk Fantasy, initially playing jazz funk and soul and then, around 1985, the first house records that were coming through. Then I was given a Monday night show which I called Fresh Start To The Week, which focused on hip-hop.

At that time Tony Blackburn was doing the daily 9am - midday show playing lots of funk, and then I was playing a mixture of funk, house and hip-hop, so it was pretty cool for what was essentially a conventional local BBC station. They even let us rebrand the late evenings on the station between 10pm - midnight, which we dubbed Nite FM. I did Mondays and Thursdays, Gilles Peterson was on Tuesday, Gary Crowley on Wednesday and then on a Friday we gave Pete Tong, who had been cutting his teeth on Radio Invicta in Kent, his first slot in London as well.

On the Thursday night show, in particular, we would always cover what was going on in clubland. I was DJing out and about myself in London by now, and Nicky Holloway was a famous party animal, man-about-town, and you kind of new that if his fingers touched anything it was going to be a lot of fun.

What interested me about Nicky's Trip at The Astoria was that a few months before that started I was playing predominantly to a black crowd. Not many white people then were interested in dance music, but there was almost like this overnight sensation. Within a couple of months the whole London scene had changed and everyone was going mad and dancing like you've never seen before. It was a real eye opening experience to go and see that. It was completely different, because, up until then, people used to dance side to side to a slower beat, and now the music sped up as the night went on, all fuelled by this new drug that hit London called ecstasy.

And it was one particular excursion to The Trip that had a profound effect on Pearce.

It's always really funny when people ask you about your memories of a certain club. The stock answer is that you shouldn't really remember if it was that good. One of my long-standing memories of Trip, however, is when Nicky Holloway played Phase II - Reachin'. I already liked the record, had heard it on import, but hadn't heard it in a club. That night I got so into it I actually climbed inside a large speaker stack. I'm surprised I'm not deaf. I just clung on for dear life to hear it in there, and it's such a positive, beautiful record. It really, really touched me, and I actually set up a rave label called Reachin' Records, on the back of that night and hearing that record at Trip.

The music business was now moving at a frightening pace and with his influential radio shows, Pearce had quickly established himself as a key player on the London club scene.

In November 1987 he had introduced US hip-hop stars Public Enemy live on stage at London's Hammersmith Odeon, with the band a year later sampling a recording of Pearce's introduction for the opening track of their seminal album It Takes A Nation Of Millions To Hold Us Back. The pioneering release went on to sell millions of copies worldwide and saw rap music break into the mainstream.

More than two decades later Pearce would interview Public Enemy frontman Chuck D for a BBC 6 Music special, in a series which also featured his old friend Frankie Knuckles.

I had an interesting role on the London radio scene in the mid-to-late '80s, because I had a hip-hop show on Monday, and then what was meant to be my funk show on a Thursday, turned into a house show when the house started to come in.

So I was one of the first DJs to play house on the radio in London. I had Frankie Knuckles on for his first radio slot in London, Tony Humphries too, all those guys. My contacts with the hip-hop community in New York were good, and a lot of those labels were playing around with dance music, so I got to know everybody, got to know people like Rocky Jones at DJ International. I got embedded in promoting house through the airwaves of London, and, at that time, there was very little dance music on the radio in the UK at all.

Around 1988/'89 everything suddenly changed very quickly. Everyone talks about the Chicago stuff coming through, but the early Detroit stuff was coming through around the same time as well, so as soon as this house music came in from Chicago and Detroit, suddenly there was this new energy. Prior to that the music had been really slow. I think it had got slower as a backlash to disco, all the hi-nrg stuff, and this was the first time since then that dance music had sped up again. It was the infectious energy in the music that inspired people.

I think that people who had gone clubbing previously at that time, if they wanted serious music, they went to black music nightclubs. There were probably some white clubbers who weren't as comfortable with that for whatever reason, and I think the other really interesting thing is that clubs before that, apart from our few specialist clubs, were essentially pick-up joints, where guys would go to pull girls and vice versa. Suddenly when the house music came along there were bunches of guys dancing together with their arms in the air, and they couldn't care less about pulling anybody. Everybody felt safe in the environment and suddenly it was fine to go up and hug a complete stranger.

It was quite a spiritual thing, and quite bizarre looking back at it now. Quite a lot of female clubbers that I spoke to at that time acquainted it with gay clubs, which they used to go to, and which up until then were the only places they could go to, to hear great music and not be hassled by guys all night.

With Trip, and acid house going overground, I think it was all a natural progression really. Nicky spotted this music, what had been going on in London at more underground clubs, and decided to take it to a bigger audience, by putting it in what was a considerably-sized venue, The Astoria.

One of my other favourite clubs was Spectrum at Heaven, which was a large club, but because it was on a Monday it was still an underground night. One night at Spectrum somebody had decided to build a maze on the dancefloor out of black material. You have to remember the state of people in that club at that time, because you went in the maze and in the middle of it there was a big strobe and it just blinded you. There were hundreds of people stuck in there, in their altered state, who couldn't work out how to get out of the maze. I was in there for about half an hour. It was a totally bizarre thing to put in a club. I also remember people kneeling on the floor and worshipping the lights. It sounds incredible, but that actually happened. It was very theatrical, actually.

When he did finally get out of the Spectrum maze there was a phone call waiting for Pearce from Polydor Records.

They had heard my Radio London shows and said they were looking for an A & R guy. I'll admit that I didn't actually know what one was, but I went along for a meeting and got the job. It was weird because they didn't tell me how to do it, or what to do, they just left me to it.

Polydor had previously been behind a lot of rare groove tracks like The Jackson Sisters' I Believe In Miracles, Maceo & The Macks' Cross The Tracks and lots of great Roy Ayres records. They wanted to bring that heritage into the new scene, and one of the first projects I did was called Urban Acid. It was the first concept album as an acid album, and also became the biggest selling acid album. I had wanted to make my mark and we put the album together during the summer of 1988 in a studio in Soho and had a whole host of up and coming producers making acid house tracks specially for it - people like Tom Frederickse, who went on to work with Sasha in the '90s, Ian Dewhurst, who later launched Mastercuts, Martin Freeland, who went on to do loads of stuff under Man With No Name for Perfecto, and Damon Rocheford who later had a massive hit as Nomad with I Wanna Give You Devotion. In fact, apart from Bam Bam, all the guys on that album were British.

Just as we were releasing the album the home affairs correspondent at ITN News called us at the label and asked us all about acid house because they were about to run an item on it.

It turned out to be the lead news item the next night, and ITN actually used our album cover as the backdrop. So the News At Ten came on, with the famous chimes, and the newsreader said "acid house is the new dance craze, sweeping the nation", with our record sleeve emblazoned behind her. The managing director of Polydor rang me at home, and bearing in mind he'd been involved in punk rock and everything before acid house, was saying "have you seen the news?". I thought he was going to say "well done", but I actually got a huge bollocking, and told that I was going to put the company in disrepute. The next day we sold about 20,000 copies, and we were outselling Polydor acts like Level 42, so the MD calmed down a bit after that.

Some of the guys in the studio decided to make a record parodying the News At Ten report, called Mr E - Acid House, and we got a then unknown actor called Steve Coogan in to play the newsreader, and cut his comments all over an acid house record.

Pearce had swiftly got his head around A & Ring and now waiters from Chicago were spending their hard-earned tips on flights to London to seek out accommodating record labels.

When the first records started coming in from Chicago, Trax Records and DJ International became a bit like that Motown machine, and they weren't just putting out records every few weeks, it seemed like they were coming thick and fast daily. Those labels went round to all the local churches in Chicago and signed up all the best gospel singers, and started making some really great records, and a few really bad ones as well.

The people who couldn't get signed in Chicago would often turn up in the UK, and one day, this guy appeared in the reception at Urban Records. He'd heard I liked stuff like Ten City, and so reception called up to me, and I said, "why not, send him up". He told me he was a singer from Chicago and he wanted to make a track, and I said, "OK, play me the track". He didn't have anything recorded, but said he could sing it to me, and so this guy belted out Better Days. His name was Jimi Polo.

I listened and I said, "OK, I'm going to put you in the studio and we're going to make the record". And we got an unknown keyboard player called Adamski, to go in a studio with him for a day. We made a Chicago house record in London and a lot of people still think it was made in the States.

With radio a constant throughout Pearce's career, he was in prime position when a former pirate station campaigned for a pioneering legal dance music licence for London.

Kiss FM had been a pirate for some time, and a lot of its DJs had helped campaign to get a London-wide dance music licence.

By 1990 the BBC had shut down Radio London and created GLR, which they also hoped would tackle a lot of social issues and I actually had Kiss FM's Gordon Mac on my new GLR show talking about the campaign, and how the station had shut down as a pirate to apply for a licence. I got involved with helping Gordon put the application together, but we didn't get the licence initially. It went to Jazz FM, but then they announced a second round, and we got one.

With the licence awarded I quickly joined Kiss and it was quite anarchic at the time, with not many people really taking notice of each other, and everyone doing their own thing.

Kiss is still there more than 20 years on, but at the time everyone thought we were mad. They were saying not enough people knew about dance music, that it would never work. When we did finally get the London-wide licence we put on a free party in Highbury Fields and 100,000 people turned up. It was absolutely incredible.

The exciting thing about Kiss in those days, and I did breakfast, daytime and drivetime in my time there, was the playlist, or more like the lack of it.

Radio stations now are run by computers and playlists, and analysts, and all sorts of weird people. God knows what they all do, but at Kiss we had a sort of playlist, which as DJs we got together to talk about, and which was largely ignored anyway. You brought half the records in from home, and people would literally give you a track that they'd made, on the street, and you'd play it on the radio the next day. And loads of them got signed.

Kiss was then responsible for driving rave culture, which some people would call hardcore, and playing SL2 and The Prodigy on the radio for the first time. All of that was really driven by us putting those records on daytime radio. Every now and then, Radio 1 would have to play one or two tracks of this awful music that was so popular.

*(clockwise) * Dave Pearce as studio assistant at
BBC Radio London in the early-'80s
* With 6 Music interviewees Chuck D
from Public Enemy, Boy George
and house legend Frankie Knuckles
* Arms in the air at a massive trance event*

Another natural progression for Pearce was club promotions, and with Kiss he had the perfect vehicle.

My involvement in the rave scene was one of the things I was keen to do at Kiss, as that next stage of rave arrived. This was after free raves and as it moved back into clubs again. I decided to put on an event, and to use The Astoria, which was a fantastic old venue, and was still the home of Sin. So I took on The Astoria with Kiss, and we did Thursday night parties there. I remember one Thursday in 1992, on the bill I had The Prodigy, SL2, Alison Limerick and CeCe Penniston, all on the same night, and all doing it for about £50 each.

The atmosphere was absolutely electric in there, and we spent loads of our budget on production, theming the stage differently for each event. We had Rob Blake, the Marathon Man, as warm-up, and also Steve Jackson, a great DJ from Kiss. The Astoria was amazing, when the crowd roared after you dropped a big tune it literally hit you in the gut. I don't think I've ever experienced that raw energy since.

With clubbing so much more organic in those days, and the movers and shakers so much easier to penetrate, Kiss provided a great platform for all and sundry.

Suddenly everybody started making dance music and people knew that Kiss was the place that would play their records, because we didn't have people telling us what to play. If it was good, you played it. If you played a bad record, you were a mug, and people would diss you, so you couldn't just play anything.

It did give an enormous democracy to people who were making the music. I was in a cab on the way to the radio station one day, and the driver said his cousin had made a track, that he had a copy in the car, and asked was it all right if he gave me a white label. I got to the station, listened to it, liked it, and played it during that very show. The track was Ratpack's Searching For My Rizla, and that got signed too.

So instead of a record label executive sitting there with a big cigar, wondering whether to sign a record because they weren't sure if they'd get any airplay, it kind of went the other way, because Kiss was what I would call an A & R station. It would play these underground records and then they'd get signed because the records already had the necessary airplay.

After pioneering hip-hop and house in London, Pearce's profile across the UK increased dramatically in 1995 when he was re-signed by the BBC to Radio 1, the highest profile broadcasting platform in the land. Pete Tong had been in place since 1991, Danny Rampling and Tim Westwood had been poached by the Beeb a year earlier in 1994, and Trevor Nelson (1996) and Judge Jules (1997) would also leave Kiss for Radio 1 as, the likes of Dave Lee Travis and Gary Davies made way, and the station reshaped and reorganised to appeal to a younger and more dance-based audience.

I had been doing my Dangerous Dave Breakfast Show on Kiss, which was massively popular and had a healthy market share of the London audience, but when I joined Radio 1 they were revamping the station. It had been stuck in a rut and they were getting stick from the press, so it was a big opportunity to try and help change the station from the inside.

The top people there, controller Matthew Bannister and head of production Trevor Dann, were really up for the change, and I signed a deal, but it was based on me doing a dance show, as well as the early breakfast slot. They had just brought Chris Evans in, and they wanted me to do the show before him. However, I had to wait nine months before a relevant slot came up for a dance show, so my first introduction to the nation was playing mainstream pop music, which I had never done before. Four months in I moved to an afternoon slot on Saturday and Sundays, and that's when I came up with the idea for a breakfast show for ravers, at 1pm on a Sunday called the Recovery Session...for people crawling out of bed, or those that hadn't got to bed yet!

That was a big success, but I wanted to do something bigger and I'd always fancied a Sunday night slot, because at that time the TV was pretty rubbish. We launched Dance Anthems, and I did that every Sunday for 13 years.

I'd been begging Matthew Bannister to let me do it for a while. It was the height of the superclubbing era and we quickly got 1.7m listeners. By the second or third week there were so many people calling the show, 200,000 people at once at one point, that it crashed the entire BBC telephone system.

The now immortal, yet slightly edgy jingle "roll another phat One Dave" was a far cry from the 'smashy and nicey' days of Alan 'Fluff' Freeman and co, but that was exactly Bannister and his team's remit.

With Pete Tong now firmly in place on Friday nights on Radio 1 with his Essential Selection show, Eddie Gordon - then Tong's manager/producer - knew that if station bosses could witness the euphoria sweeping the nation first hand, then anything was possible.

With the advent of ISDN telephone lines being able to carry digital signals without delay or loss of sound quality our next major move was to persuade Radio 1 to let us broadcast the Essential Mix live from one of the UK's big club nights.

The first big gig at the Que Club in Birmingham was attended by Matthew Bannister, the new R1 Controller, and Andy Parfitt, his head of programming, and when Bannister and Parfitt walked into the main room at 1am the place was going bonkers. The energy from the audience was so electric, you could almost touch it. The two BBC heads were sold. They wanted this audience from around the UK locked into Radio 1.

We set up West End Radio Productions to produce the new shows alongside the Essential Mix, and clubbers were touring the country at the weekend from town to town and city to city in search of another great night.

Dance music quickly took over at Radio 1. Dave Pearce moved from Kiss FM and had several long-running shows, and Seb Fontaine came over from Kiss too. The likes of Lottie, Eddie Halliwell and Annie Mac were all signed up as well.

The world was listening to the UK, and suddenly producers from around the world knew if they had a hit in the UK, it was guaranteed they would be a hero back home too, in France, Germany, Spain, Australia, Holland, Italy, Sweden, Germany and, yes, the USA as well. The UK was king of dance music around the globe.

Meanwhile, Pearce's versatility was proving invaluable.

I had a later stint on the Radio 1 weekday drivetime show, and the Mix At Six I introduced for half an hour each show was pushing the limits even further where dance music was concerned. There were stiff people within the station trying to get rid of that mix from day one. The BBC can be a very hard place to work sometimes if you're creative, and the mix was hugely influential, dropping soon-to-be massive trance tunes by people like Ferry Corsten and Tiesto. I managed to get hold of a listeners report that showed a massive surge when the mix came on, so we were thankfully able to keep it, but it was always a battle.

I was getting sent more and more music from Europe, and I just found trance really, really exciting at that time. I felt that conventional house music hadn't really changed much since those early days. I'd always liked the faster tracks, and the emotion of a breakdown, which obviously works really well in big main rooms or at outside events.

As trance continued to sweep the UK, Pearce, with the Mix At Six and his Sunday night Dance Anthems show, was able to bring all the big tunes from that scene to the trance-thirsty masses. Work on camera on several ITV1 shows followed, as did another huge clubbing platform, MTV, even if early broadcasts from the iconic music channel were less than organised.

I suppose when you look back at my particular musical journey, I grew up listening to records like Donna Summer's I Feel Love, which is probably the first trance record. You know, if you listen to Giorgio Moroder's synth in there, you can hear the trance progression, and he just got it so right on that record. Looking back, I believe that both I Feel Love and Space Base by Slick were also embryonic beginnings of a trance record.

And some of my favourite moments are at the trance end of things. One night I was working as a guest presenter on the MTV Dancefloor Chart. It was Golden's 10th birthday, and they wanted me to go up there and cover it with a film crew. Sasha was going to be playing there, and I thought that would be really cool.

I got in the van with the crew, who I hadn't worked with before, and promptly fell asleep. We pulled up outside this club, we'd been travelling for hours, the crew said "we're from MTV", and the guys on the door said, "oh, yes, come in, come in", but it turned out we were in completely the wrong club, and obviously the people at that club had gone along with it because they wanted to be on MTV. So we had to rather sheepishly get all the camera stuff out, and go and find the right club.

We got there in the end. Sasha at that time really was a 'God-like DJ', and what I miss, I think, is seeing those DJs play on vinyl because one of his arts and the true art of DJing, is keeping the mix going for ages, on vinyl. Nowadays there are computers and all sorts of tricks you can do. It's really not as hard as it used to be, but in those days you could go and watch someone like Sasha doing it on vinyl and it was pretty special. The crowds back then, well, it was just pure euphoria, and Golden sums up that era, you know, sweat dripping off the ceiling, everybody's hands in the air, just a really, really happy vibe. And one of the clubs I absolutely loved having an association with was Gatecrasher, being such a trance fan.

Pearce would go on to host a season-long Gatecrasher residency at Eden in Ibiza in 2006, the culmination of a long-running association with the San Antonio venue, the start of which saw him become one of the first British DJs to headline a club night on the island, as opposed to a brand or club night name being the focal point of the promotion.

With the Dance Anthems name associated we were able to do Dave Pearce presents Trance Anthems, so it was called that for the first couple of years, then it was Dave Pearce presents Euphoria, and later presents Gatecrasher. Also Dave Pearce vs Tidy, because we knew the Tidy Boys well, and there was this synergy with hard trance and hard dance.

The Eden thing came about when Dan Prince of MixMag fame approached me about putting on a night at Eden, weekly on Saturdays. Up until then it was promoters like Cream, Clockwork Orange and Up Yer Ronson who did whole seasons. It was always amazing playing to a Gatecrasher crowd because they were such a loyal following, who really loved and respected the music.

Back in the UK, Pearce was soon a mainstay on the trance circuit.

The music had moved on, as we'd gone from rave on to Euro-house and trance, and I got asked to play at lots of clubs around the country.

One of them was Progress. Suddenly places like Derby were on the map, and before that you just wouldn't see Derby as a No 1 clubbing destination. But when you got there, the whole club was just bouncing, a real community feel, a real happy vibe, very consistent, very infectious, and that's why people travelled to go there. Now, I can't remember the last time that I played Derby.

Pearce recognises that his journey nationally with Radio 1, as to being based in London with Kiss, was vital in optimising his DJ bookings across the UK.

Going to places like Northern Ireland, and also Scotland, was always an experience.

I still play for Colours at The Arches in Glasgow and I'm so glad it's still there, it's just a fantastic venue, with a crowd that is really, really appreciative about its music.

One of the great things about Colours is that it's like a family. Ricky McGowan has been on the scene for years and years and they are lucky to have one of the best homes and clubs in the world, in The Arches in Glasgow. And when we look back at the great days of clubbing, here's one great club that is still open.

I remember the Millennium Eve night I did up there for Colours. There had been all this hype about computers going down, the electricity, and predictions that loads of weird things were going to happen. I was doing the live broadcast in the run-up to midnight, and into New Year and 2000.

The whole thing was being broadcast on other radio stations around the world, and we were on this huge outdoor stage, in front of 25,000 people in Glasgow town centre, all in association with Colours.

The BBC were so worried about all the Millennium bug speculation that Radio 1 actually had a secret studio in a military base, in case something strange did happen. I had vinyl to play records, I had CD players, I had reel to reel tape, DAT machines and I had cartridges, which we used to play jingles on. All these formats they'd insisted on, all powered separately, in case the record decks suddenly didn't work anymore. Can you imagine it? What a headache!

It got to just before midnight and the Glasgow crowd being what they are, were all hands in the air, people literally leaping through the air, such was the big rush of anticipation. Two minutes before midnight and the chief of police appeared to tell me that I'd got to turn it down. It was the biggest night of everyone's lives, and I was having this battle with the producer, saying, "no, I'm not turning it down"...then I was told I would be arrested, and I said, "ok, arrest me, live on the radio, at midnight at Millennium, in front of 25,000 people, that will be good". Fortunately, I didn't get nicked, and we managed to get through it.

I remember one night I did with Paul Van Dyk there which was absolutely amazing, as are the Scottish crowd, who all chant at you when you're playing.... "Here we...here we...here we fucking go...". The first time you hear it, you're like what's that, but they chant it to the rhythm of the record and it's phenomenal.

In 2000, with Dance Anthems a firm fixture on the Radio 1 schedule, Pearce teamed up with BMG to set up a new record label, NuLife, and launched with a bang with Victoria Beckham's debut solo single Out Of Your Mind by Truesteppers featuring Dane Bowers, a UK garage track which went on to sell more than 350,000 singles, to this day the biggest-selling solo single from a Spice Girl.

Dozens of massive trance hits followed on NuLife from the likes of Ian Van Dahl, who scored three Top 10 singles for Pearce. Also signed were Dab Hands trio Leo Elstob, Mark Wilkinson and Richard Searle with their 2004 remake of the Lou Reed track Satellite Of Love.

Meanwhile, Pearce was signed up for the Euphoria compilation series, compiling and mixing five in total, with his Transcendental Euphoria release selling 220,000 copies.

Pearce rolled his last "phat one" for Dance Anthems on Radio 1 in 2008, and has been working since with BBC 6 Music on various "specials", including those in-depth radio documentaries on Frankie Knuckles and Chuck D, as well as Boy George and 40 Years Of Philly. More projects like his excellent 13-week series on Radio 2 are in the pipeline too.

DJ-wise, he continues to play all over the UK and Europe, and argues that if the DJ's passion is still there, it's the best job in the world.

What people forget sometimes is that DJs have an immense passion for the music they play, and to get a positive reaction when we play a record means everything. As good as it is for those on the dancefloor, it's probably better for us seeing it all go off from the DJ booth. And it's that passion which means we keep going.

I loved doing the Radio 2 series in particular. It was great to hear people's stories and to go back over all those years of dance music. Delving back in history on the Six Music specials is fascinating too, especially the Knuckles one which came 25 years after I first interviewed Frankie on Radio London.

I could sit and give you a Top 50 of One More tracks, and they'd all be really special for very different reasons, but one defining tune I guess, which really sums up a big chunk of my career, is Silence by Delirium, which is basically a record that has never left my record box. I still play it all the time, and it still gives me a buzz. I must have played it a thousand times. I've worn out all my vinyl copies, and, of course, I now have the digital versions.

I'm so gutted I didn't get to sign it. I was close, but that would have been the icing on the cake. I never got bored of playing that record, it still makes the hair on the back of my neck stand up. I've cried playing that record, and it's a record that bonds people together, and the reaction it evokes from the crowd is amazing. So for those reasons it's my perfect dance record.

TURNMILLS

The Newmans were running Clerkenwell and Farringdon a whole decade before Fabric opened just down the road...an era when, in clubbing terms, Old Street, Shoreditch and Dalston were no-go zones.

Built on a firm family foundation, iconic London venue Turnmills ran a mammoth 22 years from 1986 to 2008, closing on a high when brothers 'Tall' Paul and Danny Newman thought they had taken it as far as they could.

We caught up with Paul and traced the story back to the club's humble roots when his dad ran the site as a wine bar feasting on Margaret Thatcher's lunchtime trade of the mid-'80s.

My father John previously had a bar in Rathbone Street, just behind Oxford Street, and then he moved on to a pub that needed to be brought back to life, the Sir George Rowbey in Finsbury Park. He then had the idea he could open a nice fancy wine bar in the middle of Clerkenwell. It was tiny, compared to Turnmills the club, probably a third of the size.

It evolved over the years, basically because of how the market trend went at the time. When we first turned up, Fleet Street just down the road was massive with the all newspapers still there. It was the City, it was the '80s, it was the so-called yuppies - people had money, and they were going out spending it, drinking at lunchtimes and the wine bar was absolutely packed. You couldn't get anyone else in there.

All the tables were booked in advance so we expanded the business and we doubled the size so we could get more people sitting down, to buy more food and more wine. That area was what became the dancefloor. In later years I'd look at the dancefloor from the DJ booth and remember where the old hotplate was and where the piano was up in the corner, everyone sitting down and eating. But in the late '80s, very similar to what happened in the late noughties, it all popped, the economy went backwards, interest rates went through the roof and all the trade that we relied so much on, it all just faded away.

However, step forward a mini-cultural revolution in the making and fortunately for Mr Newman, eldest son Paul was perfectly positioned and right on the cusp of it.

Just as the recession hit there was obviously this huge sweep of acid house, raving in farmers' fields all night long and I was just coming into that myself. It really was a case of changing our spots to keep the business going. I had already been DJing at office parties at the wine bar and in 1989 my father applied for a 24-hour music and dance licence, which was unheard of at the time. However, our council, Islington, was saying that it wanted to get more in line with Europe and have less restrictions on opening times so it granted us the licence for one year on trial.

And so that enabled us to go later and the people that wanted to party and go on longer could do so. There were still very strict laws on the sale of alcohol, but back then people just wanted to stay out later than normal, so that's what triggered the whole change - the economy, the late licence and the emergence of the rave scene.

Paul, then in his late teens, was determined he was going to seize this amazing opportunity. Suddenly the prospects in the family business had changed from being a waiter at a wine bar to a DJ in a nightclub...literally overnight!

I started DJing through a combination of always loving music and taping my favourite bits off the radio, and trying to find pirate stations playing cooler music than the mainstream ones were. Then it was a case of finding the tracks I liked, so going to record shops loads and generally becoming a bit of an anorak where music was concerned.

Back then some friends of mine had mobile discos and I used to go and give them a hand with that. One of our mates was a bit of a technical wizard so we all got together to try and buy a radio rig. The idea was to set up our own pirate station, which we did do, called Touchdown FM. And if anyone knows Swiss Cottage in north west London, well, there are some great big tower blocks along there and that was our home for about three years. With our huge rig we could get down to Brighton on a clear day.

That was lots of fun and running alongside all that was Turnmills, and the big transformation happening down there. It really couldn't have worked out any better for me. I didn't really understand the financial dilemmas behind the scenes, but I was happy that my dad was getting all these parties down there. And I used to go and try and DJ at the club, that was obviously my big thing.

I managed to get the Friday slot, up until 2.30am, and then we used to shut and open at around 3.30/4am. The promoters would come in, and I used to hang around watching great DJs like Paul Oakenfold and Smoking Jo. At that time they were part of this Friday night afters session called Space and then Trade did the same on a Saturday night, in the early hours of Sunday. My dad managed to blag me the last set at Trade, which was at about 10am on a Sunday. Trade just ran and ran, and I soon picked up a residency at The Zap Club in Brighton on the back of that.

Paul would go on to become one of the UK's leading DJs throughout the '90s and into the next Millennium, DJing all over the world. Hooj Choons label boss Red Jerry came up with the Tall Paul tag, when 6ft 6ins Paul produced the massive club anthem Rock Da House in 1992. The track charted at No 11 in the UK nationals in 1997 when it was re-released on VC Recordings, while under another guise, Camisra, Paul's equally huge and anthemic Let Me Show You reached No 5 in 1998.

But in 1988 chart success and such clubland stardom was a pipe dream for Turnmills' rookie resident DJ. Brother Danny was coming through the ranks as a glass collector eyeing up the club manager's job, while Newman Snr set about installing certain standards, values that his two boys would hold firm for the duration of Turnmills. And anyone who ever clubbed or worked at Turnmills will tell you that this was a decent club, a well-run club, and one which looked after its punters and DJs alike.

The club's ethos was what my dad carried through. He loved doing the lights, doing the lasers, trying to buy more equipment, putting more money into the club, and just generally trying to create a good experience for people. And that's what we always tried to achieve, making sure the décor, the production and the programming of the music and the DJs was all perfect. That was always so important, to make sure the right DJ was on at the right time of the night, especially with such irregular opening times. And to keep pushing it forward. The whole family would be involved. My dad would be there, I'd be there, my brother Danny, who went on to run the club, would be there, and people liked that.

However, Turnmills would not have survived for more than two decades on tight family principles and generous hospitality alone. And like any successful nightclub with high overheads, it needed both the Friday and Saturday nights to be busy, at the very least.

The Gallery started in the mid-'90s because Friday was always a very difficult day. Once our late Saturday-nighter Trade became very popular, it gave us a problem with Fridays because Trade had got us a bit of a brush. It was a mixed gay night, so it became difficult to have a straight night on a Friday, with a really popular gay night on a Saturday...well, according to the critics at the time, at least. So increasingly this Friday thing became a problem, getting something different going. We had some great parties in there, some great ideas and promoters, but none of them would last longer than six weeks.

Then myself and my brother, and a girl called Samir, who worked for Kiss FM, got together and said, "why don't we try and do an in-house night, without having to pay rent to the club, and with all the door money going to the club, not an outside promoter, give it a good run, and see how it works?". We opened with a bang, we had Danny Rampling for the first night, then Paul Oakenfold over the next few weeks, and they all helped us out with fees and supported us in what we were trying to do, but it was difficult.

It started well, went up, dipped, went up, dipped again, and it continued like that for about four months, and I remember standing with my dad at the bar and him saying, "this can't go on, there are people knocking at the door, they want to pay rent, and they want to give their thing a go", and so The Gallery was nearly shelved.

Of course, many club nights may have prospered eventually if they had been given a few more weeks by the powers that be. And while The Gallery is one of a handful of high profile events that did go on to great things after almost getting the chop, there can't be any that lasted every week for the next 16 years.

We had started on my birthday in May, 1995, you know, as you do, anything to help it along at the start, with a big party and then I think we made it through the summer and instead of getting rid of it, we persuaded my dad to let us run it up until Christmas, for the next few months, and thankfully he agreed.

The promotion of the club was initially done through all your old favourites, you know, adverts in your MixMags, flyers outside clubs, etc. The Gallery artwork was a combination of my brother and my dad. My father liked his Spanish artwork, and we were trying to get together something different and he came up with something left of centre, shall we say. Then the great team that Danny had assembled, the creative people who worked with us, used to adapt it literally each week. There are still a few flyers in my collection missing, though. I remember one night Danny had Fat Tony playing and the artwork had a tin of soup on it, with the label saying "Fat Tony, Minestrone". There was lots of silly stuff like that.

I remember the arguments my dad would have with my brother when he saw the invoices for these flyers. Danny just used to spend what he thought he needed to spend to get it done. He always tried to make the flyers and promo stuff fun and I think people appreciated that.

Still going strong at the time of going to press, The Gallery, which has been at Ministry Of Sound since 2008, celebrated its 16th anniversary in April 2011, with Judge Jules, Marco V and Boy George all joining Paul and his fellow long-serving resident Steve Lee on the birthday line-up. You'll still find Steve, now a black cabbie, playing twice a month, with Paul chipping in a few sets throughout the year. The Ministry provides a fitting setting and sound system for a London clubbing institution, which prides itself on its line-ups.

But then Turnmills and The Gallery, in particular, were always all about the line-ups, and with Paul establishing himself as one of the country's leading DJs around the time The Gallery took off, attracting the big names was never going to be a problem.

I knew a lot of the guys through meeting up with them at various gigs all over the UK and indeed the world. My brother Danny had a great relationship with a lot of the agents too. And Fridays wasn't a big deal, especially in London, as there wasn't a lot of choice in the south of England on Fridays. There seemed to be a lot more going on up north, in fact.

Also, there were only so many times guests could play one club, maybe every three or four months, and once the circuit had revolved we'd get the guys that we wanted coming back around again. Danny had a vision of how he wanted to do it. He wanted to have two headline guests and you could see that worked because the times that we did only have one headliner, the numbers would drop.

So we were lucky in the way that fees wouldn't be ridiculous, because it was a Friday. So, especially with our contacts, we could get two headline guests pretty easily and cheaply. I genuinely didn't realise how big our line-ups were at the time. It was only when I was away DJing abroad and I'd get asked, "so who's playing at The Gallery this week?", and I'd say, "oh it's Judge Jules and Sister Bliss this week", or "we've got Paul Oakenfold and Seb Fontaine next week" and people would be amazed. It would be hard for other promoters, especially in other countries, to get those line-ups at that time. So that used to bang home to me how successful we were.

We used to pride ourselves on our line-ups, especially around the birthdays and other celebrations, and a lot of the other promoters I met were scratching their heads, asking how we managed it. We also used to look after the DJs and make sure they had fun, and either me, Danny or my dad would be there to have a drink with them, embrace it and have a crack too.

With so many of The Gallery's guests personal friends or peers of Paul's, picking his favourite in this instance is even more difficult. His most cherished memories are easier to discuss.

I get asked this a lot, who is my favourite DJ? And it's almost an impossible job. The DJs we booked were the ones who came down with the right attitude and did their job. The ones that didn't - and those moments were rare, just a small handful - simply didn't get invited back. We booked people who would do their hour-and-a-half or two-

*(clockwise) * Tall Paul at home* Turnmills fan Danny Rampling
* The iconic Gallery 'bust'/logo * Tall Paul at Turnmills with dad John
* A typical Gallery line-up * The building, which house Turnmills,
on the corner of Clerkenwell Road and Turnmill Street*

Tall Paul. **Luvdup** Nancy Noise. **April 5th** Steve Lee. Paul

Tony De Vit. Tall Paul. Lottie. **April 12th** Jim (Shaft) Ryan.
The Gallery exhibiting Miss Moneypenny's   The Gallery exhibiting M

...eased Wimmin. Tall Paul. Lottie. **April 19th** Seb Fontaine. St...
...RST BIRTHDAY   FIR...

...kin Jo. Brandon Block. Steve Lee. **April 26th** Lawrence Nelson.
The Gallery exhibiting Love To Be   The Gallery exhibiting L...

hour set, raise the roof and get stuck in. It's difficult to pick one in particular. A regular Gallery DJ would always perform.

Favourite memories? That's another difficult one. But I always used to look forward to the birthdays of The Gallery because it was more recognition of how difficult it had been at the start and how it almost never happened. We had a lot of regulars who used to come down at least every month and to see those regular faces, people on The Gallery membership, at the birthdays was always a pleasure. We always had a good relationship with our punters and we used to listen to what they had to say too. And for the birthdays I used to make sure I got to the club early, checked out the queue, made sure we got everyone in as quickly as possible, especially if it was raining out there, and get the party started a.s.a.p.

And Paul will always chuckle when thinking about the last set each week at The Gallery and how a certain resident was happy to play what some would regard as the graveyard shift.

The last set at The Gallery? Well, we used to get complaints from residents as time went on, because of people leaving the club, cutting through Clerkenwell Green opposite. Also down on Turnmill Street around four or five in the morning, making a load of noise, etc.

When we started in the mid to late '80s, all the properties around the club were pretty much offices and when we closed 20 years later they were mostly all residential flats. So throughout the club's existence there were a lot of exchanges between us and local residents. The only way we could get round this was by keeping the club open until the Tube and trains started running again, around six or seven in the morning, when the security could chaperone people down to Farringdon Station. In fact, a lot of The Gallery crowd used to come on the train from outside of London, the suburbs and all over the place. Our regulars certainly weren't inner city kids.

So we pushed back the closing time later and later. A couple of times I did do the later slot, but that does make it a much longer session so step forward our faithful resident Stevie Lee, arm raised. "I'll have some of that," he said, and in he went. So that was Stevie's weekly grim reaper hour, and he loved every minute of it.

And no doubt, Steve Lee would have played Danny Newman's own track, 5.55, under the guise Durango 95, which was released on Turnmills' own label, Duty Free Recordings. It became one of the tracks intrinsically linked with the club.

Danny made 5.55 because he reckoned 5.55 in the morning was the time you'd finally got rid of the wannabe ravers, and just the hardcore clubbers were left to see it out to the end. That track became a big anthem for the club. And so did some of our other productions on Duty Free. You know, my track Precious Love, well, if it wasn't for The Gallery crowd always asking for it, I'm not so sure it would have actually come out. The first few times it was played, it didn't really work, but it always worked at The Gallery, and people would ask for it and then it took off. I always look back fondly at the little helping hand that The Gallery crowd gave that track.

Also massive was anything by Sister Bliss (or Faithless) because Ayalah, well, she was always a big DJ for us, and she still guests for The Gallery at The Ministry. And then there's the track I used to play loads, a Thin White Duke mix of Depeche Mode, a fantastic record, called A Pain That I'm Used To, with every element that I like in a record. For certain tunes I would get the key to the sound system and turn it up that little bit more than anyone else could. Turnmills, as a club, had many anthems down there. The Gallery had numerous ones too. I suppose, you could say Jam & Spoon, anything by them or Storm, which was also Mark Spoon, God rest his soul.

Danny Rampling has the highest praise for Turnmills.

I heard about Turnmills long before it became, for me, probably THE greatest club in London. A friend told me about this wine bar/ restaurant/club in Clerkenwell in the late '80s, but I didn't actually go down there for a year or so after, until Craig Daniel, from Trax Records, invited me down there to play with him and Paul. It was still early days for the club, I walked in there and was gobsmacked that there was this amazing venue on my doorstep. I'd been doing my own nights in London and also travelling around internationally, but just hadn't had time to check out Turnmills.

I think Laurence Malice was instrumental in the success of Turnmills by running Trade there as an after-hours club in the early days, and one of the most notorious and wild club nights in London at that. Laurence had a strong influence in the direction Turnmills took, alongside Paul, who was travelling the country as well. He initially played at Trade, and I saw Paul play there and I thought he was a great DJ, and Danny Newman, who later went on to run the club, he was just a kid at the time, 12 or 13 years old, in his dad's club. John, God bless him, was a great guy, a larger than life character, a huge man, with a real rock solid vision of what he wanted from his club, and he really achieved that with that space.

And during the after-hours was where it really came into its own. I'd go and party at Turnmills after coming back down from wherever else I'd been DJing in the country. Or after The Leisure Lounge, just down the road in Holborn, where I used to DJ a lot too. It was a booming time for the after-hours scene in London. Through the night you could get a couple of thousand people down at Turnmills. You had The Gallery, and my nights, Metrogroove and London Calling, which I promoted with Danny, more on the house tip. Turnmills was my home in London, there and The Cross, the two clubs I loved playing most in London. For many years you would find me DJing in London every month in one of those clubs.

Turnmills was all about the energy, this great long basement, with the lazers, a booming sound system, a great crowd of up-for-it party people. It was a free state really, people were left alone to have a good time in that club, with no overly-oppressive security, a great management team, and it was always "stay as long as you want".

Back in the day, when I used to party, I'd go to Turnmills on a Sunday morning, stay till lunchtime, go to another club, and then come back to Turnmills, to whatever Sunday night club was on, and party until Monday morning. You know, they were wild times. It was the '90s, it was also Brit-pop. It was party-central for eight to ten years and the UK was the No 1 nation in the world for partying at that time. 'Excess All Areas' in fact. Whether it was the clubscene, Brit Pop or the festivals, it was just one long party.

Judge Jules knew the Turnmills set-up well, but was glad when one particular obstacle was removed at the venue.

I was very close to Paul Newman at the time Turnmills took off. His girlfriend had been a big mate of my other half, and I always found the concept of Paul being born and raised into a family that owned a club as very unique and an unusual route into DJing.

I'm not gay, but I used to go to Trade because it was one of the first late night clubs, and I don't know how they got away with it. They managed to do what the Ministry Of Sound couldn't, and stay open all night, maybe because they were just on the borders of the city. If you were in London and you wanted to go out late you would have heard about Turnmills at the time.

The Gallery went on to about eight in the morning, so I would always arrive in the early hours, having played somewhere else, and could get there from virtually anywhere in the country. I'd usually had a few hours kip in the car, so for the first ten or fifteen minutes I really didn't have a clue what was going on. However, Turnmills always had a crowd which helped you along the way. It was like a double expresso, walking through that door.

And Turnmills for a number of the years had this glass fronted DJ booth, like a goldfish bowl, so there was little interaction with the crowd. You could tell people were going mad, you just couldn't see them. I think they got rid of it in the end, because so many people used to smoke in the booth at that time. They took away the glass and suddenly the DJ was no longer an exhibit, and it just went off...bang! Suddenly the atmosphere was so much more tangible.

Thankfully The Gallery still exists at The Ministry, and is still a very successful night. When it finished at Turnmills we knew it was going on to pastures new. Clubland does have a bit of an ebb and flow about it, with the summer always dipping because of festivals, people being away and students not being around, but The Gallery was and is just so good all the time.

And as the The Gallery continued to deliver the goods on a Friday, another iconic London night was about to grip Turnmills, and a whole new dance music genre would add a further twist to the proceedings.

The Trade faithful had long feasted on a diet of high-octane nu-energy dance music and at The Gallery a main room trance direction had evolved over the years, with house or breaks in the second room, later dubbed T2. Then in 1996 Danny Newman was instrumental in bringing a new left of centre weekly Saturday session to the club - a promotion that would run until 3am, and perfectly precede the Saturday night/Sunday morning early hours Trade session.

The Heavenly Social, a label night for Jeff Barrett's seminal Heavenly Records, had begun life in 1994 on a Sunday night in the basement of The Albany pub in central London. Attended frequently by indie royalty like Oasis, Primal Scream, The Charlatans, et al, the night soon outgrew its modest home and a deal was struck with Turnmills to take The Heavenly Social there. It would become the springboard for the likes of Fatboy Slim (Norman Cook's new guise of that year), The Chemical Brothers (who would be weekly residents on their way to superstardom) and Jon Carter, who with his Monkey Mafia productions on Heavenly Records, would become Mr Big Beat himself.

Paul continues:-

That was the other night that helped put Turnmills on the map - the whole Heavenly Social movement, which was masterminded by my brother. The whole Chemical Brothers, Jon Carter, Wall Of Sound thing, which was a real musical shift from all the dancey, fluffiness of the house scene that was dominating things at the time.

Heavenly Social simply just left that all alone and was almost the rock and roll of its era. The Chemicals played down there all the time, Fatboy Slim used to love playing down there, and we used to have some big heavy nights and all, of course, before Trade started.

Norman Cook remembers:-

The Heavenly Social was a gathering of like-minded DJs who, at the time, were fed up with house music. People like Richie Fearless, Jon Carter, Justin Robertson, the Kahuna Boys, Dan and Jon, and, of course, The Chems. And there always seemed to be at least three of us on the bill each week.

I got involved because a friend of mine told me about the night, saying that "you'd like it, they play the sort of music you're into".

And so I went down there and Tom and Ed Chemical were like, "oh yeah, you make the music we like", and vice versa, and so on. And that was the start of big beat.

There was definitely a feeling that we were a gang, and like The Escape Club in Brighton in the mid to late '80s, this was my clubhouse of that era. Yeah, I have very fond memories of the Heavenly Social.

With Fridays eventually becoming Turnmills' flagship night, there was now a constant need to find successful Saturday night events to complement The Gallery and a couple of years later when the Social moved on, other in-house successes came in the shape of London Calling and Metrogroove nights hosted by Danny Rampling, Toni Tambourine's City Loud - which Masters At Work, Tony Humphries and CJ MacIntosh all guested at - Together New Year's Eve parties with The Chemical Brothers, and Roger Sanchez's huge one-off Release Yourself parties, when he would play the entire eight hours in the main room himself...joss sticks, huge revolving S-Man logos and all. Various Clockwork Orange nights at Turnmills, run by Danny Gould and Andy Manston, were also massive for Turnmills.

Paul remembers that Turnmills' unique policy of shutting one Saturday night promotion in the early hours of Sunday morning before opening another minutes later threw up interesting logistical issues for the club's door team.

Saturdays became a heavy night for Terry, our head of security, in particular, because it was a 9pm start for Heavenly, and Trade would be queuing up around the corner for a 4am start. That actually became a problem for us because as Heavenly got bigger, they wanted to stay open later and there was this clash with Trade. But it all meant business was booming. I was down there one night when Jon Carter recorded the second Heavenly album live and I thought it was one of the greatest sets ever played at Turnmills. I just stood back in the box and watched Jon at work.

Yeah, Heavenly was big for us, a big deal. A night where you could hear stuff like The Stone Roses' Fools Gold thrown in from nowhere always scored big marks from me. I wish I could have been there more, but by then I was up and down the M1 every Saturday.

After the original transformation from wine bar to club the Turnmills capacity was initially around 700, but the venue underwent many refurbishments and extensions over the years as the Newmans continued to plough in more investment. At one point it was as if they unveiled another room each year.

We had a gym that we owned at the back, a big dance studio, which we could open on busy nights and at a push we could get the capacity up to 1,800 – 2,000. It would start to get a bit uncomfortable when you were approaching those kinds of numbers, though.

And as Turnmills' popularity continued to soar as the '90s unfolded, just down the road, Shoreditch and the surrounding areas were undergoing a urban/clubbing regeneration, which would take many punters and promoters away from the traditional haunts of London's West End, as east London slowly began to build its creative and clubbing reputation.

Then at the end of 1999 Fabric opened and became Turnmills' nearest competitor on that kind of scale.

Paul continues:-

It was difficult to admire the other clubs at the time, when you were so involved in what you were doing. But there was a bit of an unwritten rule that, for instance, if someone locally was trying to do a big drum and bass night, we wouldn't try to go after the same crowd on the same night.

And with our Trade night, people tried to stay away from what we were doing on that night, you know - The End, Fabric, even the Ministry. All great clubs, and I've DJd at them all. I remember the first time I heard a house record through that great sound system in the main room at The End. Fabric always did the business too. I guess you could say there was always a rivalry, but I suppose we all understood the rules.

And the Newmans were well aware of the rules concerning their lease, which was due to expire in 2008. With hindsight, with another massive recession looming, they could not have a picked a better time to bow out.

Turnmills finishing was a combination of factors. Our landlords had big ideas about what they could do with the property and Danny wanted to do something that had more of a weekend attention, because Turnmills wasn't just a club, it still had a wine bar and a restaurant and there was a health club out the back too.

There were a lot of rates, lot of bills and expenditures and it was a lot of work for a lot of people. And I know Danny wanted to concentrate on doing new things on the weekend, which he was good at, and had done with the Get Loaded and SW4 festivals in Clapham.

Constantly looking for new concepts and nights at Turnmills, Danny had, in fact, launched Get Loaded at the club in 2004, a midweek indie night which he had persuaded a down-on-his-luck Shaun Ryder to be resident DJ at, with Ryder's Happy Mondays sidekick Bez and New Order's Peter Hook also guest jocks.

The night actually gave birth to the Clapham Common festival, Get Loaded In The Park, and Danny was instrumental in the Happy Mondays reforming to headline the event in 2005. The festival would run annually until 2009, with Pete Doherty and Babyshambles headlining in 2006. After a year's break, Get Loaded returned in June 2011 with Razorlight the star 'turn'. Danny's collaborative Lock 'n' Load events were by now responsible for the SW4 festivals at Clapham every August Bank Holiday, the huge Cardiff Calling events, Electric Gardens in Kent, and among other club promotions, the various Swedish House Mafia parties in London too.

Paul explains:-

Danny couldn't do all that and devote his time to the day-to-day running of the club as well, so that was a factor. And my father passing away a couple of years before almost meant Turnmills didn't have the same excitement anymore for me and, I know, for Danny too.

The landlord was talking about putting all sorts of floors on top, and all that became quite awkward. There were lots of arguments and then they were going to give us some money to go and open somewhere else and we did start looking, but then Danny's health took a bit of a turn.

At the end it didn't feel there were many more directions we could take it. Sure, we could open a new club or start a new brand, but we did continue The Gallery at The Ministry Of Sound, where it still is today, several years after we actually shut. All in all, I guess closing Turnmills just felt right really.

As for our legacy? Well, I'd like to think that the people who drifted in and out of Turnmills over the years, particularly the clubbers from '89 onwards, the Trade lot, the Dance Cult lot, The Gallery people and everyone since, I hope they all appreciate that it was a unique place. Yes, it was a bit of a dungeon, it wasn't glitzy, no big VIP lists or queues or loads of cocktails and champagne, but I hope it's remembered as a decent place, where people could come and have a party, straight down those stairs and then we'd look after them. And that we weren't going to take the piss with the drinks prices, we weren't going to make them feel unwelcome, we wouldn't have big lumps of security all over the place making them feel uneasy, that there was a bit of a warehouse feel to the whole thing and that we always did our best to give them all that. I hope that came across.

Sonique is another who holds Turnmills in the highest esteem. The DJ and singer enjoyed a renaissance behind the decks in the mid-'90s, but at the age of 16 had already enjoyed solo success in the mid-'80s on Cooltempo Records, and five years later was also a member of Mark Moore's chart-topping S'Express. The 360 degree shift in her career was complete when she scooped a Brit award in 2001 for her No 1 single Feels So Good.

For me, in the '90s there were only two decent clubs in London - The Cross and Turnmills. The Cross was a bit more "looking goody"... and Turnmills was a bit more "yeah, yeah, let's have it". And the thing that I thought was really cool about Turnmills was that the DJ booth was completely separate. You couldn't even see anything, there was just this glass panel. You couldn't see me, and I couldn't see you. It was just the strangest thing. You felt alone but you could somehow pick up on the vibe from the lazers. And if anyone was going to get mashed it was in that booth, because that was THE private DJ booth.

I really liked Paul (and his brother)...I didn't even know their dad owned it. Paul was just a really nice guy and he always played decent music. His music always had a bit more soul to it than most people. If I hadn't seen him, just heard him out on the floor, I'd have thought he was a black guy. I used to look at him and think "Hmmm? A tall white guy can do that? Quality!". When Turnmills went, The Cross had already gone, and it was devastating. That was a sad time.

In Turnmills' case the planned last record was swallowed up because like most of those great Turnmills nights that 24-hour licence meant the party could simply carry on.

Paul adds:-

It was supposed to be a remix of This Is The End by The Doors and it was much deliberated over and Danny Rampling was going to play it. He'd got hold of this mix, but it just didn't happen that way, because Danny must have gone on and played something like an extra hour that night. Well, I say night, because it was about two in the afternoon when the thing finished.

I think it was Balearic classics all the way for the last hour. In the end nobody wanted to go home. There had been a plan and none of the various anthems seemed capable of ending a whole era, as such. We threw it out to a lot of people and the ideas we got back, well, none of the tracks seemed to sum up 22 years, so I think the haunting Jim Morrison vocal and a dancey mix of that dark track would have been quite fitting.

Danny Rampling was probably better equipped than most to deal with Turnmills' closure. He had recently brought down the curtain, somewhat abruptly as it turned out, on his own career. And for him, there was only one club to host his retirement gig.

It was a very sad time when Turnmills closed. I went through a period just before that when I decided to make an exit from music myself. I was going through some changes in my life, and decided to make a change out of music, and I played my so-called last night there, a 12 hour set, and that's the club I chose to say farewell to DJing, or at least I thought so. However, once a DJ, always a DJ. I love music, and I did gravitate back towards music. Then I was very privileged to be asked to play the last set at the actual Turnmills closing party, which was an incredible night. So I've had two last nights at Turnmills. The last record that I played there was a great electro mix of This Is The End by The Doors.

As much as we didn't like that it was the end of Turnmills, that Doors track worked perfectly. The clubbers were crying, the staff crying, it was a really emotional night. So many people had shared so many good times inside that club. It was the end of the road, "This Is The End", it had run its course and I guess the owners wanted to move on. It was my choice to play something with a bit of sentiment, people were taking stuff from the club, anything they could get their hands on, really. And there was a hardcore of 300 or 400 people who were going nowhere, they just wanted to party on.

Without the hindsight of not yet actually playing his last record (and for the record, as one of the several hundred who braved it until 2pm to hear it, I can tell you Rampling's was Missing by Todd Terry) Paul Newman, like many we asked, ummed and arred when asked what record he would play to mark the end of his career.

If I was playing my last record in my last set ever? Well, it would have to be something people know, it would be the biggest record of the moment, the biggest record of the year so far or a bootleg that I've got, which not many other people have, but which I know is going to work. You don't want to be playing something that is too far ahead of everyone, that hasn't been out properly yet.

For instance, when I did the Camisra record, Let Me Show You, I had that for four or five months before I could get any legal issues resolved, so there were only a handful of people who had it and on a big night I could end on something like that.

But it's not quite the end for me. I'm still doing the odd gig for my brother down at The Gallery at the Ministry and I enjoy that. I take bookings here and there, as long as it fits in with what I do now. I'm doing a bit of property developing and other stuff in that field, which is a business, and which I started doing on a much smaller scale when I was out on the road, DJing.

It's a pretty boring world, and not as glamorous as the old days, but I've got a family now and they need looking after and I've got my weekends back, which I love. What I really like now, about where I am at this moment, is that it's gone completely full circle, because when I DJ for whoever, it feels like it did initially when it was a hobby. It has that feel to it again.

There was a time a couple of years ago when I was on a tour in America when I thought, "that's it, I'm not enjoying this anymore". I'd done the circuit for so many years by then and had been exposed to the club scene from such an early age. I was literally 16, still at school, when I was dabbling around, practising at Turnmills when I was supposed to be doing the cleaning for my pocket money. I was a long time in the game, if you like, and I had a little bit of a moment a couple of years ago, when I thought, "OK, let's wind this down now". And over the last year or so, with the gigs that I've done, especially for Danny at The Gallery, it feels that I'm doing it again because I want to, not because I have to.

COLOURS

"Running" with Motherwell casual firm Saturday Service in his late teens surely gave Ricky Magowan the confidence to launch pioneering Scottish Sunday all-dayer Streetrave in a huge rundown pavilion on the remote west coast of Scotland.

Previously inhabited by rockers, Magowan took a punt at the sparse 1,500-capacity Ayr Pavilion and football skirmishes quickly took a back seat.

We were already putting on this little soul night, and we were used to running buses and travelling to other parts of Scotland to follow Motherwell away, so all that helped us believe we could pull off Streetrave. We were going to the football each week, we were the local go-getters, we ran buses already for the matches, so we knew we could get people in and out of Ayr, no problem.

The football thing was more of a fashion thing as far as I was concerned. We were young kids so of course there was a bit of aggro, but it was mainly about oneupmanship...trying to out-do the rival supporters with the trainers or clothes we were wearing, whether it was Fila or Kappa or whatever.

The Motherwell supporters used to be among the best dressed, and we always had a good rivalry with Aberdeen. The Rangers fans in those days were still mainly skinhead neanderthals, who didn't know anything about what to wear. We would go to Ibrox and they'd have these small tins of Airfix paint and they would throw them over us from the stands to try to ruin our clothes.

We took a Sunday at Ayr Pavilion because we couldn't get a Friday or a Saturday, and on that first Sunday we put 1,200 people in there.

Back then, Magowan had aspirations to be a graphic designer but soon started to make some money out of his new Sunday service.

When I was aged 18 I was putting on a soul and jazz night called Club 9 at various hotels in and around Motherwell. Our DJs started playing a bit of house around 1987.

We had the chance to do a big party at the Ayr Pavilion, which was a massive old ballroom, with a balcony going all the way around it. The venue at that stage was being used for a rock night and Bob Jefferies, the Southport Weekender stalwart, had been down to have a look at the venue the week before us, and he saw all these big beefy rockers there and decided it wasn't for him.

The all-conquering Streetrave all-dayers in the small seaside town, 30 miles outside of Glasgow, would go on to earn legendary status among Scottish clubbers. The fun and games there kicked off on Sunday, September 10, 1989.

Jon Mancini was installed as resident, and would play every Sunday for the next four years, including, at each party, the closing 1am – 2am set.

Ayr was chosen, because Ricky and Jamsy (aka James McKay) were mates through Motherwell, and Jamsy came from Ayr. Ricky was from Motherwell, just outside Glasgow, and the pair of them had met up through various soccer hooligans. They were casuals and they both ran for Motherwell.

They couldn't spell the word music, between the two of them, if I'm really honest, but like most of the kids then, it was something fresh and new. They weren't promoters, they were part of a group of pals who wanted to put on a party and have a good time. A few of them had been to Ibiza and had seen what was happening, and the papers and magazines were bringing up the acid house thing all the time, and that was like a red rag to a bull.

The Ayr Pavilion, this huge old ballroom which sat next to an esplanade, used to be full of old bikers, and Ricky and Jamsy just grabbed it and started Streetrave.

And the age-old theory of football hooligans coming together because of acid house, almost a cliche these days, was no more poignant a reality than at Ayr Pavilion.

Mancini continues:-

There were lots of different casuals at Streetrave - Celtic, Rangers, Motherwell and Falkirk. They were all in their own wee groups, but the violence never ever erupted in the club because of that wonder pill called ecstasy. They'd be fighting on a Saturday and cuddling on a Sunday.

We weren't the original or only promoters in Scotland. There were other guys who had done stuff. The Slam boys had been doing their thing, The Sub Club was happening, you had Fever in Aberdeen with Jackie Morrison, and the Sweatbox nights in Arbroath. We all had these small pockets, but they were healthy pockets.

And because Scotland isn't that big, people would travel and do them all. It would be Friday night and the bus would be organised. They'd go 60, 70, 80 miles to a club, come back, and then go somewhere else the next night. Our opening line-up at Streetrave included guests Graeme Park and Mike Pickering. They were probably the biggest known DJs for us in the UK at that time.

Magowan adds:-

That first night we paid Pickering and Park £400 each. We spent £80 on a couple of strobes, and that was the extent of our lighting rig. We also put on Bob Jefferies and DJ Yogi Haughton, who played soul at the start, and our other resident Iain 'Boney' Clarke, but we didn't have a clue what we were doing really. There wasn't a book called How To Put On A Rave, Part 1...we were writing that as we went along.

I don't know what Graeme Park thought he was going to find up here. We always had that Motherwell/Aberdeen banter with him, and on that first trip I think we managed to put him and Mike up in the worst B&B in Ayr. But when they got to the venue they were like "fucking hell, this is all right".

Like so many iconic clubs, Mancini is adamant Streetrave would not work in modern times. And both he and Magowan feel the promotion never got the 'props' that it deserved.

You would never get away with Streetrave now. It started at two in the afternoon and finished at two in the morning. It was twelve hours, had a capacity of 1,500 on a Sunday afternoon in a small seaside village. You had kids outside licking cones, and kids inside licking their eyebrows. People came from a 150 mile radius. And there was no build-up during the day, they were having it in there from the start.

You would drive up to the venue and there would be a queue right the way down to the beach, and that was a sight to behold, especially in the summer with all the tourists walking around and all the ravers in line ready to go. It was just a fantastic place to be. Often the party would carry on outside once the club had finished, and through to Monday.

Murray Richardson, a DJ/producer who has promoted his Rebel Waltz nights worldwide and released music on leading house labels like 20:20 Vision and Low Pressings, says Streetrave had a profound effect on his life and career.

Streetrave at the Ayr Pavilion was an institution, but I agree that it has always tended to be overlooked when people talk about classic UK clubs or parties at the very beginning of the scene.

It had a massive effect on people's lives, and personally I consider myself lucky to have been part of a scene that would change my own life forever. As I stood in the middle of the dancefloor at Ayr Pavilion I realised that I wanted to become a DJ, and having spent the last 14 years DJing all over the world, I can honestly say that if it wasn't for experiencing Ricky Magowan & Jamsy's Streetrave parties as a young lad then my life would have ended up very differently indeed.

My first Streetrave was a far cry from previous nights out with my mates. We had spent most of our youth hitting dodgy nightclubs in Ayrshire and the surrounding areas in search of booze and birds, having not taken any real drugs before. Apart from smoking a bit of hash, we were what you would call extremely green behind the ears.

Then someone said there were these "west coast jams" going on at the Ayr Pavilion, down the beach on a Sunday afternoon from 2pm for twelve hours non-stop - that it was some kind of acid house party. Any 19-year-old lad in his right mind would be up for that in a flash. And so began the task to find some acid as, naturally, if it was an acid house party then you have to be on acid, right? Or at least, so any 19 year-old-lad in his right mind would think, right?

Off we went loaded up on purple ohms for the first time ever, going to a rave for the first time ever and experiencing along with hundreds of others something that was quite magical and really special. Something that was also going on up and down the land in little pockets all over the country. It was all there, a huge sound system that resonated right through your chest and nose, flavoured smoke, lights and strobes, DJs playing amazing music you had never heard before and loads of people who you didn't know and who you would go on to form friendships with that would last to this day. It was a paradise in a way, our own little paradise, in an old rundown skanky 1920s ballroom dancing hall.

The list of DJs who graced the decks reads like a who's who of underground DJs including Pickering and Park, Stuart & Orde from Slam, Jon Da Silva, Nightmares On Wax, Forgemasters, DJ Mink, Eddie Richards, Rythmatic, Fabio & Grooverider, LFO, 808 State DJs, Homeboy and Hippie & Funki Dredd. Even the mighty Sasha was a regular there, among many, many other top quality DJs and live acts from all over the world.

As Streetrave began to grow and grow, the all-dayers led to all-nighters all over Scotland, but it was always that family feeling with Streetrave that made and still makes it so special. Whether it was the tiny intimacy of the Kitsch club in Ayr, the massive New Year's Eve celebrations at the Prestwick Airport parties or the yearly birthday parties at The Arches in Glasgow that are still going strong to this day, and which me and my pals still attend.

Mancini fortunately mentioned "sweaty jocks" and "southern softies" before anyone in the "southern softie" One More team could, so the ball was quickly in his court where the so-called north/south divide is concerned.

The southern thing was really strange to us. We went and played at The Ministry Of Sound in the early days - myself and Boney, the other resident. We were pretty nervous, and we got a shock because we didn't feel the real energy that we got in Scotland. It seemed all very safe to us. We just didn't get the London thing, but to be honest, we didn't give a fuck, because we had our own scene up here.

We always felt the further up north you got the madder it was. Through the Midlands, clubs like Shelley's in Stoke, then to Manchester, the Hac', etc, and up to us, the so-called "sweaty jocks". The first DJs who actually came up hadn't experienced anything like it, and all the DJs and the punters will vouch that we had, and have, an incredible crowd. We were, and are, an incredible club and an incredible brand.

And the Scottish faithful needed little encouragement to travel across their native land to see English, European and American guests. Mancini continues:-

As for the Scottish DJs, I've always thought we've never got the recognition we deserve. There have been obvious notable successes. Slam played at our events way back in the day. And you should obviously class Graeme Park as Scottish, as he's from Aberdeen. Even if he was working in Manchester, our crowd always loved him coming up and playing for us. Scottish people will always latch on to anything that is Scottish.

Generally, the type of DJs we booked from the start, well, I think we were pretty upfront. We gave Carl Cox his first booking up here, Laurent Garnier, Fabio & Grooverider too. We also went down the live route as well. We gave Prodigy their first booking in Scotland. Inner City, K-Klass and M-People too. Americans like David Morales, Frankie Knuckles and Tony Humphries also came to Scotland to play for us.

In the early days I don't think many clubs had a music policy, because the DJs were basically playing all the same records - just not necessarily in the same order. And we were no different. There weren't hundreds of tunes out at the time, and most of those records became anthems because they would get played four or five times in one night.

Later the scene did split, as the music matured, but I don't think that was a good thing. I think it was better when everybody played

(clockwise) * Early '90s dancefloor action at Ayr Pavilion
* The flyer for the first Streetrave party in September, 1989
* Jon Mancini outside the Ayr Pavilion site in 2011
* Put your hands up in the air, Streetrave style
* Colours head honcho Ricky Magowan

STREET RAVE'S
WEST COAST JA
ALL DAYER, THE PAVILION, AYR, SUN 10th SEPTEMBER 1989 · 2.30pm
M.C. DUK
AND HIS DANCE TROOP
GRAEME PARK + MIKE PICKERIN
(KICK OFF AT 4pm ON THEIR FIRST LIVE APPEARANCE IN SCOTLAND)
BOB JEFFRIES, YOGI, ORDE + STUART, BONEY, GIBBY and BAT
SCOTLANDS FINEST EVER D.J. LINE
BUS DETAILS OR FOR FURTHER INFO: Tel (0292) 611676 or (0698) 35

everything. Things became slightly more snobby, as people picked their genre and went to their preferred night, and then wouldn't alter from that. We've always played across the board, from start to finish, through Streetrave and Colours. We've always played every genre of music.

And somehow a bit of Italian disco crept in as well, a retro genre which bizarrely spawned the weekly Streetrave One More track.

Mancini reluctantly explains:-

I was playing the last set one night at Streetrave, and Jamsy came into the booth and said, "after you finish tonight, that's us done here". He and Ricky had had a falling out with the people who ran the club. You know, the usual. The people who run the clubs know better than the promoters, it's always been the case. They think they can do it themselves, that they can do it better, when they know fuck all. Jamsy told me to announce that this was the last Streetrave, and I had this sinking feeling, because I had had so many great nights there, and made so many good friends, and I'd suddenly been told it was all over. It was like chopping my arms off.

And when you're put in that situation it's obviously a tough decision as to what to play at the end. If it was my last ever gig, or I really need to choose my ultimate One More track, my personal choice would be Joe Smooth's Promised Land. It's one of the ultimate anthems. It's got soul, it's got heart, it's just a phenomenal tune, and it brings back so many great memories from days gone by.

But the last tune that I played at Streetrave, well, there was only one tune I could play. It was the same tune at every Streetrave and, if I'm really honest, I fucking hate the tune now. It was called Energy by Beautiful Ballet. It was an old Italian disco thing, it was down the BPMs, around 112. And that record, up here, to this day, is a fucking anthem. I must take the credit because we made it into an anthem. The crowd loved it, because they thought it was a good tune, but they hated it because they knew it was the end of the night. We still do the Streetrave birthday parties once a year in Glasgow, a notorious night at The Arches, which the old crew all come out to. And I have to play that tune last, or my life wouldn't be worth living. I know people who have had it played at their weddings.

A quick check on the track's YouTube comments backs up Mancini.

colinsinnett72
absolute classic - the last song played at all the streetrave all-nighters at Ayr Pavilion from 89 - 91 or thereabouts....absolute class....happy days!
eh82007
and then the main lights came up. STREETrave ..... christ if i could go back i'd do it tomorrow.

Ricky Magowan admits the decision to leave Streetrave's spiritual home in Ayr was a tough one, but argues that it was one that was quickly vindicated.

As we were leaving Ayr Pavilion in 1993 we could see that there was a sea-change. The drug situation at the Pavilion was getting out of the hand. Because of the acts we were breaking - M-People, Prodigy, Moby and Utah Saints - a lot of record company execs were coming up and drugs were getting offered to the wrong people. Some of the security had started selling the drugs, and that was it, their dealers were in there, the old "who wants Es? Es Es, who wants Es?" everywhere you went in the club.

It was time to move on. It wasn't an easy decision, and financially, it was a bad one at the time. But six months later, two or three clubbers had died at Ayr Pavilion, after the club management decided to put on their own nights and change the venue's name to Hanger 13, in what was a move into the hardcore, Scottish rave scene.

It was all over the papers and the press, and if we had still been there, I may not be sitting here talking about Colours now.

In 1994 Magowan and co took Streetrave to the Fubar venue in Stirling, where it remained monthly for a year. But before Streetrave left its spiritual home, sell-out events at the Livingstone Forum and at Ayr Ice Rink, as well as those intriguing one-offs at Prestwick Airport, had already shown that there was life after the Ayr Pavilion. Magowan reflects:-

Between '91 and '93 we put on six Streetrave presents Eurodance events at Prestwick Airport, which we saw as the ultimate unique venue. The airport had shut down for financial reasons. The parties were in the concourse with people actually dancing in the old ticket halls. I'm told the money the airport made from those parties helped them open up again a year or so later. Again acts like M-People and Prodigy, and DJs like Coxy all played there. Big one-off Saturdays for 5,000 people, and if someone had done that at Stansted Airport or somewhere else in London, they would have been the best parties ever. We didn't get the press or recognition for those parties, either.

In late '94 we launched Salsa at The Tunnel in Glasgow, big one-offs on Bank Holiday Sundays, featuring big American jocks like David Morales, Frankie Knuckles and Inner City/Kevin Saunderson.

And then on February 25, 1995, we launched Colours, every Saturday at The Vaults in Edinburgh, the first night with Masters At Work and 2000 people through the door. This one was also more on the US house tip, with the likes of Roger Sanchez and Boy George headlining.

A year later we moved to The Arches in Glasgow, which would become Colours' spiritual home. We started on the second Saturday of the month, the worst one, and eventually got the first Saturday of the month, and became the biggest night there.

Colours is still all those things more than 20 years later, a reassuring testament to all the bravado of the people behind it.

Mancini reiterates:-

The Scots stick together, especially the clubbers. They like us promoters to get people to come in from outside so they can show them how they do it. They work Monday to Friday, and they just go for it at the weekends. That's how it works up here. Anyone that did come up was shown a good time and if they liked them, they let them know they were liked. If they were shit, however, they were told they were shit. It did feel like a siege mentality at the time, but most of the time incomers were welcomed with open arms.

Around 1994/'95, with the major sponsorships, and the likes of Cream and Gatecrasher really coming through, we decided that if we really wanted to go down the route of being a big club, and to create a big brand, Streetrave wasn't the right name. The word "rave" was frowned upon. So we came up with a new concept. We called it Colours, and Colours still goes to this very day.

And after the halcyon days of Ayr Pavilion, Colours did not restrict themselves to parties in Glasgow, or indeed to regular events purely held in clubs, as they expanded considerably to host a series of massive (and on-going) one-off and outdoor live events.

Edinburgh venues Club Mercado, Potterrow and Honeycomb have all played host to Colours over the years. While those huge events have included Live In The Capital at The Royal High Centre in Edinburgh, Summer Exposure at Glasgow's Tramway Theatre, prominent roles in the Scottish Homelands events in both Ayrshire and Aberdeen and parties at The SECC (Scottish Exhibition and Conference Centre).

Colours tour nights have also taken place all over the world, and then there's that annual Streetrave birthday event at The Arches, and, since 2002, the Colourfest party at the Braehead Arena and Waterfront in Glasgow, on the first Saturday of every June.

Mancini adds:-

We weren't ever tagged with one genre of music. We have always gone right across the board, and we give the people what they want by bringing them the biggest names. In the past twelve months we've had Armin Van Buuren, Tiesto, David Guetta, the Swedes (Swedish House Mafia) and Deadmau5 - probably the top five dance acts in the world right now. But we also like to keep bringing in the new guys like Max Vengeli and Wolfgang Gartner. We deliver what the public want, and we're versatile, and that's it in a nutshell. We put on the best parties in Scotland by far, and we're the biggest promoters up here by far. There's a lot of good nights up here and a lot of great DJs up here, but I feel we are just that bit further up there than the rest of them.

Magowan reckons he is lucky if the £1,500 he used to spend on an entire Streetrave line-up in 1989 would cover the agent fees of one of his headline acts in 2011.

We still put on events at The Arches, but it's more of an open diary. As we speak, I've got Tiesto coming up on Bank Holiday Sunday, and in April just gone we had Guetta, Van Buuren, and the Swedes twice, all in the space of three or four weeks. Nowadays it really depends on when the big boys are available.

And the reason those guys continue to come back and play for us time and time again is because we have looked after them from day one. They love the Scottish crowd and our crowd never let them or us down. David Guetta was being interviewed on Capital Radio in London recently, and the presenter asked him who the best crowd was on his UK tour... suggesting "London, Manchester or Brighton?" The radio host didn't even mention Scotland, but Guetta said immediately... "Glasgow".

These days there are seven or eight DJs who bring in big numbers and generate big sales. We're now part of this events-based business.

Back then there was no booking fee, no production costs and no tour manager to sort out. The DJs came by themselves, there wasn't this whole pop stardom thing.

We were charging £15 - £20 a ticket 22 years ago, and the entire DJ bill was £1,500 - £2,000. These days, you can't even charge as much as £15 - £20 for people to get in and the headline DJ's manager's fee is £2,000 alone.

One thing that hasn't changed, fortunately, is that our crowd always used to live for the dancefloor, and they still do.

VENUS

It is hard to believe that the man behind one of the most lauded and pioneering clubs in the UK began his working life as a teenage miner in a Scottish coalfield.

Venus creator James Baillie is a colourful character to say the least, and one of the most celebrated by the various clubland luminaries quizzed for the One More project. But by the time he launched the legendary Nottingham club he already had six years' experience of promoting in his adopted home town.

Baillie rocked up in Nottinghamshire in the late '70s when his pit in the small mining village of Kelloholm in Dumfries was closed.

My dad was a miner, and I started down the pit when I was 17, in 1976. Music was always my passion, though, and the first record I bought when I was 13 was David Bowie's Life On Mars. I didn't have anything to play it on, so I used to walk around the village with that seven inch single under my arm, knocking on people's front doors asking if I could come in and use their record players.

And Baillie has been blagging his way into nightclubs to use their record players ever since.

The first album I bought was by Glen Campbell, who I'd heard when my mum and dad brought some records back from the Miners' Welfare Club. After a couple of years of working down the mine, and developing my record collection, and also being seen as the weirdo in the village, they suddenly closed our minefield. I was 19 and I had the option to transfer to a pit in Hucknall in Nottinghamshire, for which I would receive £6,000 in "disturbance money". That was a lot of cash in those days, so I agreed, did a couple of months down the pit in Hucknall, and then when the money arrived, I left mining.

I'd got friendly with some people in Hucknall who had a company, called Olto, making made to measure clothes, and that's how I met my ex-wife Heather. This was the early '80s and myself and Heather broke away and set up our own company, making clothes for rich ladies in the area. Heather went to college to study pattern cutting, and we were both out and about most nights in Nottingham - which was pretty fashionable at the time - at various events and gigs.

Then around 1984, Soul Train with Jeffrey Daniels was on the TV, and I thought, "you know what, this could be set in Nottingham".

There was a small club in town called Pieces, and I put on a Saturday night party called The Kremlin Goes To Pieces. The group of friends I had at the time were all into hi-nrg, go-go and funk. We made handmade flyers and a few of us DJd on the night. I put banks of old black and white TVs all over the club and did stupid things like put toilet paper with Margaret Thatcher's face on, in all the cubicles. The capacity was about 300 and we filled it, and then, on the back of that success, a guy who owned a club called Food For Thought, asked me to take that place over. So I did, and renamed it Barracuda. It held around 350 people, and I got interior design students from Trent Polytechnic to redesign the place, and ever since I've always tried to involve students in whatever I've done.

In 1985, the same year that the BBC launched EastEnders, Baillie started a Friday night at Barracuda called The Queen Vic - after the famous pub in Albert Square - with Michael Murphy and Martin Green, DJs with links to Leigh Bowery's iconic Taboo night in London. The music policy was trashy/Italo disco, and again Baillie involved local students. Pioneering Nottingham city centre venue The Garage had opened in 1984, but after the success of the Kremlin party, Baillie claims he was barred from there, charged with pinching punters.

At Barracuda, I ran Fridays and Saturdays, and also put on student fashion parties midweek, and local bands. Then in 1986, I was asked to take over another venue called Eden. The student that I got in to design that went on to sculpt the huge set of metal wings near Angel Tube station in Islington in north London. A lot of the people I gave an opportunity to have gone on to great things, and that's always rewarding. It's always nice to hear and see what they're up to now.

Back then I was actually taking this all pretty much in my stride. I just felt like a bloke who was doing his job. And that now my job was to have my finger on the pulse, to be creative and to encourage other people to be creative. I did feel fortunate, though, that I was involved in the music business without being able to play a musical instrument. I had been given this platform to be creative, and I was happy bringing in whoever else I thought could be creative too.

With Heather, who has since gone on to be head pattern cutter at Paul Smith, I then opened a fashion shop in Nottingham called Pax, and, as a couple, where music, clubs and fashion were concerned, we quickly became well respected in the Nottingham area.

I was involved with Eden until around 1988, and then I was approached to get involved in a bar on the edge of town called Papa Binns, which was Nottingham's version of the Hacienda's Dry Bar in Manchester, and where loads of people would meet with their brick phones to wait for details of raves in the surrounding areas. The bar became a really popular meeting place, we had DJs playing most nights and we did really well. Then I was asked to go back and do something at Eden again, and so I launched a night called Return To Eden.

By now Graeme Park had left The Garage which had been renamed the Kool Kat, a title it first held in the 1960s. Allister Whitehead had taken over as resident DJ there, and although a regular at the Kool Kat, at some point, Baillie was also barred from the venue - probably, he thinks, for supposedly taking business away from them too.

By the end of the '80s, Baillie's rise through the clubbing ranks had certainly been eventful, but he soon upped the stakes when he took over the reins of a venue, unimaginatively, called The Club. The swiftly re-named Venus would not be Baillie's last venture in the town either, as he continued to shimmy around the city centre from club to club, right up until 2004, when he completed 20 years of promoting 'service' in Nottingham.

I was obviously doing other clubs before Venus in the mid-'80s and I went on to do others after as well, but, like with all of the clubs I've done, I just saw a gap in the market to do something a bit different. There was a big northern rave scene, which I wasn't into, so I was going down to London a lot and I took bits and bobs of all the influences there and put them into Venus.

The Club was owned by brothers Phil and Steve Kirk, and run by a guy called Sam Bowery. They asked me to take over, we gave the club a makeover and renamed it Venus, which was actually a suggestion from Heather's dad. We had a capacity of 520 on two floors, with 180 in the bar room, and then the bigger room was downstairs. I stood on the door most of the time, and it was quite easy for me to get the balance right, between the casuals and the fashion kids, because I knew so many people in the town. I knew the bad heads, as well as the good heads.

And things were just in place, really, because of the emerging house scene and the chemical influence with what people were taking at that time. As well as my various events, our punters had been going to The Garage, the Hacienda, the raves down south and also the raves in Blackburn. It was quite funny, because we did get a lot of football lads from Derby, Leicester and, of course, Nottingham, but there was never any trouble.

Many Venus regulars were also travelling great distances in search of the right club, but Baillie was already a past master where that was concerned too.

Around that time I had been frequenting Full Circle, the Sunday after-hours club in Staines, and Gosh at Dingwalls in Camden (promoted by Clive Henry, later of Circo Loco fame, and Rocky from X-Press 2) and, of course, the legendary Boys Own parties in London and wherever else. I also liked going up to the Sub Club in Glasgow, and Spice and Most Excellent in Manchester, as well as Chuff Chuff in Birmingham, and I got all those guys involved at Venus at the start. I had certainly been getting around the place and I think that's one of the reasons Venus exploded. In my head, without naming it, I guess Friday quickly became my 'inter-club' night, when I started to invite other promotions and their DJs to the club from wherever they were based in the UK. It was the first time a club had done that, and the first people I brought up were Flying, first on a Friday, and then I started booking the guest DJs and club nights, wherever they were from, on a Saturday too. That policy has since been credited with kickstarting the guest DJ circuit, and even for helping to bridge the north south divide, because clubbers from Manchester and London were suddenly partying together in Nottingham.

My favourite DJ was, and is, Andrew Weatherall, and I've always booked him since for whatever I've done. You have to remember that when I started Venus, there was no Back To Basics, no Cream, no Golden and no Progress. They called it the Balearic Network, and at Venus, it wasn't all about house. I was one of the only promoters taking Norman Jay's High On Hope night out of London, as well as people close to Norman like Gilles Peterson, all the acid jazz stuff. We also put live acts on like Barry K Sharp, Brand New Heavies and Galliano.

The good thing about Venus was the venue. It was a beautiful club compared to all these other places I used to go to, which were basically dives. The guys who ran the Kool Kat were my friends, but it's true that I did get barred from there soon after we launched Venus.

Sam Bowery was manager at The Club and played an integral part in the transition to Venus. He says:-

We wanted to make some changes at The Club so we went to see a night that James ran locally and I couldn't believe what he was doing and the atmosphere that he had created. I couldn't work out how he was doing it, apart from the music being very different to what we were playing then, which was very much middle-of-the-road R&B. A few weeks later James approached us and asked us if we were prepared to change the name and decor of our club, reorganise the place. So that's what we did and changed the name to Venus.

However, Bowery was shocked by the invoices he was now dealing with in the office.

Suddenly the costs were sky high. Compared to the one DJ that we had playing all week, who was getting £100 for that whole week, we were now paying DJs from out of town £200 or more each and more for just a couple of hours. Fortunately, we soon realized that while the operation was becoming more expensive to run, the amount that people were paying to come into the club more than covered the expenses.

I knew there was a change in the music, but before that I'd never really got into the music side of things and had never really even been on the dancefloor that much. One night in the early days at Venus I was standing to the side of the floor, having a bit of a jig and James

Baillie came over and put this small half a pill in my mouth. Within half an hour I was kissing and hugging everyone and suddenly everyone at the club that I didn't like was my best friend. That really got me into the whole environment of Venus and the whole culture. It was just fantastic. Suddenly I understood everything.

Mark Moore was one such London DJ who enjoyed the trip to the Midlands to see what all the fuss was about. And is perhaps testament to just how much clubland in those days changed people's lives.

Venus was a club I'd heard a lot about really, and which was essential in kicking off things, and putting that northern scene on the map, mixing the debauchery of acid house with a bit more glamour, where people would dress up and really let rip. Once James Baillie knew I was playing Chuff Chuff he got me down to do the bar at Venus and I remember Terry Farley from Boys Own saying at the time, "the thing about DJing in the bar at Venus is that you've got to get them dancing on the bar".

Years later I was playing out somewhere, and Samantha Morton, the wonderful actress, came up to me and said, "do you remember me Mark?", and I said, "yeah, of course, you were Oscar nominated in Woody Allen's Sweet and Lowdown and you snogged Tom Cruise in Minority Report. Yeah, I remember you" and she said, "no, from Venus, I used to dance on the bar for you at Venus".

A quick check on Morton's wikipedia page reveals the actress, born in 1977 in Nottingham, would have been aged around 16 at the time Moore played at Venus, and that *"at the age of seven, Morton was made a ward of court and never lived with her natural parents again. The next nine years were spent in and out of foster care. Under the effects of drugs, she threatened an older girl who had been bullying her, and served 18 weeks in an attendance centre. She said in an interview, "as a child I had a serious anger problem, but from the age of 16 I've been trying to turn bad things into positives".*

Maybe, dancing on the bar at Venus helped Morton turn bad things into positives. And when you are dancing on top of a bar, circa 1992/93 at a legendary club like Venus, in your teens (let's remember) then surely the positives outweigh the negatives, if only for those few hours.

Moore adds:-

Music-wise, at Venus in those days, there was a whole load of great stuff coming out, so I'd be mixing up a lot of British progressive house with New York stuff like Clivilles & Cole's A Deeper Love - amazing soulful vocals mixed in with mental progressive electronic house music.

Ian Tatham was resident DJ at Venus, and midweek promoter of the Ask Yer Dad Thursday session there from 1992 through to when the club closed in 1993.

I had been DJing for a few years before I came to Nottingham as a student and we always used to go to Venus on a Saturday. I wanted to do my own midweek night there and bring the Saturday vibe to the students during the week so we brought the travelling DJs in on those nights as well.

The night that made it for me was Flying, and the DJ from that lot that I liked most, who I felt created the best atmosphere, was Terry Farley. But he would be just one of fifteen of the best DJs in London, all with Flying, who would come up with friends on five or six coaches. It was an absolute riot. People had big afro wigs, playing inflatable guitars stood on speaker stacks. In most clubs if you got on the bar and started dancing someone would come and pull you down, but at Venus you used to see James Baillie actually helping people up on to the bar!

As well as Farley and other Flying DJs like Brandon Block and Dean Thatcher, James had all these contacts from the London and Manchester scenes, and the likes of Justin Robertson, Jeremy Healy, Darren Emerson and Jon (Pleased Wimmin) would all come and play at Venus too. Darren Emerson played some great sets down there, and through James Baillie's contacts we pretty much had everyone who was anyone at the time.

Now it kind of all blurs into one big night. My favourite memories were the atmosphere that was created, the early '90s Balearic vibe, being brought in from Ibiza, and in turn the clubbers from London who had been to Ibiza. All that really helped redefine what was going on in

Nottingham at that time. It was a chance for us in Nottingham to be a link between the London and Manchester scenes. It was about as hedonistic as you were going to get at the time in a nightclub in Nottingham. And it was basically like nothing else happening then, certainly outside of London and Manchester.

The Flying party coaches to Venus were too much for Danny Rampling. On the one occasion he braved it up on the bus from London, he decided to take refuge in Nottingham after his set rather than risk the journey back home.

My first trip to Venus was a real eye-opener. I was running a club at the Milk Bar called Pure Sexy, with my wife Jenny. James Baillie was at Pure Sexy one night and said "you'll love our club in Nottingham, it's rocking", and it was absolutely rocking. It was really so connected to what we were doing, the baggy look had gone out, people had started dressing up again, the rave scene had tailed off and people were feeling good again about going to a club. It was an exciting time, the glam time of clubbing, walking in seeing people dancing on the bar, and really pretty girls dancing on the bar, and with Nottingham, and its high population of good-looking females, it was like "wow". It was clear this was a really sexy club.

Sasha was DJing there at the time. The basement was a small club like the Milk Bar, with this bar area on the top floor, and it really was the leading light in Nottingham at the time. It was such a pleasure to walk into that environment and it feel like it was a home from home.

I think my second trip there was a Venus meets Flying night, promoted by the legendary Charlie Chester. He said "why don't you join us on the coach, come up with us?" I got on the coach, but it was absolute carnage. The bus had only just left Hounslow, but there was a full scale party going on. Everyone on the bus had been out for two days already and with the greatest respect to Charlie and the people on there, the stuff going on was actually quite scary. It was a case of what didn't happen on there. I actually opted to get a hotel for the night in

(clockwise) * A visiting London crew at Venus, with a certain Chris Good, front centre * James Baillie interviewed for the * One More documentary at Dalston Superstore, 2010 * A Venus newsletter, June, 1991 * Sasha promo shot * Mark Moore filmed for One More, 2011

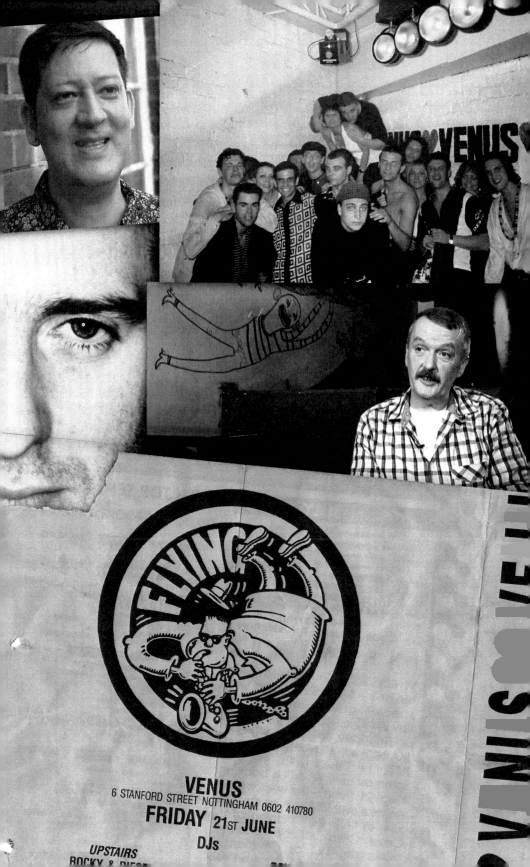

FLYING

VENUS
6 STANFORD STREET NOTTINGHAM 0602 410780
FRIDAY 21ST JUNE
DJs

UPSTAIRS
ROCKY & DIESEL

Nottingham rather than go back to London on that bus.

But they were amazing times, and Venus was an amazing club. The set there was uplifting house, lots of piano house, lots of vocals. That was the Pure Sexy sound too, lots of US house, Italian house, British house. It was party time, it was "come on, let's celebrate our lives". The post rave scene had gone back into the clubs, people would go out and buy something new to wear every week, get glammed up and have the time of their lives.

Baillie was in his element and his preferred DJs were also the nation's favourites.

As well as Andrew Weatherall, there was a young Darren Emerson, while Danny Rampling also floated my boat. And, of course, there was Sasha, who was seen as a northern rave DJ. I took him under my wing and became his manager for three years. When he played at Venus he tailored his music to the Venus environment and the Venus crowd.

There are so many amazing memories of Venus. I always used to like the Ducksoup parties, which I held on Bank Holiday Sundays. I used to do a joint ticket with the nearby Royal Hotel, where they had 200 rooms...202 to be precise. On those Sundays I block-booked the hotel and if you had a room at the Royal, we had a sound system in the bar downstairs and you could party down there until about ten in the morning after a Ducksoup.

I realised Venus was a success when I used to turn up to open the doors on a Saturday, and we started to see the queues around the block were already in place. The capacity of Venus was exactly 508, and it was a bit bigger than some of the other places in town. You also had the bigger 'Mecca' clubs in town, but Venus was the perfect size for us. I've always thought it was best to turn people away, rather than to try and fill something bigger.

There are a few tracks that sum up Venus, but, to this day, and it's still very strong, it's probably Joey Beltram's Energy Flash that stands out. Also up there, JayDee's Plastic Dreams and Weatherall mixes of Love Corporation's Give Me Some Love and My Bloody Valentine.

And Weatherall's pioneering mixes were certainly causing a stir, and still do on YouTube. Of the aforementioned mix of My Bloody Valentine (The Glider EP), 'UnePlanetedeGopak', comments:-

This record was/is/always will be visionary. It stood for an intersection in music where so much was possible. But it was the expression of the possibility in itself. That sounds pseudo-intellectual I know, but hey!

Ian Tatham's favourite Flying DJ was conveniently behind his favourite track at Venus.

The tracks that sum up Venus for me, was Bocca Juniors' Raise, which Terry Farley was involved in. I liked the Balearic vibe, but also the ho-down piano and the Italian vibe; Ginny's Keep Warm and SLD's Keep Out was also where I was at - anthemic piano tracks that still kind of retained some kind of credibility.

Months after opening and with Venus in full swing, Sam Bowery was by now well used to punters travelling from all over the UK to Nottingham, and had even started venturing further afield himself.

I used to travel down to The Milk Bar in London on a Monday night to Darren Emerson's Recession Session, specially to hear him, and then travel back to Nottingham. Suddenly driving miles just to see a DJ seemed to become the norm. My friends thought I was mad, but it was well worth it because I heard all the tunes I wanted to hear.

I have to say that initially the local Nottingham guys were a little averse to people coming in from outside of the area, but that soon changed. They seemed to have this football mentality during the day at the matches and then in the evenings at the club they'd be fine with everyone there. That's what I found amazing - the friendliness between all the people from different cities.

My favourite two tracks were Degrees Of Motion's Do You Want It Right Now and Future Sound Of London's Papau New Guinea. We actually had Degrees Of Motion perform live in the basement. I got so carried away that I ended up on stage with them, only to be quickly ushered off by James Baillie.

And it wasn't just the predominantly underground 'Balearic Network' who were travelling from out of town to Venus. Pete Tong's manager/producer Eddie Gordon quickly pinpointed Baillie's celebrated club as a key conquest if Radio 1 was ever to shatter it's cheesy reputation.

We identified Venus in Nottingham and Back to Basics in Leeds and as two potential guest spots, but were knocked back on the first calls, with Basics boss Dave Beer saying, "I don't need no fooking Radio 1 DJ in my club, we play house music mate, not hits".

And that was totally understandable, given Radio 1's image from the '80s. So I decided to drive to Venus to speak to the promoter James Baillie in person. I already knew Jonathan Woodliffe, a fantastic DJ from Rock City, who was co-promoting there, so I was confident I could get Pete in there as Jon knew Pete from London Records, his day time gig, along with writing for Blues & Soul.

Venus blew even my calculating mind. It was everything we had tried in the '80s - two rooms, big sound, unique decor, and a crowd that were having a great time. However, this was so much better, largely because of how the Venus-ites were dressed. After years of seeing punters in jeans, baggy T-shirts and boots or trainers, the Nottingham crowd were dressed to kill.

Everything from the music to the decor and attitude was super sexy. James Baillie agreed to try our "Radio 1 lad" on the say-so of Jonathan and a date was set.

I drove back to London thinking "I'm going back to Venus with or without Pete" - this was love at first sight. Then the fashion and design syllabus at Nottingham University was the best in the country so half the clothes being worn in Venus were self made and after a night of ecstatic dancing, hanging off everyone, punters half naked but with huge smiles on their faces. Amazing scenes.

As we pulled up to Venus for Tongy's debut in his little 320i BMW, Baillie told me the place was already full and hundreds of girls had turned up to see who Tong was. He blew them away with his set, we had a celebratory spliff, hung out afterwards and the motion was set. We were going to hit every cool club in every town in the UK.

James Baillie let other promoters know of Tong's pulling power and now everyone took my call.

We started teaming up with promoters all over the country - Russell and Pete at Progress in Derby, Brian Andrews and Charlie Chester at The Arena in Middlesbrough, Lakota in Bristol, Geoff Oakes at Renaissance in Mansfield, Nigel Blunt in Birmingham, Paul Taylor at Angels in Bolton, Jon Hill at Golden in Stoke, the legendary Ryan brothers at Moneypenny's and Chuff Chuff in Birmingham, Richard Carr at Slinky in Bournemouth, John Digweed in Hastings, Darren, James, Gill and Jim at Cream in Liverpool, David Vincent at Sankeys Soap in Manchester, Ricky McGowan at Colours in Edinburgh, the Reid brothers at The Tunnel in Glasgow and The Arches in Glasgow, The Warehouse in Leeds, The Leadmill in Sheffield, Pacha in Rotherham, Scott and Simon at Gatecrasher in Sheffield, the two Barrys at Sugar Shack in the north east...every weekend up the M1, M6, M62, M4. Anywhere but London, except for the odd Friday night at The Gallery or the Ministry Of Sound.

Ian Tatham remembers the fashion of the early '90s fondly, but still laments the demise of Venus in 1993.

The owners of the clothes shops in town would all be in Venus too. They could see what all the cool kids from Manchester and London were wearing and they'd begin to stock all that stuff in their shops. Back then it was men in leather trousers, women in fluffy bras and loads of waistcoats all round.

Then people who went to Venus started their own nights using the same formula, not just in Nottingham but in Sheffield and Leeds and Derby... which meant they no longer travelled to Nottingham. The club also had run-ins with the police due to overcrowding.

Pushing the limit on the club's capacity meant an awkward court appearance for Bowery. Although, he has few regrets.

Unfortunately when we were being successful we were overcrowding the venue, and we had to go to court. Myself and Steve Kirk lost our licences and we weren't able to be involved in the club towards the end. From working at Venus, though, I met loads of people from other cities. I met the guys from Moneypenny's – Jim, Lee, Michael and Dermot - I went on to work with them, and in Ibiza. And then I met my wife in Ibiza. In some ways Venus gave me a lot of my future, and the girl I ended up marrying, so I have a lot to thank the club for.

Like many of the clubs featured in this book, Venus would come to an abrupt end after just three years. It would be one of the shortest documented here.

Its influence, however, is probably immeasurable. As far as Baillie is concerned, though, there is still some unfinished business, because he had big plans for Venus.

Venus wasn't supposed to finish. We had already talked about the possibility of adding an extra room. Phil Kirk decided he was going to buy the whole building, and I had been taken upstairs to discuss ideas for a third floor. With all the pressure from the police, and with Sam and Steve losing their licences, it was agreed that Venus would shut down temporarily, so the heat could be taken off it, and we would open something else in the meantime. We also had to shut down because there were so many people trying to get in the club, much more police were needed in the town centre, and that meant the costs for the police went up massively.

Baillie, naturally, already had the name and concept for his new venture, a holding club until Venus was ready to reopen. And aptly enough, Rockadero was the name of a popular haunt of fellow miners Fred Flintstone and Barney Rubble in legendary cartoon series The Flintstones.

The plan was that myself, Steve and Sam, would briefly open a club called Rockadero. Then one day Steve told me that Phil had sold Venus to the solicitors who had the building next door to the club. He never told me and to this day I still haven't had a call to say it's finished. I'm still waiting. I had big ideas for the new version of the club, and I planned to call it Venus still. I believe it could have gone on for many years because there was so much more scope to develop it. And it's sad because the last night we did have there, I couldn't take it. I had to leave early, so I guess I sensed something wasn't right. It was very frustrating, because I wasn't just doing Fridays and Saturdays there, I had really strong midweek student nights too. The likes of Pulp, Blur,

Spiritualized, Paris Angels and Northside had all played live at Venus during the week.

One such "student" is Ian Tatham. When his degree finished, he stayed in Nottingham, and promoted nights for James at both Rockadero ('93/'94) and Deluxe ('94 –'96).

My last track at Venus, personally at Ask Yer Dad, was Ce Ce Rogers' Someday. We had Al McKenzie from D-Ream guest for us that night. I think Darren Emerson played the last ever record at Venus, one of his Underworld tracks. I can't quite remember what it was, it's a bit hazy.

Baillie is immensely proud of the part Venus played in the history of British clubland.

The club's legacy was bringing a lot of people together and people coming from all over the place to go to Venus, not just from the UK. I remember the likes of Jerry Bouthier, who now does Nice in London, coming over from Paris once a month as a punter. People came from Amsterdam once a month too. Because we had a membership policy we knew exactly how far people were travelling to get to the club.

Baillie also had a management agreement with Sasha, a business arrangement he says he "stumbled upon", and, which later, he was glad to stagger away from unscathed!

Sasha just loved the music he could play at Venus. It opened his mind, because it was different from all the stuff he'd been playing at the raves. I was able to take him out of the rave scene, and got him bookings at things in London like Kinky Disco, Pushca and Boys Own, because those were the people that I knew.

However, after a couple of years, I stopped managing Sasha because of the death threats I was getting from promoters who I wouldn't let book him. There were also loads of promoters who put him on their flyers, because they knew his name would sell out the gig for them. Then Sasha would get a reputation for not turning up to gigs, which he'd never been booked to play at in the first place. Eventually he went over to be managed by Seven Webster at Seven PM, and by then I'd really had enough. I was standing up to these promoters and they were saying, "we know where you are, we know which club you're going to be at tonight", and I just didn't need that.

However, with those often unavoidable sinister elements of clubland thankfully now a distant memory, there are nothing but glowing references when Venus is brought up in Baillie's presence... and it regularly is.

I still get bombarded about Venus wherever I go. It's amazing. I was at a pool party at Shoreditch House and this girl - who was with the DJ Neil Macey, from Birmingham, back in the day - came running up to me and said, "You're James Baillie, aren't you? You changed my life". And she was literally standing there crying. I was with my new partner at the time, who just couldn't believe it. And it's funny, because my promotions and events straddle a couple of generations. I went to a party Andrew Weatherall put on recently (2011) in Stoke Newington, and there were the older lot from Venus there, as well as the younger lot from The Bomb.

Before The Bomb, his longest-running Nottingham venue from 1996 - 2000, Baillie had the Rockadero from 1993 onwards to help him get over the sad demise of Venus. But he wouldn't settle easily.

I did Rockadero after Venus, and then a night called Deluxe (which was later at a gay club called Neros), again with Steve and Sam. I remember one line-up I had at Deluxe was The Chemical Brothers and Monkey Mafia (aka Jon Carter) downstairs with Death In Vegas and Daft Punk upstairs. The whole line-up probably cost around £800 and included Daft Punk's travel expenses from Paris. My problem is that I've never kept any flyers, and don't have any record of these events. I then had a fall-out with Steve there, and moved on to do a club called Essence in 1996, which had previously been a ritzy club.

Baillie says he got "stitched up" at Essence, because he refused to book the likes of Jeremy Healy, alleging that a well-known local player on the scene, not a million miles away from this chapter, agreed to book Healy instead.

I'd booked Jeremy for Venus, but by 1996 I was over all that, and wanted to book people like Angel Moraes, DJ Pierre and Eddie Flashin' Folkes, as well as all the British shakers and movers on the deeper and more underground house scene. The owner at Essence wanted me to book people like Jeremy, but I refused. Then I went on holiday to San Diego, and got stitched up by this person who said that if they were given the run of the club, then they would indeed book Jeremy, before, allegedly adding: "I think James has had enough of Nottingham, by now".

Which could not have been further from the truth, because, unrepentant, Baillie left them all to it at Essence and accepted yet another offer to take over The Hippo Club in Nottingham town centre, which he quickly renamed The Bomb.

Kelvin Andrews was a resident for me at The Bomb, but had also played for me at Venus, Deluxe and Essence, before that. When I started at The Bomb I booked people like Harvey, who played for me each month for the first year. Other early guests included Faze Action, Idjut Boys and Jools Butterfield, as well as the likes of Kenny Hawkes, Luke Solomon and Stuart Patterson from the deep house scene in London, and, of course, Andrew Weatherall played for me throughout. Kelvin would play in the main room some weeks, and in the second room, which would be slightly more alternative, other weeks. During my time at The Bomb I also curated The Social Bar from 1998 - 2002, and then I was asked to open Stealth in 2002 and ran that until 2004.

DJ, producer and songwriter extraordinaire Kelvin Andrews received a somewhat frosty reception from Baillie when they first met at Venus.

My brother Danny and I had been doing well with our Sure Is Pure production guise, and I was resident at Golden in Stoke at this point too. We had been booked for a PA at Venus, and I was also due to play later that night too. But we turned up late for our soundcheck, and were greeted by James who told us "you can fuck off, you're not doing the PA now". We hung around anyway for my DJ set, and by the end of the night me and James had made up, and we went on to become great friends. I played at other stuff he did in Nottingham after that, and became a full-time resident at The Bomb for the whole time James ran it. The Bomb was an amazing club, and James stuck to his guns with that club when most of the club scene was going very commercial and trance was everywhere. James went the other way, always underground. He is a true lover of music and had a vision for The Bomb, which he always stuck with. James will always be recognised as one of the most important people in UK club culture.

Baillie's promoting career in Nottingham was coming to an end but, significantly, he had finally addressed the question of his sexuality.

I came out in 2001, and people ask why I stayed in the closet for so long, but, you know, I've worked in the music business all my life, and, certainly in those early days it was mainly run by blokes. And to be honest, I never thought they would have understood.

And I was with Heather too, who I had married, and who I loved. She had been a rock to me from the start. When I came out, we'd been together 21 years, and married for 17 years of that. I'd known from a very early time that I was gay. In the end, though, it got to the point where I thought I was going to kill myself, and where I was drinking and taking drugs just to stop myself hurting inside so much.

I had put a brave face on it all for so long, and I actually stayed with Heather until she found someone else. And she has. She is remarrying and that's marvellous. I come from a mining village in Scotland, lived there in the '70s, and I've always been a feisty, I suppose, angry guy, and it's because I was always bottling everything up. I've lost count of the amount of people who have said what a different and nicer person I am now since I came out.

After Stealth, Baillie severed his ties to Nottingham, and headed down to London, working on the nationwide Club NME brand, putting on nights all over the UK, and also programmed the Rizla tent at festivals. In 2006, he became music consultant for Fred Perry, also putting on Sub Culture events at the 100 Club in the West End through the iconic clothing brand's Heritage range.

But in London the club offers were still coming in thick and fast. He took on the role of live manager at the ill-feted Matter at The 02 in

North Greenwich, and then accepted a position setting up a new warehouse-style venue called Cable, in London Bridge.

In 2008 I was approached by Fabric to be the live manager at their new club, Matter. It was a fantastic venue, a great club...just in the wrong place. And it barely lasted 18 months. Shortly after I was asked to help launch Cable, which was set in disused railway arches at London Bridge, but that whole project was a total nightmare. And, that's how and why I think I had my heart attack. I was 48.

The Cable experience drained me, shook me up, and for the first time in my life I was disheartened enough not to want to be involved in clubs anymore. I'd been putting in serious hours and it just wasn't a pleasant experience. I was having a particularly unsavoury phone call at home on the day I first got the pains. I stumbled out in the street to try and flag down a taxi and the cabbie who pulled over took one look at me and drove me straight to A&E. I was wired up, they did loads of tests, and told me I'd had a heart attack.

I took some time off, to recharge my batteries and to decide what I wanted to do. Then I went to Lovebox in Victoria Park with a friend, and just wasn't feeling it. He asked me what I would do with the festival and, I said, I'd do a gay friendly day on the Sunday, because Sunday clubbing is so associated with the gay community. And then, through a friend of a friend, I was asked to do exactly that at the Lovebox 2010. I booked Grace Jones and Hot Chip, among others, and I was really happy with my first year's involvement - I'd always thought the best clubs were polysexual.

I'm now employed full time by the Mama Group, who run Lovebox, and through that I was asked to programme Gay Pride in central London, which is scheduled to be part of World Pride in the near future.

So finally, after a career in the club game spanning four decades, James Baillie is content in his own skin. It counts for barely 36 months of those hugely eventful 30-odd years, but at the time of going to press Venus is surely his most career-defining achievement.

MISS MONEYPENNY'S

Much has been made of the glamour of Miss Moneypenny's, the scantily-clad models, the general hedonism at work, their exclusive Sunday Chuff Chuff parties which rolled effortlessly into Mondays... and, believe me, it's all absolutely true!

Indeed, those one-off Chuff Chuff parties, for so long the hottest ticket in town, often had more lingerie on show than a Victoria's Secret catalogue.

In fact, if Sid James and Barbara Windsor had stumbled across one in their heyday, Carry On DJ might just have been added to the iconic British slapstick film series. And with Chuff Chuff, just like the Carry Ons, there was always a theme.

It was that other legendary UK film series, James Bond, of course, which spurned the Miss Moneypenny's name. And it was Miss Moneypenny's, just like the flirty, yet dutiful secretary of the same name, which did the business for its founders week-in, week-out.

Jim Ryan, and his brothers Dermott and Mick, and their pal Lee Garrick, were the four lads about town behind the Moneypenny's empire, and Jim explains exactly how it all came about.

We ran Miss Moneypenny's from 1993 to 2006 at Bonds, which later became HQ, at a site in Hampton Street in Hockley, Birmingham. It was a result of another party that we used to put on called Chuff Chuff, which itself had started, basically, because we were in the right place at the right time.

The Moneypenny's brand itself evolved from a clothes shop that my brother Mick and I opened in Birmingham in 1986 called The Depot. Lee worked in the shop and Dermot would also help out during his holidays from university.

The Depot, I guess, became the epicentre of dance music club culture in the west Midlands area. We sold tapes and tickets for all the events, as well as club wear and other paraphernalia like videos, and we were actually taken to court by the Greater Manchester constabulary for selling tickets for the "illegal acid house parties" at the time.

In '88 we decided to put on some of our own parties. Initially on boats on the River Severn in Worcester, these evolved into boat trips on The Thames in London, and also parties at Venus in Nottingham and at The Milk Bar in London. These were, in fact, all early Chuff Chuff parties. Dermot would handle the marketing, Lee the promotion, Mick the organisation and the music was my domain.

We were influenced by the raves, so used a lot of those strategies for the early Chuff Chuffs, such as not releasing the venue until the day of the event. However, we felt that our locations should be a little more off the wall, so the very early Chuffs were in venues such as Baskerville Hall, Oliver Cromwell's ancestral home in Huntingdon and Peckfortan Castle, to name but a few. Musically, we felt more attached to the Balearic sound of the time.

As well as Venus, I was also influenced by going to parties in London like early Pushca events, and saw an opportunity to put on similar things in the Birmingham area. I was a DJ and I wanted somewhere to play.

Jim Ryan argues that Moneypenny's was one of the first post acid-house clubs in the UK to consistently focus on the glam side of clubbing on a weekly basis.

In the early '90s at The Milk Bar in Soho, Danny and Jenny Rampling had launched Pure Sexy, and then its successor, a night actually called Glam, two relatively short-lived weeklies that had followed on from the couple's pioneering Shoom night in the capital, which had been all about bandanas, dungarees, smiley face T-shirts and acid house.

So they had been smartening up their act down in London, while the likes of Renaissance in Mansfield had also stuck their necks out where a door policy was concerned as the post-rave northern clubbing era unfolded, but Moneypenny's and Chuff Chuff quickly became renowned for a crowd that was, for want of a better word, sexier.

For many, Miss Moneypenny's was as much about escapism as it was the music. And whereas Renaissance would become known for a harder, more epic brand of house, which later became progressive house, Moneypenny's adopted the funkier side of things, with plenty of vocals. And plenty of vocals always equalled plenty of girls.

And with one clever use of the title name of cult 1971 blaxploitation film Shaft and The Theme From Shaft, this particular Ryan brother was even able to make an average Brummie name sound exotic.

When I first started to DJ in the mid '80s the name was bestowed upon me by my partners as a bit of a piss take, really. In fact, in those days I was just DJ Shaft. I decided when we started getting a little recognition I wanted to use my own name, but the Shaft moniker remained to maintain a link with those early DJ years.

The club's mission statement and ethos was essentially glam clubbing. It was about people dressing up and being extrovert. It was a crowd with a gay mixed feel to it. It had evolved as a result of Venus in particular, and we took that ethos through to Miss Moneypenny's.

Like every club in the early stages of our club culture there wasn't really a music policy. DJs just played what was available really. There wasn't as much music being produced in those days, so quite often you would hear three different DJs play half a dozen of the same records in any one night. There was a format of DJs that were travelling all over the country, the likes of Sasha, Paul Oakenfold and Jeremy Healy who were, essentially, the travelling oracle of dance music and they regularly played alongside myself at Miss Moneypenny's.

I think it was in the late '90s that things became more defined in terms of music. Because we were a glam club, we quickly got labelled a little bit with that handbag house tag, and a lot of that early uplifting Italian piano house music was played at the club. That was probably true, though, for pretty much most clubs and DJs at the time, because many were tapping into that stuff in the early to mid '90s.

Back in 1993, in terms of promotion, Miss Moneypenny's was no different to its counterparts all over the UK, but the guys soon realised that the brand they had created could effortlessly lend itself to rather more elaborate and outrageous publicity campaigns.

In the early stages promotion was pretty straight forward. Firstly, we had our base in town so we always had access to people who were interested, clubbing people who would be in and out of the shop, getting flyers, buying stuff to wear at parties and looking for somewhere to go. So we had an audience that we were catering for on a day to day basis.

And secondly, in the early days it was very much flyer-led. There were teams of people all over the Midlands and the country who would do flyering so we tapped into those resources, and then as it became a little bit more sophisticated we had to think of different strategies. We were putting out mix albums regularly so we were looking to tap into more mainstream audiences, who would in turn tune back into the music of Miss Moneypenny's.

On-going, one of the biggest ideas we had was to put a transvestite up as candidate for the 1997 General Election in the Tatton constituency, which at the time was one of the most talked about constituencies, because it was the Neil Hamilton/Martin Bell contest. We decided, as a blatant publicity stunt, to put up this colourful and outrageous character who looked incredible and captured people's imagination very, very quickly. As a result the amount of press that we got for £500 - the cost of putting up a candidate - was phenomenal.

We had Radio One following us, we were on the front pages of two of the national tabloids and all the broadsheets did something on it, too. NBC News in America even followed us around for the day, and we were featured on loads of other TV news items. That, in particular, helped spread the concept of Miss Moneypenny's, and what we were about, all around the world.

When Miss Moneypenny's started, Birmingham had become one of the main clubbing areas in the UK, certainly for house music. Pretty much at the same time as us there was Wobble down the road, there was Fun at The Steering Wheel and there was Crunch. There was the latter part of the Snobs thing, and as a result of all this there was a big travelling scene of people who were coming to Birmingham so we were all very important to the Birmingham entertainments economy at the time, and our involvement in the '97 General Election certainly added to all that.

Importantly, the thousands of clubbers passing through were networking just as much as promoters and DJs.

In the early days of clubland there was this network of DJs and everybody pretty much knew everyone, so it wasn't a case of banging on agents' doors to try and get someone to play, it was fairly easy to get who you wanted. It was a case of getting on the phone, and more often than not the DJ would have heard of the club and knew it would benefit their career to play in another part of the country.

We were one of the more high profile clubs and it was fairly easy to get who you wanted. Paul Oakenfold, Nicky Holloway, Mark Moore and Sasha all played for Moneypenny's on a regular basis. As a DJ, my early influences were people who were around the Birmingham area at the time, guys like DJ Dick, Lee Fisher and Neil Macey. DJs were soon more than just people who played records. There were people, including some of the big American DJs, who got the mixing of those records off to a fine art, and to evolve in the dance music scene you suddenly had to take the idea of mixing records on board. In the UK the likes of Graeme Park and Sasha were particular influences, in how they used to put music together. So we would listen and study the way they played and try and copy and emulate the way they mixed records. As a result, we learned the trade.

Miss Moneypenny's, I'd like to think, was pretty much an instant success, and that was because we had done our homework. We'd already done our other one-off Chuff Chuff parties. We had our audience for that, and Miss Moneypenny's went on to become the weekly Chuff Chuff event on Saturdays, with Chuff Chuff moving to a Sunday promotion held every three or four months.

S'Express producer Mark Moore's first DJ booking at an early Chuff Chuff was as much of a surprise to him as anyone.

I first heard about Chuff Chuff when my friend said I was on the flyer for one. I didn't even know what it was but my friend said, "they're not massive yet, but they're really good parties". So I went along with my records and they said, "oh, we thought you couldn't make it" and I said "yeah, well you've put my name on the flyer, so I'm playing now". That night was amazing and I pretty much played every one after that.

Chuff Chuff was the first one to really start glamming it up outside of London. They had these amazing drag queens, an amazing mix of people and then you would have what my friends and I called "Stepford Wives On Acid" and they would just look incredible, beautiful girls, identical... literally looking like they were on acid.

I remember at that first Chuff Chuff I started with this new record that had just come out by Felix, called Don't You Want Me, so it must have been some time in 1992. And I remember I was in a tent in these amazing grounds, and there were people sunning themselves out by the pond, but as the track kicked in suddenly everybody just gravitated to the tent like zombies. The ice machines went off, and the party had started. Incredible.

My overriding memory of Chuff Chuff would have to be the after-parties in the hotel rooms, wherever the event had been held. There were different parties going on in each room, and each one would be like a different universe. There would be a bunch of mad girls in one, next door to a bunch of mad geezers, with a bunch of mad drag queens just along the way. You could experience the whole of humanity in one hotel corridor.

Manchester likely lad Adrian Luvdup also remembers those Chuff Chuff parties well, and still feels fortunate to have been able to attend.

Moneypenny's always had the reputation as THE glamorous club, all about style, glamour, beautiful women and class, whereas the Luvdups had a rep of being complete mental northern monkeys, always leathered, half the time playing, half the time passed out behind the decks.

Although we only played Moneypenny's a couple of times, even if we'd been DJing in another part of the country on the Saturday night we'd make the effort to try and go to Chuff Chuff wherever it was. And also to find out what the theme was and dress accordingly.

One particular Chuff Chuff was called Bedtime Stories. So we assumed the theme was characters from bedtime stories you were read as kids. We went as Tweedle Dum and Tweedle Dee from Alice In Wonderland. The big bellies, the big hats, we hired all that and got an Alice outfit for one of the girls too. When we arrived we realised the tag line was "baby dolls and silk pyjamas", and everyone was dressed in sexy outfits, smart dressing gowns and cravats. There we were looking like a pair of clowns as usual, so we got leathered as usual.

I think Moneypenny's epitomised the whole handbag house side of things in the mid-'90s, with DJs like Jon (Pleased Wimmin), but people

Miss Moneypenny's

Miss Moneypenny's

Miss Moneypenny's

like David Morales would play there too, and the music was always spot on. Chuff Chuff was simply something else.

After launching Chuff Chuff first, Jim Shaft Ryan had seen Moneypenny's come to the forefront of his operation, but those one-offs were always special:-

Chuff Chuff had actually preceeded Moneypenny's by five years and by 1993 when Moneypenny's started we had developed quite a national following and that's why we believed we could do a weekly club night. Chuff Chuff had created the infrastructure and network in which Monneypenny's could evolve, and we would then go on to hold around four Chuff Chuffs up and down the country each year.

My favourite one was called The Enchanted Fairytale at a venue called Hinchingbrooke House in the deep countryside of Hertfordshire. It turned out to be the hottest day of the summer and everyone was sitting outside. There was a Punch & Judy show as well as a harp player on the lawns and I remember some guys playing football. Justin Robertson was playing and dropped Rock The Kasbah by The Clash and everyone just rushed the dance floor. It was magical.

Jon (Pleased Wimmin) was a perfect fit for Miss Moneypenny's, and got his first big break after Danny Rampling spotted his drag act on the London club circuit.

I was always into music, spent all my pocket money on records, then went to fashion college in London, and started going to mixed/gay clubs. I never wanted to be a DJ, because at that time it didn't seem like a job. I ended up doing drag with a couple of friends, and we called ourselves The Pleased Wimmin. We used to do stupid cabaret acts, in shell suits, and just take the piss really.

We did a lot of work for Kinky Gerlinky, which was massive in London in the early '90s. Danny and Jenny Rampling gave us a card one night there and said "call us, if you want to come and work for us". They were just starting Glam at The Milk Bar, and we became 'dancers' for them. We'd turn up at Glam and get paid to sniff poppers, get drunk, fall over and snog all the straight men.

I always used to speak to Danny about music, and then he said "I'm off to Ibiza next week for six weeks, do you want to do the warm-up?", and I said "all right then". I had loads of records, but I didn't have any decks. I literally had to learn to play for that first night.

Through doing that, other people asked us to play at their night, and before I knew it I was going up and down the motorway every weekend. It just happened really quickly, completely unplanned. Rick and Debbie, the couple who put on Pushca in amazing film studios all over London, used to come to Glam, so I got booked for those. Then James Baillie from Venus was at a Pushca and asked me to play for him in Nottingham, where the Ryan brothers came up to me and asked me to play for Miss Moneypenny's. That's how it worked.

My trademark was chucking in pop or old glam rock records, and that's what I loved, that people were so openminded back then. It was like doing a really great collage, or someone putting a great outfit together. It wasn't just a two hour mix of the same music. That excited me and made me want to take things further. It was like a conversation with the crowd.

Birmingham was always quite famous as far as I was concerned, because of the New Romantic scene up there in the '70s, and the Rum Runner club, which the Duran Duran management used to own. And Birmingham people were always up for getting dressed up. Moneypenny's was like a fashion show and sunbed shop all rolled into one. As for Chuff Chuff, which I also played at, they were like Sodom and Gommorrah.

Judge Jules was another Chuff Chuff regular in the early days.

I DJd at quite a few of those parties, and it always felt like you were away for the weekend, because of the combined hotel/dancefloor experience, of wherever that particular event was taking place. The girls wore next to nothing, and the guys went out shopping weeks before to work out what they were going to wear, and all in an era when clubbing was a lot less about dressing up. I remember one Chuff Chuff when John Kelly, one of my best DJ buddies, had brought two bottles of Dom Perignon with him. There was about ten of us in one of the hotel rooms after the party, but we had no glasses so John decided to use the small kettle that came with the room. We were drinking this expensive champagne out of a hotel room kettle, and it just seemed such a waste of money. Now it's a good memory, and good memories are priceless.

With most of his best and most notorious work done towards the end of the weekend, at the likes of FUBAR (at The Milk Bar) and Space terrace, in Ibiza, Brandon Block knows a decent Sunday party when he comes across one. So Chuff Chuff was also completely up his street.

There was always a theme and the girls would always be in sexy outfits and, to be honest, that just made your night. The Chuff Chuffs ran for a long time, but like many great things they came to an end and become great memories. I always remember Chuff Chuff was an institution in itself, the whole mystery tour thing made it different to other parties. Not knowing where it was going to be until the last minute was certainly reminiscent of the old Sunrise raves, but in the early to mid-'90s the Chuff Chuff version was a lot more organised and legal.

After we all moved back to nightclubs from the raves, Chuff Chuff were events that weren't in a normal nightclub again. And this was when promoters started adding more imaginative drapes and other visuals. The various themes also made the punters feel they were being offered something more. Chuff Chuff and Moneypenny's will always be remembered for all the gorgeous girls. The best, in fact. Musically, it was more on the vocal garage, funky house, soulful tip, and this is when girls started dictating what music was being played. And we all know girls attract boys.

Progress boss Russell Davison cannot speak too highly of Chuff Chuff.

It never ever got as good as Chuff Chuff. Total hats off to those boys. I believe the atmosphere during the first two years at Progress was definitely up there with anything at the time, but nothing could match Chuff Chuff. They were the first to do the boys and girls tickets, the % split in favour of girls. And what amazing women they attracted. It really was phenomenal. And with all the DJs there it was both a promoters' and punters' dream.

Miss Moneypenny's continued to thrive on a weekly Saturday night basis, and with Chuff Chuff its cheeky little sibling, the two promotions were helping to perpetuate each other's success. And like many successful promoters, it was a humbling experience for Jim Shaft Ryan and co.

In the early days Moneypenny's was only for about 500 people and we regularly hit that on a weekly basis. I probably realised it was a success when we started on the international circuit.

We began in Ibiza in 1996 doing weekly parties at Pacha and then moved to El Divino. By then it had become more than just an extension to our social lives, which in the early days it definitely was. That's when we started to have a reasonable business on our hands.

It's very difficult to pinpoint favourite moments, when you've put on a club event from 1993 to 2006 every Saturday night, and you've travelled around the world with that brand too. It's obviously very hard to say. Rather than naming one or two events, I would say that the fact that something that did extend out of our social lives to become something that entertained so many people all over the UK and the world, is in itself my overall favourite memory.

For instance, when people say they got married or had kids because they met at Moneypenny's, well that's got to be more important than any one particular memory, the sheer fact that you potentially impacted so much on people's lives just because you wanted to play music and put parties on.

As the '90s wore on, for many, that Moneypenny's music policy of funky, soulful vocal house was becoming a more palatable sound than the likes of Detroit techno or Chicago house. Dezire Dubfire, the renowned drag queen DJ who cut her teeth with the Ryans in the early to mid-'90s, likens Moneypenny's and Chuff Chuff to a certain world-famous American theme park, but argues the parties were anything but Mickey Mouse.

Moneypenny's and Chuff Chuff gave me a launch pad to be a DJ. And being involved in so many of those parties reminds me of the calibre of the production the boys put on - big, expensive and extravagant. Going to a Chuff Chuff always felt like going to

Disneyland as a seven-year-old. The crowd was always so gorgeous and diverse. Everything was glamorous and, as Barbara Tucker would say, it was for the "beautiful people" - everyone kitted out in designer clothes, everything just magical. Clubland was magical at that time, though.

Rather than naming specific tracks, for me, it is the sound that I can remember, that of uplifting, sexy, funky, happy party house music. If I had to be pinned down to one tune, though, my final One More ever, it would have to be Turn Me Out by Praxis featuring Kathy Brown, a great vocal with a big dirty bassline, which for me symbolises what the mid-'90s was all about.

And for me, house music in general broke down so many different sexual and racial barriers, smashing them down, in fact, welcoming gays, lesbians, blacks, whites, and celebrating diversity. The boys in Chicago who kicked things off have a lot to be hailed for, I think.

In 1997 Moneypenny's released a high profile three CD mix package, compiled by Ryan, Mark Moore and Tony De Vit, with the latter, the late great De Vit, including many of his own trademark pumping hard house tracks.

A year later came Too Glamorous, a Moneypenny's compilation featuring on the cover a tastefully topless Melinda Messenger, the page three girl turned TV presenter, who was one of the club's celebrity fans at that time. Vocal anthems came from the likes of Doug Willis (aka Dave Lee) with Get Your Own, Cevin Fisher's Freaks Come Out, several Jocelyn Brown tracks, plus David Morales' Needin' You and Give Me Luv by Alcatraz.

Then, for the 2000 release of *Funky House – The Sound Of Miss Moneypenny's*, tracks were included by the likes of Robbie Rivera, Joey Negro, Richard Grey and Eddie Amador, and were typical of the filtered, sampled, disco house sound that labels like Erick Morillo's Subliminal had thrived on at the end of the '90s.

Shaft Ryan continues:-

Musically, I think we became totally defined when the funky house sound came about in the late '90s. I would probably argue that we coined the phrase 'funky house', because we put an album out at the time with funky house in the title. It was 2000, it was the turn of the

Millennium and at that time it was the given music of Miss Moneypenny's and Chuff Chuff.

Meanwhile, I think the track that would sum up me as a DJ was a track that was used on many Moneypenny's albums - one I produced myself, called Happy Daize, which came about because I got my head around how to use a musical idea to my benefit. It was a remake of the Edwin Hawkins choir 1968 hymn Oh Happy Day, which was big track back then.

It was originally written in the 17th century and I saw there was an opportunity to recreate the recording, and not only recreate it, but own it, and own it from a publishing point of view, because the recording was so many years old. I like to think that summarises not only how I evolved as a DJ, but also as an opportunist within the club environment - by being able to claim some sort of ownership of it.

As Miss Moneypenny's was going for so long, to think about one record that would end the night is extremely difficult. As a DJ playing the last set of a night, you always had to think how you could make the perfect ending.

And sometimes things happen which mean there hasn't necessarily been a happy ending that day. Events bigger than any one record, any one night, any one promotion and any one drug or high.

One particular night that really stands out, when I really had to think about that 'end-of-night' record carefully and how to end the night, was September 11 in 2001, the same night we were doing the closing party in El Divino in Ibiza.

Firstly, the effect that 9/11 had on Ibiza was phenomenal, because you just take it for granted that everyone in Ibiza, whether they're on the beach or in bars, that there is a sense of partying endlessly throughout the day and night, whatever is happening in the rest of the world.

However, on this day, Ibiza just closed down, the beaches were empty, people just went inside. Ibiza is an incredibly dramatic place anyway and I think that there was a sense that this really could be the end of the world.

We were confronted with having to do a party, but not just any party, one that wrapped up the season for us, and would hopefully sum up what had been a successful season, too.

But instead of promoting the party, like everyone else, we were stuck indoors talking about the catastrophe that had happened in New York, watching it all unfold on the TV.

Eventually, by 11pm, things started ticking over again. However, ironically, it had been decided - possibly two or three days prior to the event by the girl who looked after the dancers and parades through Ibiza Town - that the clothing would be of an Arabian theme, and when the parade took place at the start of the night there were one or two incidents. One of the dancers was physically attacked because of the clothing they were wearing, while others were applauding.

I had to do the last three hours of the night, and I had to think how I could really sum up how people were feeling that night, and I decided to play as many tracks as possible that mentioned the word 'love'. I just thought it would be appropriate at a time of incredible hatred, and so to try and spin it on its head.

I was astounded. It was one of the moments as a DJ where I thought I'd had a real effect. From 2am to 8am the club was really heaving. It came to the last record and I was thinking "what do I end on? How can I touch people emotionally and spiritually?". And I had this record, that was always tucked away in the back of my box. It was a track by John Holt called Tribal War, and it had lots of anti-war elements, and it summed up how people should be a community rather than be defined by their tribes. I played it, and it's a reggae record, so in club terms it probably wasn't appropriate to play at a Moneypenny's party then, but in terms of the theme it summed it up, and people took to it, and it got to the point that people were singing along and pretending they knew the words. It was a very poignant evening indeed.

Miss Moneypenny's as a brand continued touring throughout the Noughties, and its 12 year residency at El Divino - until the port side club closed in 2009 - remains something of a record for a British promoter.

Our first season in Ibiza was 1995, when we were invited to host a couple of Moondance parties with Jose Padilla at Pacha. The following year we were offered the Sundays in Pacha, and Lee (Garrick) ran those parties and very much became the face of Moneypenny's on the island, We moved to El Divino in 1997 and embarked on a long-running residency there. That partnership was very symbiotic with both brands developing together. I was the resident DJ alongside high profile jocks such as Danny Rampling, Ron Carroll and Joey Negro.

Miss Moneypenny's lives on, and the brand still tours the UK, and, as brands go, it's surely one of the strongest built among the promoters in One More.

Recent collaborations have included Brothel, a Chuff Chuff-esque promotion which has seen the latest generation of Birmingham's pretty club babes out in force. And, maybe even some....the daughters of...

As for what Birmingham's fab four are up to now? Dermot runs a management agency looking after a number of signed bands, including Hitchcock ('Black Sabbath meets Chase & Status'), Lee is developing a new bar/restaurant concept, Mick is 'in property', while 'Shaft' Ryan, as well as still being the face and resident DJ of Moneypenny's and recording as Zoned Out, is writing a musical "very much focused on dance music".

In terms of the legacy that the club has left, Jim Shaft Ryan believes the influence Moneypenny's has had is far reaching.

As a weekly glam club we influenced so many others, including the likes of Hed Kandi, who really just used the Miss Moneypenny's model. We look back feeling they pulled the rug from under our feet a little bit, because they had more financial clout, firstly being owned by the Guardian Media Group, and then by the Ministry Of Sound. I would argue that we were influences behind all that, the idea of getting dressed up and being surrounded by like-minded and beautiful people.

In terms of being a DJ, I was part of that circuit of DJs who were playing four or five clubs each weekend in the early to late '90s and I know I was very fortunate to play some of the really big clubs at the time. Particularly in the early stages of my career, clubs like Venus were so influential and where I made great friends along the way, people like James Baillie and Sam Bowery, who are still very active in clubland today. I also feel very fortunate in the early days to have played Back 2 Basics for Dave Beer, who is just a legend and was even crazier in those days. Later on, clubs like Lamerica in Cardiff, where Craig Bartlett was always very hospitable to me.

I guess I was very fortunate to pass through a lot of doors and experience those really heady early days when you were doing too many gigs to really take it all in.

GOLDEN

Such was the personal success of Golden founder Jon Hill that he was the subject of a unique mid-career transfer to Cream in Liverpool which still allowed him to oversee his own empire... and that's like Stanley Matthews signing for The Reds, but being allowed to play for Stoke in the cup too.

And while British clubland has certainly thrown up some unusual situations over the years, this was probably one of the strangest.

Years later Hill would receive an honorary doctorate from Staffordshire University for "services to the local cultural industries and entrepreneurism" and that was just about the icing on the cake for him.

Being recognised like that by the university was pretty special, certainly for a nightclub promoter. Staffordshire University also did a poll of in-coming students during our reign, if I can call it that, and asked them what they knew about Stoke. No 1 was Alton Towers, No 2 was Robbie Williams and No 3 was Golden, and to me that was recognition. I'm a Stoke man, my resident DJs were from Stoke and I'm proud of what Golden means to Stoke.

Golden started in March, 1992, as much an attempt by Hill to fill the gap left by Shelley's as a chance for him to settle down clubbing-wise, after the legendary venue's closure forced him to travel out of town for his clubbing kicks.

I'd been a dedicated clubber for a while and my formative clubbing years had been spent at Shelley's in Stoke, which featured an up-and-coming DJ called Sasha, who obviously went on to great things when he left the club in 1991.

Me and my friends used to go there every Friday night, Sasha's night, so when he moved on we were stuck for somewhere to go. We spent about 12 months trawling the country, doing the Balearic network, travelling up to Liverpool, to Manchester, to Birmingham and to Nottingham, and we had enjoyed all that, but we felt that the time was right to try something ourselves in our home town, which we did with Golden and which we started on Saturday, March 7, 1992 - one week, I think, before Renaissance and six months before Cream, and we then ran in tandem as a business model with clubs like that.

Allister Whitehead was delighted when he was booked for the opening night of Golden.

I heard about Golden through James Baillie, who got me into the office at Venus and said he'd got me a gig at this club in Stoke. I knew loads of people in Stoke, the crowd who used to go up to the Hacienda for the Nude night, and Golden wanting me to play the opening night was great for me. Sure enough, when I got there, all the old Hacienda lot were out in force. One of them even gave me a capsule from 1988, from those Hacienda days, after he'd recently found a batch tucked away somewhere. I had been playing at Venus, and had also played in Liverpool, and would soon play Renaissance in Mansfield, so it was nice to DJ in another local town, and spread my name further.

I remember that night the big record was Pamela Fernandez - Kicking In The Beat, and I think that got played about two or three times in total, by myself and the resident Kelvin. The Golden crowd always had this amazing combination of being both knowledgeable and mad. They weren't just getting out of it for the sake of it, they were really into their music too.

And Hill knew exactly what he wanted as well.

In terms of mission statements and ethos, we had two main ones, I guess.

Firstly, to try and mould the big northern club night out, the big Hacienda, Shelley's-type event, with the Balearic network, with the DJs that were happening in other cities - especially the London DJs, like the Boy's Own and Flying lot and people like Danny Rampling and Paul Oakenfold. So the idea was to book the DJs that we liked into a club that we liked.

Secondly, in terms of the ethos for the customers, it was quite simple - I just wanted to throw the best party in town, something I would want to go to, something I would want to pay to go to, that my friends wanted to go to. And I think that's what we succeeded in achieving.

However, for the first year of Golden, Hill had been juggling a career as a teacher at local sixth form colleges, unwittingly creating something his students wanted to go to as well. After studying English and American literature at Manchester University, Hill had been teaching for several years before he started Golden, but, financially his day job had quickly become surplus to requirements.

During the months where the two things overlapped I always had it in my mind that I would come back to teaching at some point, because nobody knew how long this thing would last back then. So I wanted to finish the last few months on my contract and didn't want to burn any bridges. That did stand me in good stead when I did eventually go back.

However, before I left, one of my students came in on a Monday morning and said she needed an extension for her homework. I asked her for a good reason and she said "because I was at your club on Saturday night, sir". I dutifully gave her the extension.

Hill was determined to involve as many people from Stoke in his new project and that meant securing the services of local DJs Pete Bromley and Kelvin Andrews.

I wanted a strong basis of residents and we had the two best residents in Stoke-on-Trent in Pete and Kelvin. As co-writer on some of Robbie Williams' big hits, Kelvin has since gone on to worldwide success, but he still does a night in the Staffordshire area called Wonk from time to time, and I always go down and see him.

As well as the residents, we wanted to bring a different guest DJ in each week playing a different style of music, so we didn't stick to US house, we didn't stick to progressive house and we didn't stick to handbag or Balearic house. We wanted a DJ who could come and deliver a two-hour set which was different, week-in, week-out, doing their own thing and then we'd always end up with our residents at the end of the night. And that's a policy we always stuck with right until the end.

The initial promotion of Golden was the good old-fashioned way of going around handing out flyers. I always felt that at the start of Golden that hand-to-hand flyering, the personal contact, was the way to do it and we obviously graduated to posters, press ads, radio ads, etc, etc. We started with the grassroots, though, and myself and my friends, our girlfriends even, would go around to bars or stand outside bars, talking to the customers, telling them what we were all about and what they could expect if they came to us.

Hill will never underestimate the impact that Shelley's had on his own clubbing institution. And Shelley's is certainly right up there with Venus in terms of an iconic club that people, and especially Midlands promoters, talk about as hugely influential.

It's quite simple, without Shelley's there would have been no Golden! I was about 23 when I started going to Shelley's, quite old for a fledgling clubber. I sort of missed the initial wave of acid house. That didn't really get me. I was still into indie music really, but I went to Shelley's when Sasha was there in 1990 and I was just blown away by the whole atmosphere and vibe of the place, and soon I just lived for his night. In my opinion, it was the best club ever. I know I'm biased and a lot of people will have their own opinion, but for me, it was.

The moulding and the mixing of a brand new DJ playing a completely different style of music - phenomenal mixing skills, happy vocal party music in a big old-fashioned club was just unbeatable as far as I was concerned. I would say that with Golden we did strive to recreate the Shelley's feel, even more so than that of the Hacienda. I loved the Hacienda, but my formative years at the Hacienda was more of an indie thing. I saw The Smiths there in 1983, but Shelley's was year zero for me where house music is concerned, and when that started to go down the drain a little bit, we decided to have a go at creating something ourselves. And although without Shelley's there would be no Golden, I do think we evolved into something different.

The other clubs that I admired at the time were Venus and things like Most Excellent in Manchester. I admired the music policy of Venus and the atmosphere, although at times it was quite chaotic, and I admired the eclecticism and exoticism of the Balearic network in general. This was before so-called corporate clubbing and superclubbing. Golden did come after the Ministry Of Sound, but I wouldn't say the Ministry Of Sound was an influence because I'd not been there at that point.

Golden's early existence was a nomadic one, quickly outgrowing venue after venue, and Hill was even forced to leave Stoke at one point as he literally ran out of clubs.

Our first ever home was a very small venue in Newcastle-under-Lyme called Peppers, which operated across two floors with a total capacity of 200. Downstairs was a rock night, and upstairs was our night. The bouncers at the top would ask the customers "rock or rave?" when they came in and they would be pointed to the relevant floor.

That initial start was a huge success and we then moved to a club called Regimes in Hanley in Stoke, which took us up to a 500 capacity. That's when we started booking people like Pete Tong, Jeremy Healy, Farley & Heller and Mike Pickering. Again, the night lived out its natural lifespan until, in January 1993, we moved to The Academy, which wasn't a custom-built club, but it was a custom-converted club to our specifications, with a proper DJ box, a proper sound system and a proper chill-out room. We existed there for three years, and in 1994 we won the MixMag Club Of The Year, voted by readers of MixMag, which was an extremely proud moment for us, after 12 months of opening at The Academy.

In 1995, however, things didn't go too well for us and towards the end of that year I decided to move cities and we went to Sankeys Soap in Manchester.

At the time people thought that I was a complete madman to do this and friends even counselled against it. I was heavily advised not to do this, it was deemed to be a disaster-in-waiting, mainly because of the incipient gang problem in Manchester. I admit it was a risk, it was a huge risk, in fact, and we initially encountered a lot of problems with the DJs, because they had had a lot of problems in Manchester, with the gangs. But I liked Manchester, I'd done my degree in Manchester and I liked the people we would be working with. I really wanted it to work.

It was a struggle, the first six months were a real struggle actually, but after that it really kicked in. And we soon found that we could book who we wanted. The DJs loved it, the gangs stayed away and we had all sorts of fantastic nights there. We stayed there for three years, until we came back to The Academy, which, by then, had been re-named The Void.

The Void had a capacity of 1,320, which I can remember vividly. But if I'm honest, and I can obviously say this now, we exceeded that every week. We had a full house each time, people coming from all over the area, the country and even people from mainland Europe. And one of my best memories of that time was having 10 coaches booked in and turning another 10 more coaches away.

There was another club in town called The Place, which was bigger, but much more commercial, so in terms of what we were doing, Golden was the biggest credible club night.

Judge Jules, for one, was pleasantly surprised at Golden's success.

Golden, considering it was in Stoke, which is not the biggest city on the clubbing map these days, was just so consistent. And it was always such a surprise that it was so good, particularly at The Void, which was such a big club to fill in a relatively small clubbing region. Golden always felt like a family atmosphere, with the same resident DJs and backroom staff working there throughout its tenure.

Jon Hill, the promoter, was this English teacher, who abandoned education for his love of tunes, and I always like it when people have a career, but follow their hearts instead. I've got a law degree and I went on to be a DJ so I suppose there's a parallel there. I always arrived at Golden early because there was a nice social area behind the DJ booth there. And you could tell which clubs I liked most at that time by how early I turned up for my set. At Golden I always had a good hour there, drinking, and talking the proverbial crap before I went on.

For Hill, pinpointing his favourite DJs is an easier task than for some interviewed for One More. And it simply comes down to those two local residents, and his two biggest guests, both constantly name-checked throughout this account.

*(clockwise) * Main room action, Golden-style (and bottom)*
* John Hill at the former site of The Void, now a car park

golden

golden

golden

. manchester. 1995

ip / coaches 01782 821454 (office hours only)

golden

golden. manchester.

I've got to mention the two DJs that started it all for me, Pete Bromley and Kelvin Andrews, who were two superb resident DJs. But in terms of guests, my two favourites were Sasha - who started with us at Golden, and had obviously inspired me so much in the first place - and Jeremy Healy, who was the biggest DJ the UK has ever seen, certainly in terms of bums on seats. Such a nice guy too. His music was always so uplifting, the crowds he pulled were so vibrant and he just created such a great atmosphere. Jeremy played beautiful music for beautiful people and was a pleasure and joy to work with. He was our biggest DJ for about five years and is still my favourite DJ to this day.

Kelvin Andrews had already flirted with chart success, through his Raspberry Ripple Mix of brother Danny's reworking of the Beatles Strawberry Fields Forever, as Candy Flip, which had reached No 3 in the Top 40 in 1990. The duo would go on to achieve more national top 10 success on the back of one of THE anthems played at Golden.

The brothers have since gone on to work on several solo tracks for Robbie Williams, including Rock DJ, but following that one hit wonder with Candy Flip, the prolific pair spent the early to mid-'90s producing under the Sure Is Pure guise. Their version of Golden anthem We Are Family reached No 8 in 1993, and the subsequent Sure Is Pure mix of another Sister Sledge anthem Lost In Music reached No 5 in the same year.

Sure Is Pure would go on to produce more than 90 remixes in total, with other notable highlights including their versions of Doobie Brothers' Long Train Running and Who Keeps Changing Your Mind by South Street Players, while they were also behind the stand out mix of Blueboy's Remember Me in 1997.

However, Kelvin had certainly done the Stoke circuit before his time at Golden, which included wowing Take That star Robbie, then still a schoolboy, who was snuck into local gigs by friends of friends.

I started DJing in Stoke in 1983 in a two-storey bar and discoteque called Quenchers, playing soul and jazz funk, and locally I also went on to play in Joels and, for many years, a place called Freetown. In fact, myself and Pete Bromley were residents at a night called Juice at Freetown, when Jon Hill came down and asked us to come and do Golden. I had noticed a big change around 1985 when what we now call house music started to appear. I used to get my records from an import shop in Burslem in Stoke called Davo's, but it wasn't called house, the tracks were referred to as "US imports". It was the tail end of boogie and electro and the kick drum was becoming more noticeable. A local DJ called Trevor M had been playing house at an under-18s night at The Place in 1987/88, so by the time Golden came around those kids had been primed for house music, and were ready to go.

Like the rest of the country, house music would engulf Stoke too. With his apprenticeship in DJing complete, Kelvin Andrews was himself in a prime position.

I knew something was happening with house music when I was able to buy my mum an oven with the door takings one week from a Wednesday night acid house party I was putting on down the road in Newcastle-upon-Lyme.

Later when the Hacienda first closed down, the Stoke lot that used to go to the Hac' naturally ended up at Shelley's and when that finished, there was definitely another void and Jon Hill was able to fill that with Golden. Sasha had played at both the Hacienda and Shelley's and went on to play Golden loads, so he has always been a hero in Stoke.

Golden became massive in Stoke very, very quickly. There was the core local crowd mixed in with the out-of-towners, who came by the coach-full, but it was the local crowd, who always made it, the family, as we called them, and that's why, I guess, We Are Family became such a massive track. I was playing the DMC mix of the track one night, when Jean Branch from East West Records asked me to remix the original, and it was amazing getting the original Chic parts and working on them. It was an amazing time all round. Golden had been voted number one club in the country, we had remixed a Chic record and had got in the Top Ten with it, and the club was heaving each week. Yeah, Golden back then was about as good as it got. In fact, for a while Stoke felt like the centre of the universe. I'd just like to apologise to Kathy Sledge, though, because the morning after she came and performed at Golden I was due to meet her for breakfast but got so carried away partying afterwards that I forgot. Sorry Kathy.

The Sister Sledge performance provides Hill with his overall Golden highlight.

The first opening night of The Academy, when we booked Sister Sledge to play for us, if I had to narrow it down, that would have to be my favourite memory. We had played We Are Family as the last record at the very first Golden in 1992 and it was the last record at every Golden for the next three years.

Then in 1993, when we moved to The Academy, we wanted to do something really, really special, to put on a show for our regulars, and we managed to book the original line-up of Sister Sledge with Kathy Sledge, before they had splintered off their own separate ways, and they performed We Are Family live.

The other one I'm quite proud of is again from the early Academy days, when Paul Oakenfold played. Even by that stage he had been there, done it. He was THE first DJ in many respects where our scene was concerned, the ultimate DJ, who had played in every club in the world. He played for us in 1994 and his first record was Robin S, Show Me Love. I remember him playing that track, the bassline kicked in and the crowd went 'whoosh' and Oakey turned to me and said: "Fuckin' hell." I thought: "This is Paul Oakenfold in Stoke-on-Trent... amazed." And that will always stick with me, too.

The track that best summed up Golden's spirit was obviously We Are Family and the record that, due to a remix by one of our resident DJs, Kelvin, was propelled into the top 10 of the UK charts, purely, I'd like to think, because it was the most popular record at the most popular club in the country at that time.

Other tracks included Jump Around by House Of Pain, tracks that you wouldn't necessarily expect to hear in a house club and then, as the '90s moved on, another Balearic track, Doobie Brothers' Long Train Running, which a DJ called Raphael, who is now a bigwig in the music industry, but was then one half of a DJ duo called Trannies With Attitude, dropped one night. It tore the roof off, an old funky guitar track from the '70s - again not what you would expect to become a club anthem - and again that became a big track for us. Kelvin went on make a very a successful Sure Is Pure mix of that as well.

Later in the '90s came that fascinating approach from Cream in Liverpool, which took Hill by surprise, and in the end was just too good an opportunity to turn down. It was further proof of the influence that a small number of club promoters were having on the whole of country.

Most of these pioneers, people we have interviewed for One More, had already taken their brand out of their home town or wherever it had started for stand alone events or tour/"vs" nights. But getting poached for a high profile job at one of your rivals, and still being able to run your own club, was certainly an interesting take on the whole proceedings.

I did have a brief sojourn away from Golden in 1998. I was offered the job of Head Of Music at Cream in Liverpool, not just for the Liverpool club, but their worldwide operations too, booking the DJs and setting the musical agenda for Cream worldwide, which was a huge brand, and at the time, they would argue, second only to Ministry Of Sound.

I initially turned the job down, but my ambition just got the better of me so I struck a deal with James Barton, who I have nothing but respect for and who is the only boss I've ever had in the dance industry. It meant that I could still keep Golden going, and I did the job at Cream for two years.

I made sure I kept ownership of Golden, but I handed the day-to-day running to Nick Dean and Mark Adams, who had worked for me for some time. I threw myself into the Cream job and only went to Golden once in the next two years, for the 9th birthday, in March 2000.

I'd known Darren Hughes for some time. My girlfriend at the time had studied at Liverpool University with his girlfriend. I had a lot of respect for him and I knew the Cream camp, James Barton and co, and, without being big-headed, I really felt that when Darren left, James would offer me the job.

It was the summer of 1998 and I was in France for the World Cup when I got a call from my office saying James Barton had made contact. I actually said: "Has he offered me the job?" And they said: "Not quite, but we think he is going to".

And I really was very honoured to take the Cream job. I'm a big football fan and it was like a manager being offered the biggest job in the game. Cream was the biggest job in clubbing at that time.

Hill had big boots to fill at Cream, though, because Darren Hughes had just left to set up Home in London. He had taken Paul Oakenfold with him and Hill's brief was to replace Hughes and Oakenfold.

I brought in a rising DJ in Seb Fontaine and he went on to great things, becoming a Radio One DJ during that time. I changed the music policy a little bit - I brought in a night called Bugged Out on a Friday, Johnno Burgess and co, friends of mine from Manchester. I had a two-year contract, which I fulfilled. We won five awards, and I like to think I left Cream in a better position than when I found it. I also oversaw Cream's Ibiza residency. I wasn't out there all summer, but I went three times a season and booked the DJs. I made Paul Van Dyk the resident at Amnesia and he's still resident for them there to this day.

When I did leave Cream, I was offered a similar job at the Ministry, which I turned down. I'd had two years working for someone else and I wanted to go back to Golden and that's when I bought the nightclub.

Shades of that classic Remington advert from the late '70s, though, when American businessman Victor Kiam uttered the immortal words: "I liked it so much, I bought the company."

Looking back it would be easy for Hill to wish he hadn't "bought the nightclub" and had, instead, taken that job with The Ministry Of Sound. But he has no regrets. Jon Hill wasn't the first, and he certainly won't be the last, where successful promoters, ambition and nightclubs are concerned.

Yes, I bought The Void nightclub and in retrospect it was a mistake. By no means could it be judged a success. At the time, however, it was the right thing to do.

The clubbing industry was in a bit of a dip, but I did a very conservative business plan, building in a 30% dip in trade. I raised the finance, put a lot of my own money in - it was most of my money, in fact - and took it on seven nights a week, trying to fill it every night of the week. We put bands on. Different things - rock nights, etc, but unfortunately the clubbing industry was about to go into terminal decline.

We didn't have a 30% drop in trade - we had a 60% drop in trade. We kept it going for nearly 18 months, but by that point it was all over. It's not something I feel guilty about, because there are not many decent nightclubs left anymore. There used to be 10 nightclubs in Stoke and now there is one. So we bought the nightclub at the wrong time. In hindsight, we shouldn't have done it, but we did and I don't regret it.

So it was the beginning of the end for Golden, but Hill is able to look back on a glittering decade, with the accolades and awards reminders of that success, happy with the part he went on to play.

Golden finished in 2003 and there's a common theory that the Millennium brought an end to our club era. I think that's true to a certain extent, but it didn't for us.

We had two parties on Millennium Eve, one at the Manchester Academy and another at The Void in Stoke. I initially bid for loads of DJs, people like Brandon Block and Sonique, but I was outbid and I'm so glad I was. I finally saw sense and instead of charging over the odds, we basically set the ticket price pretty much as we would on a normal New Year's Eve, £35 to £50, and went with our excellent residents and the odd guest, like DJ Disciple.

And we didn't do as badly as most people that night, breaking even on the Manchester gig, and I think we made around five grand in Stoke, which might not sound much in the scheme of things, but it wasn't bad comparatively.

Meanwhile, 2000 was actually our most successful year, with a full season in Ibiza, two club tours, arenas at both the Creamfields and V festivals, and we also had sister nights running at Sankeys. The year 2000 was phenomenal for us, in fact.

Hill believes it was 2001 when the rot really started to set in, citing a delayed reaction which gathered pace. December 31, 2000, was also poor and gave further confirmation that NYE and the scene itself would never be the same again.

Also, the change in the licensing laws between 2003 and 2005, with bars allowed to open until 2am or 3am and those bars not charging on the door, but playing the same kind of music, with DJs, well, it helped create a perfect storm for British clubbing, and many clubs just couldn't recover from that. So when we went, we weren't the only ones. We lasted longer than Cream on a weekly basis, but we went in May, 2003.

The last record played at Golden? Well I know who played it, it was Sasha, and it was an Unkle remix. I can't exactly remember of what and that's because I had left. It was the last night, the party was over and the club was half full. We had Sasha playing at the end and my clubbing career had started with Sasha at Shelley's, but no hard feelings, it was nothing to do with him, it was the climate at the time. And when that last record was played at 6am, I was at home licking my wounds with friends because I knew it was all over.

I think Golden's legacy is that for 10 years we gave people so many fantastic nights and even now, when I go out for a drink in Stoke, and other places, Manchester, and London, occasionally people who I don't know come up and shake my hand and say that I gave them some of the best nights of their lives. If I don't go on to achieve anything else in life, the fact that people can say that to me leaves me with an immense amount of pride, pride in myself, but also in all the DJs and the other clubbers who really made the club what it was.

Hill was more than happy to return to teaching once his Golden era was over. Clubland's loss was indeed the City Of Stoke-on-Trent Sixth Form College's gain and Hill reasons that he ran Golden for 11 years and has now taught for a total of 12 years, feeling fortunate to have had two contrasting careers.

Teaching English lit' might seem like a bit of a jump, but not really, because that's what I did before Golden. I had obviously worked in further education previously and when the club folded in 2003 I went back into it, trained again, and I've been doing it for six years now and thoroughly enjoy it. It's a completely different job to the club business, but it gives me an amazing sense of satisfaction and, again, I'm working in my home town, which I love.

I'm from Stoke-on-Trent and my heritage means so much to me. Golden became an internationally renowned clubbing brand and I'm very proud of what we created and achieved in Stoke-on-Trent.

RENAISSANCE

When Geoff Oakes persuaded the UK's leading house DJ Sasha to become the marquee signing for his new night in the unfashionable former mining town of Mansfield, he was either the bravest man in Britain or completely bonkers.

Two years later, with John Digweed firmly at the Renaissance helm alongside Sasha, Oakes managed to sell 200,000 copies of the duo's groundbreaking CD, The Mix Collection.

And in a fitting tribute to Oakes, that infamous stickler on the door, the cover of that iconic album, courtesy of Michelangelo, features the earliest ever recorded image of a fussy door picker flicking through his guest list…well possibly, anyway…

And what a stickler Oakes was, prowling the massive queue outside Venue 44 in those early days, weeding out those he deemed not right for his club. I once witnessed him turning people away from a Renaissance party on New Year's Eve at The Que Club in Birmingham at a quarter to twelve. With the group protesting that they had bought tickets, Oakes whipped out a wad of cash and instantly refunded them. OUCH!

Digweed has since referred to *"Geoff's strict regime on the door"*, but Oakes was not content with simply setting standards on the way in. Inside the clubbing Tardis that Venue 44 became, Renaissance raised the bar and set the level for the next decade with venue production of the highest order - the like of which had never been seen in house music clubs, let alone a working men's club in Mansfield.

Running for a relatively short time in One More clubbing terms - just 16 months between March 1992 and June 1993 - its success was short, but extremely sweet.

Oakes told One More:-

One of the key things was to create an environment in which people could get lost, in all sorts of ways and, although it's the norm now, we were the first to create lavish production and beautiful decor with cutting edge graphics. Somewhere really special, and where combining that with cutting edge music was also the key.

I actually promoted the club in a different way, a way which hadn't been done before. You have to remember that this was at a time when the whole rave scene was fading out and people were starting to come back to clubs. I wanted to inject a bit of style and, although it's a bit of a dirty word now, a bit of glamour into clubbing too.

We deliberately chose to advertise in some of the style mags at the time, The Face and ID, something nobody else had really done then. It helped create an aura around the brand, and although I didn't set out or intend to create a brand, it did just that, and just really worked.

Legend has it that the designs came first, then the name. Chris Howe, then MixMag's art director and now a leading television director, was asked by Oakes to come up with some ideas.

Howe has since pointed out:-

It was about a reaction to that computer generated hard-edged techno thing, big fucked-up Renaissance paintings, destroyed and remade. Sometimes with those projections it almost looked like a gallery in the club.

And nobody who went to Renaissance at Venue 44 will ever forget the first time they shuffled past the membership queue, catching a whiff of the chips and gravy - on sale for late licence purposes – as they navigated the stairs, then through the double doors, to be greeted by those fluffy cloud installations…literally into clubbing heaven.

But that was the easy bit. Queuing up outside for up to an hour, slowly creeping towards the front door of Venue 44 along the raised Belvedere Street parade, above the busy A6009, past Peter Taylor's MOT centre and Maria's hair salon, would not necessarily guarantee you entry.

A certain DJ called Sasha certainly cannot forget his first visit to the club in a hurry, revealing the backdrop behind the Mansfield launch in an official Renaissance interview in 2004 when Oakes released the 10th anniversary limited edition box set of The Mix Collection.

After Shelley's, I'd been doing loads of raves, but Renaissance was the first time I'd settled for a while so I guess it was a big deal. I wanted to do a new residency and Geoff took me to Venue 44. We both walked in, turned the lights on and it was like "come on!" With the high ceiling it had a vibe to it even though it was filthy and empty.

The idea of doing it in Mansfield was that people would have to travel so the people there were really into the music. The club was intense, it was special, the last half an hour/40 minutes you would play there would be so special the whole room would shake. It was definitely a special moment when you walked into that club, the way there were lots of different levels. You would just see people stacked up, all the way to the back.

Finding this venue was a masterstroke by Oakes, and Derby promoters Progress would later enjoy success at Venue 44 also, with their monthly Hot To Trot nights.

There seems to be little video of Renaissance nights at the Mansfield site, but there is extensive film of one particular Hot To Trot night, in February 1994, on YouTube – 10 parts in total, and around 90 minutes of grainy footage which, although not the best quality, still manages to bring memories flooding back for anyone who has clubbed in that legendary room. It particularly captures the sheer depth of the dancefloor and the different layers to the main room that Sasha discusses, largely created by the various podiums and pieces of staging strategically dotted around the room.

Before Renaissance, Oakes had been a regular at Shelley's in Stoke where he had forged a close friendship with the club's hero Sasha. The seed for this new venture was sewn at one of Oakes' infamous after-parties.

Renaissance started as a result of a conversation between myself and Sasha. We used to have these crazy parties back at my house in 1991 after Shelley's, when Sasha had the residency there. Stoke is where I'm originally from and we used to migrate to my house with about 40 people for these mad three-day sessions. It inevitably got a bit messy by Monday morning and on one occasion Sasha turned to me and said, "look, why don't we try and do something together?".

I think he was looking for a new residency and had become tired of travelling the length and breadth of the UK for gigs that weren't always that great. We decided we'd try something and I found a venue in Mansfield, of all places. The trump card was that it had an all-night licence, which very few places had in those days, and for me it all seemed to come together at the right time - Sasha wanting a new residency and me finding that space.

I didn't have any particular mission statement or ethos, other than to create a party that I would want to go to and, in that sense, I lived it from the dancefloor.

Digweed adds in the 2004 Mix Collection interview:-

People would come into Venue 44 and go straight to the dancefloor. You always had the vibe that it was going to be a great night. The British were becoming good at their own sound without looking to America, and there had been all the big raves, for 25,000 people, etc, and suddenly you had exclusivity. It was when people wanted to dress up a bit to go clubbing. We'd gone through the whole period of dressing down.

So Renaissance launched in spring 1992 and Oakes and his resident duo of Sasha and Digweed, as they quickly became known, became three powerful figureheads. Other regular and semi-resident DJs included Ian Ossia, Marc Auerbach, Nigel Dawson, Mike Pickering, Dave Seaman, Allister Whitehead and the inimitable Jeremy Healy.

Oakes remembers a clubbing apprenticeship, which, for him, began at the Hacienda.

I got into the business through a natural progression of being an enthusiastic clubber and those clubbing days started at the Hacienda in Manchester. I got to know a lot of the DJs who are now household names, because in those days they were next to me on the dancefloor. It just seemed a natural progression from that to becoming a promoter.

For Renaissance I didn't set out to adopt a music policy. I think my tastes from my days at the Hacienda were probably initially centred around the influences of American house music, although the darker, more dubbier end of that, so the Redzone mixes of various American house classics. Then, by a twist of fate, Renaissance launched at a time when the whole British house sound was coming through.

I vividly remember an article in MixMag at the time that dubbed the new wave of British house music that was coming from the likes of Leftfield and Guerilla Records as the "Renaissance sound". It later became known as progressive house, so almost by default - because my tastes evolved with the music that was coming through the UK - we became synonymous with the most current sound of the time.

Around that area there were several key clubs, all of which had an influence at some time. Shelley's is the obvious one, but Venus in Nottingham was also a massive influence, musically. And the energy that James Baillie managed to create in that place was amazing. The other club that I had a lot of respect for was Dave Beer's Back To Basics in Leeds. All those clubs were based on the passion and the personality of the promoters involved and that's something that I tried to take with me to Renaissance.

I remember the opening night when myself and Sasha were driving up to Venue 44. It was raining, it was in March and we were asking ourselves, "have we done the right thing here, it's in the middle of nowhere and it's a mining town...is anyone going to turn up?". And then we turned the corner into the cul de sac where the club was and there was about three or four thousand people outside a 900-capacity club, so we had a different kind of problem then, a much nicer one.

Attracting the DJs that we wanted to play at Renaissance was remarkably easy. I think that when you have personal relationships it helps massively. It was before the days of agents to a large degree, so it was based on meeting people and being introduced to people, and once you've got those relationships and you've spoken to people and got across your passion for music and knowledge of it, things all flow quite easily from there.

Of course, as soon as the club became established, which was very quickly, then everyone wanted to play at Renaissance anyway. It all fell into place and it got to the stage where people were calling me and asking to play the club.

I would have to say that my favourite DJs were Sasha and John Digweed, just for what they created and because they were the two main residents. John was an unknown DJ who had sent me a mix tape when we'd been open about a month. I was just completely blown away, it was like nothing I'd ever heard before. I played the tape to Sasha and we decided we'd get John to come and play. And the rest is history.

So Hastings-born Digweed proves to those millions of budding DJs who never received a call, or as much as a recognition of receipt, that sending a mix tape, CD, or, these days, a link to Soundcloud, can actually pay off. Reflecting on that life-changing mix tape he explained in 2004:-

I was always doing mix tapes and Nick Gordon-Brown from MixMag said I should send one up to Geoff at Renaissance, that my sound would really work up there. I sent the tape on a Thursday and got a call on the Sunday from Geoff, asking if I wanted to come and play. I was a bit in shock because I'd seen all the adverts with Sasha, Frankie Knuckles and Morales on them. It was a great buzz to get the phone call out of the blue and I actually went up to the club the week before I was due to play, just to go and check out the venue.

Sasha is clear just how important that innocent C90 cassette was for Digweed.

That was the mixtape that changed John's life. I don't think I'd heard mixing like that before. It was so seamless. Me and Geoff actually listened to it over that weekend and that was the thing that really grabbed us, the mixing. And for me Renaissance was the first time I started to have some kind of coherent sound and where I actually got to polish seamless mixing. It was a defining time with lots of influential labels like Guerilla and the rise of acts like Underworld and Leftfield.

Local lad Allister Whitehead was a perfect guest for the Renaissance set-up and both he and Oakes went back, clubbing-wise, to the halcyon days of the Hacienda.

*(clockwise) * Sasha at Colwick Hall, 1995 - image: Matt Trollope*
* The Renaissance 'R' lights up a stately home
* Geoff Oakes being filmed for One More at Fabric, 2010
* John Digweed Destiny: The Cream Clacton Pier, 1993
- image: Matt Trollope

Renaissance
"The Mix Collection"
3 x CD

Sasha & John Digweed with

R Renaissance

NEW YEARS EVE BALL
COLWICK HALL, COLWICK PARK, NOTTINGHAM
SUNDAY 31st DECEMBER 199
TICKET ONLY EVENT £36.50 (MEMBERS ONLY
LIVE PERFORMANCE: JUDY CHEEKS
DJ's THE FATHERS OF SOUND, DIGWEED, OSSIA
SEAMAN, DAVOLI, AUERBACH, DAWSON
CHRIS + JAMES, PAPPA, TABBERNER
8.30pm - 4.00am
STRICTLY NO ADMISSION AFTER 11.30pm
Fully Licenced Bar until 2am
VERY SMART DRESS ONLY!
(FANCY DRESS OPTIONAL)
SEE REAR OF TICKET

I lived in Nottingham, so not far from Mansfield, and I heard about the idea behind Renaissance from Geoff and some other friends. I'd known Geoff from the Hac' days a few years earlier so I was part of that kind of scene anyway. The fact that it was going to be based around Sasha, who was at the peak of his powers at that time, and the idea that we would have this club that finished at 6am, created a lot of anticipation. All the clubs in our part of the country, up until 1992, and including the Hacienda, had closed at around 2am, and the idea that this club, with a main room which was basically a take on the Paradise Garage, was going to be weekly in Mansfield really was a big deal... the concept behind it all, the artwork, etc, it just sounded great.

I was quite friendly with Sasha, and I used to go and stay with him in Manchester quite a bit and the idea of him with a new weekly residency, with a lot of American guests coming over, and the likes of Graeme Park also guesting, made everybody so excited. And the big surprise, I guess, was that they were able to pull it all off.

I was lucky enough to be asked to play Renaissance on a number of occasions, and it was a step up for me, because, although I was a jobbing DJ, with a residency at the Kool Kat in Nottingham, I had been used to playing much smaller rooms. This was a much bigger canvas, though. You couldn't do the typical early doors approach to your set when you played in the main room in Mansfield. It was a much bigger crowd, and you really had to signal your intentions from the start. I had done huge raves, but this was the first time I'd played a big main room, and this was a big room set, which may sound like a cliché now.

The DJ box was in the Gods a little bit, overlooking the crowd, and there was this distance, and it sounds like it would be intimidating, but actually it wasn't, because for some strange reason, it was as if you were connecting with every single person in the audience. People weren't coming up and asking for this or for that. They were there to go mad, and you were there to give them what they wanted, while being as creative as you could within your own style. And as a DJ you can take all the risks you want with a crowd like that. They're not going anywhere, you can play with them in a way that you can't if you're in a club simply trying to keep them on the dancefloor.

This was clubbing of the highest order and it's just what every DJ wants. And with the records around at that time, you knew exactly what to do. It was like being a kid in a sweet shop really.

I think one of my favourite memories of Renaissance was after Mansfield had been running for a while, and just the anticipation of going to the club, when there was a queue all the way around the block, and you knew it was going to be an amazing night - the sheer sense of anticipation, that's a memory in itself. And then about an hour into the set, you've got the dancefloor in the palm of your hands, and you realise for the last hour of your set you've still got all your best tunes to come.

When it comes to memories we all have great ones of people and events at one time, but as a DJ, when you're performing, you just cannot beat that feeling. It's just you and the crowd and you've got these immense records in your box, these bullets, that are going to take the lid off the place. It's like an hour-long orgasm, really.

Danny Rampling is not a DJ you would naturally associate with Renaissance, but he was a regular in the early days and would go on to play all over the world for Oakes at various nights and residencies.

Renaissance at Venue 44 in Mansfield was another great Nottinghamshire club night. My first time there, I'd already played another club in the north of England, and then headed over to Mansfield, of all places, and there was this club, this great big club in the middle of nowhere, with more than a thousand people, and an energy that was just amazing.

Geoff and his team really made an effort with the decor, branding and identity of the club. It wasn't just some dark, dingy after-hours club - which is basically what it was - it was this amazing place where the crowd would stay until six or seven in the morning. I remember playing late there one night with Sasha, after having a great night somewhere else, and, you know, you could get there late and it would still be going off. From there, Geoff did lots of one-offs, and I played for him loads, including at Pacha in Ibiza, and in Russia too. I also loved what he did with Media in Nottingham, with that great Richard Long soundsystem, which, at the time, rivalled the Ministry Of Sound.

There was definitely a distinctive sound that emerged through Renaissance, and it was really where John Digweed showcased his sound. I think John shaped that whole Renaissance sound more than anyone really. Dave Seaman and Ian Ossia were other favourites of mine there, and the music was good chuggy stuff around 126/130

BPMs, but I didn't tailor my sound to Renaissance when I played in the early days. I was playing American house and at the time that was appreciated there as well. Back then it was still about variety, and whether it was American house or more progressive house, at the start it all went down well in Mansfield.

With Sasha and Digweed his weekly headline acts, Oakes was well aware of the sheer DJ talent he had on his hands. It was time to record and document this for prosperity.

Although The Mix Collection would not be released until October 1994, by which time Renaissance had moved to The Conservatory in Derby, it included many of the anthems which shaped Mansfield and its success, a heady mix (with the emphasis on the fact it was mixed) of Italian piano house, British 'progressive house' and contemporary 'trance'.

The moment that I realised that we had something really special was when we released the very first Renaissance compilation, mixed by Sasha and John. I think at the time the Ministry and Journeys By DJs were the only two people releasing legitimate compilations and they were selling about 10 or 15,000 units each in total.

We put our album together with real passion. It was a true labour of love and represented all I wanted about the club. In the first week alone it sold 50,000 copies and went on to sell 200,000 units in total. It's widely regarded and referred to as the compilation that launched the compilation market and I'm very proud of that, although ironically from that day on we almost created our own competition because by the time we released our second one there were about seven other clubs who were releasing comps that week. We had created a bit of a monster there.

A couple of tracks that really sum up and epitomise Renaissance? Well, if I had to choose two and, of course, there are so many, I'd go for Farley & Heller's Boy's Own mix of Perfect Motion by Sunscreem and Age Of Love by Age Of Love, the Watch Out For Stella Mix, which was a massive, massive anthem at Renaissance.

Oakes signed a deal for The Mix Collection with Birmingham independent label Network Records, which had been importing

Chicago and Detroit house since 1987 in its previous guise as Kool Kat. Distribution of the album, however, would be through Sony Music, and with units literally flying off the shelves, Renaissance would need that major label backing to meet the huge demand.

Presented in an ambitious cardboard digi-pack format, and available in cassette as well as CD, it is unusual these days to find a pristine copy not coming away at the seams.

The three disc, three-mix album famously kicks off with three versions of Song For Life by leading 'Brit-prog' house duo of the time Leftfield – aka Paul Daley and Neil Barnes. Digweed's own Bedrock guise and the track For What You Dream Of picks up the pace, while other disc one highlights include Moonchild's V.OA.T, that Boy's Own mix of Perfect Motion and the X-Press 2 mix of River Ocean's Love & Happiness, plus the excellent segue of Remake's Bladerunner and the Brothers In Rhythm Perkapella mix of Inner City's Till We Meet Again.

Two mixes of Fluke's Slid open disc two, with Sasha's seminal Full Master Mix of Talk To Me by Hysterix, a cast-iron Mansfield anthem, and the all-conquering Perfecto mix of Grace's Not Over Yet stamping their authority mid-mix, before the David Morales mix of Kym Mazelle's Was That All It Was fittingly closes.

Sasha's mix of How Can I Love You More by M-People, the club collective formed by a post-Hacienda Mike Pickering en route to commercial chart success and money-spinning TV car adverts, is first up on disc three, with two tracks by Havana - Sublime Theme and Ethnic Prayer - the ever-uplifting D-Ream Dream mix of EMF's They're Here and Oakes' favourite Age Of Love mix all dominating, before proceedings are brought to a close by Underworld, the celebrated Essex-based Brit-house trio steered by one Darren Emerson.

Sasha believes The Mix Collection served as a valuable piece of quality control for him and Digweed. In 2004 he explained:-

The album was a landmark because the tracks were all just stand-outs and we played them out a lot. A lot of the mixes that John and I had played, the segues and sections on the album, were key parts of our sets. Renaissance had such a sound, didn't it? And a lot of those records were the sound of Renaissance.

At the time the bootleg cassette market was flourishing everywhere. It was such a huge part of building our names, but at the same time they were always really bad copies. Some of the sets you really wouldn't want out there, some of them weren't even ours. So the album was an opportunity to do something properly and it was like 'this is proper now'.

Digweed agrees and believes the sheer drama of the playlist will live forever.

The whole beauty of that album is that it jumps up, it jumps down, it's got darkness, it's got vocals. It's a rollercoaster ride of a club night. You've got the cream on there and you're going to have to search hard to find another 30-odd classic tracks that are so good.

As the album hit the shops, Renaissance was thriving once more at The Conservatory, but the short hop to Derby was nothing compared to the global reach the club would eventually achieve.

Back home, at the end of 1993, Oakes had upped the ante even more, with his stately home party at Colwick Hall in Nottingham. He was leading his punters back out of clubs again, but this time not to farmers' fields illegally, instead to the grounds of the landed gentry, and with the co-operation of the local authorities.

More Colwick Hall events followed, as did sell-out shows at Allerton Castle in north Yorkshire and, in 2004, the 8,000-capacity Shugborough Hall in Stafford, which saw the Scissor Sisters make their UK festival debut at an event titled Wild In The Country.

Back in the early to mid-'90s, the one-offs at The Que Club in Birmingham were always theatrical events in their own right, and as the new millennium unfolded, Renaissance settled back in Nottingham at the purpose-built Media venue, which in more recent times has been owned by Simon Raine and run as Ultra Gatecrasher.

As early as 1995, Renaissance were putting events on in Tokyo, at The Womb, and would go on to host parties in more than 25 countries around the world, as more and more territories tapped into the opulence it became famed for.

Ibiza had the Renaissance treatment throughout various seasons from 1995 onwards. Their launch at Ku was a joint party with

Manumission. Privilege, the huge venue Ku became, played host in 2000 to a series of groundbreaking Renaissance shows featuring live performances from the likes of Kylie Minogue, Moloko, Leftfield, Moby and All Saints. Amnesia in 2002, saw the likes of Danny Tenaglia and Deep Dish headlining. And several residencies at Pacha, possibly the club the brand most suited, included a season in 2004, which featured four specials with Sasha.

Brave gambles like that 'live' season at Privilege, which had never been done before, and the launch of the night itself in Mansfield, show that Oakes has always liked a challenge, but the step up from nightclub to stately home on New Year's Eve, 1993, was as big a gamble as any.

We became known for one-off spectaculars at country houses, stately homes and other unique buildings. I think the brand was really born at the first night we did at Colwick Hall because we'd moved from clubs to these beautiful environments and it just seemed to become a brand at that point.

I couldn't have ever imagined that Renaissance would go on to put on typically around 200 shows a year in all those countries. It's certainly been a fascinating and interesting journey. Our monthly residency at The Cross in London, for example, lasted for 13 years alone.

Internationally, the clubs that I admired were Pacha in Ibiza and later Zouk in Singapore, which was just one of the most amazing clubs I'd ever seen. Later Twilo in New York, when Sasha and John took their residency there. Those were all key clubs.

Ever since the success of The Mix Collection back in 1993, the compilation side of the Renaissance operation had been bubbling away in the background. John Digweed had the unenviable task of compiling and mixing The Mix Collection Volume 2 on his own and, released in September 1995, it understandably failed to reach the dizzy heights of its predecessor. Third and fourth volumes by Fathers Of Sound and Ian Ossia & Dave Seaman both followed in 1996, and again both on Network Records, but over the next few years Renaissance Recordings, a stand alone label, with Oakes and his team at the helm, took operations in-house, handling not only the brand's comps, but also stand alone productions by the various affiliate DJs and artists.

The Masters Series, which kicked off Renaissance Recordings in 2000, was the label's most notable collection with 16 releases in total. Long term collaborator Seaman, of Brothers In Rhythm fame, aptly fronted the first one, going on to be involved in four more. Argentinian Hernan Catteneo headed a further four releases, while others came from Deep Dish, Sandy Rivera, Satoshi Tomiie and James Zabeila.

With the Renaissance sound still straddling what had become modern-day progressive house and trance, as well as tech house, Oakes was able to tap into a steady stream of international DJs and live acts who had graced the Renaissance decks and stages over the years, so a host of other compilations followed from the likes of Danny Tenaglia, Faithless, Sander Kleinenberg, Roger Sanchez and Steve Lawler, as well as the newer breed of UK big room DJs coming through in the noughties like Zabeila and Nic Fanciulli.

Other titles included The Sound Of Renaissance, while John Digweed launched a new series called Transitions, with four albums released between 2006 - 2008.

No release, however, could ever recapture the success and innocence of The Mix Collection, so the chance to release a 10th anniversary edition in 2004 was impossible to pass up. And interestingly, the mix released on the anniversary album was an entirely new one by Sasha and Digweed. Accurately based mix by mix on the pioneering original, the 2004 version was recorded on Apple Mac G4 laptops by the duo, apparently keen to show what new technology could do. Inadvertently, they had made the original even more unique, with the only difference the omission of the two M-People tracks for licensing reasons.

Oakes realises that the total Renaissance journey would have been a much shorter one without Mansfield or The Mix Collection.

There are so many last track moments at Renaissance, because obviously it went on to become a global brand and we did parties all over the world for many years. However, I would have to hark back to the original Renaissance in Mansfield and so my favourite last track memory is Was That All It Was by Kym Mazelle, which was the 1990 Morales version of Jean Carne's disco classic of the late '70s. It was the quintessential end of night track for Renaissance at Mansfield and virtually from day one it was always played as the last record. It's amazing what a shelf life tracks had in those days. They stayed around for a lot longer back then.

Renaissance at Mansfield had been weekly every Saturday for about 15 months and it was clear at that point that we had outgrown the venue. We had started doing shows worldwide - Australia, America, Singapore and all of Europe - so my focus started being on developing the Renaissance brand internationally and it just felt like the right time to go out on a high.

Shelley's and the Hacienda both ended on highs. Yes, the Hacienda re-opened, but for me their original last night was THE last night, so it was really important to end the whole Mansfield thing on a very strong point so people would have fantastic memories of it.

Personally, there are so many special memories of Mansfield, week-in, week-out, in fact. Sasha used to finish at about six or seven in the morning and we'd go and sit in the pokey little office in the corridors at the back of the club. The crowd would still be chanting and screaming for about an hour, they just wouldn't leave. Each week a few people would literally end up carrying him back out of the office and back into the booth for another half an hour of music.

Allister Whitehead is philosophical about Renaissance leaving Mansfield.

When something ends it's always sad, but I think during its time there Renaissance achieved all that it had set out to do. There was a sense of disappointment, but I think they had already given everybody more than enough from that Mansfield gig.

These days the now fabled Belvedere Road parade is battered and bruised, much like the club scene itself. Venue 44 and the four or five shops next door stand derelict and boarded up, with the legendary old club's windows all smashed in. It was never the most inviting parade, it has to be said. You can easily drive through Mansfield without realising you just did.

Geoff Oakes, two decades after the Mansfield glory days, is looking to draw a line under his Renaissance journey, intrigued at what the future may hold.

Primarily, the club's legacy has to be our series of mix compilations and in particular the first one. I would add to that, extremely strong production and musical values because as the brand established itself we were very fussy about the music we played and the DJs we booked.

The Renaissance brand has been around for almost 20 years now and that's a very long time in terms of electronic music so there's almost a natural end to Renaissance, with its 20th birthday in March 2012, and just like the end of Mansfield all those years ago, it feels like the right time to end the story.

I've been working on a new venture and will be launching a new brand which we intend to take globally in the same way we did Renaissance, but with a fresh approach, because after 18 years, inevitably people perceive a brand in a certain way and maybe it collects a little baggage on its travels too. It feels like the right time to put it to bed and move on to something new, which is really exciting for me.

WOBBLE

It was very simple. Wobble started because me and my partner Si Long wanted somewhere to play out. We weren't particularly good DJs and nobody would give us any gigs, so we needed to start up our own thing.

Yes, Wobble co-founder Phil Gifford is frighteningly honest about just why and how his particular clubbing institution unfolded. But then the former hairdresser has never been one to pull any punches.

An outlook which, in fact, mirrored the night itself. You knew exactly what you would get at Wobble, and you got it. As the night wore on, the music got tougher, the crowd got messier and sweatier... and you wobbled.

When we first started out we used to try to put on little nights here and there, and then we did a tiny Sunday night thing called Naughty But… at a small strip club in the back end of Birmingham called The Hot Spot. It was a real old school strip club - so nasty, in fact, that it often had feminists outside with banners trying to close the place down.

We did all right at the strip club, though, and then we got a call from this guy who had a venue called Branstons in the Jewellery Quarter in Hockley, on the outskirts of the city centre. He said he wanted to turn his attic into a separate nightclub for us.

It sounded too good to be true to Gifford. He was working in a "random hairdressers" in Birmingham, opposite the UK's first Red Or Dead franchise, which had been secured by Long.

We were like, "so you've got an attic above a club with an all-night licence and you want us to do a Saturday night in there? Not arf, let's do it". Someone else had tried to do a party in that room with Dean Thatcher, from Flying - who was really big at the time - but nobody turned up. The owner had seen that we were putting 150 people into the strip club down the road and so approached us instead.

His room had most recently been used as a ladies' gym and there was a jacuzzi, a couple of exercise bikes and some equipment in there, so we had to clear that lot out before we did anything.

But the all-night licence really helped our success, because there weren't many places in the town where you could dance legally until seven in the morning. So us wanting to DJ and the luck of the draw of this very nice man offering to turn his loft into a disco, made Wobble possible.

The Wobble story is indeed one of good fortune, but it's no coincidence that both Gifford and Long were well schooled in dance music. There was, however, more to the name Wobble than most believed. Gifford chuckles as he sheds more light on that particular urban legend.

We weren't really clever enough to have a mission statement, as such. It was literally get the decks in, get the sound system in, get some flyers out, tell your mates, get all your people in and bang it off. We really were in the right place at the right time. We got the lucky break and I think mission statements and ethos came a bit later when you thought you were a bit cleverer with marketing and stuff, which we never really were.

At the time people were using names like Slippery When Wet and cheesy stuff like that. We'd been brainstorming for a while about what to call the night, trying to think of something different and then someone suddenly mentioned the musician Jah Wobble. I said, "Wobble, what a good name for a club."

And then on the first night we were really busy and the floor upstairs was wobbling. So everybody assumed that's where the name came from. It was a great theory and we obviously kept running with that, but the secret is out now. It was just a name we'd come up with and the floor coincidently bounced up and down when people danced on it because it was a wooden floor on RSJs.

And while we're at it, the decks weren't hung from the ceiling from chains for effect either. It was because when we did the soundcheck the night before, the wobbly floors meant all the records were jumping. People always thought that was a style thing too, but that was a case of the club's handyman putting hooks in the ceiling and finding some old chains to hang the decks on at the last minute, purely out of necessity.

So Wobble was wobbling on its weekly way, launched on Saturday, March 14, 1992, the same night as Renaissance opened its doors in Mansfield.

A flyer for two weeks later explains that guest DJs were Jon Da Silva and Neil Macey, alongside residents Silong, Phil Gifford and Toni-C. Doors were 10.30pm – 6.30am, admission was £6 before 11.30pm, £8 after. It also adds "this week there will be a large chill-out room downstairs from 2.30am, and the club will be fitted with cooling fans in the ceiling. No trainers, no baseball caps".

Gifford and Long installed a policy of quality house and dance music across varying sub-genres, but how did the Wobble team promote the club, and what had been their inspiration? Once more, Gifford is refreshingly honest when reflecting on the outlook at the time.

We were arrogant young DJs and not really sussed about club promotion. We didn't really admire any other clubs at the time because we thought they were all rubbish. Which they weren't, of course. My inspiration at the time were the clubs that I went to when I was 17, 18 and 19 in 1986, '87 and '88. There were several really great places in Birmingham and DJ Dick was the main man. He used to run a place called Dial B. There was also a club called Rococo.

And our other stomping ground when we originally started promoting was Cake and Breathless, which was at Snobs, just down the road from where Wobble ended up. That was where all the cooler people went to listen to house music. And that's probably where we got our blueprint from - house music in one room and something else in the other room.

Like many of the promoters featured in One More, booking DJs for Wobble in the early '90s was not exactly rocket science. Gifford and Long were both DJs, they knew what music they each liked and the local DJs they had grown up listening to. Quickly pairing those local heroes with DJs, and later producers, they admired from the burgeoning house scene, soon provided the basis of their line-ups.

When we first started, we simply put on the DJs we wanted to put on - the DJs we liked. And, obviously being naive about getting people through the door, we just booked people we'd heard out, without worrying whether they would pull any people in.

We used to book Jon Da Silva a lot because we'd heard him out at Breakfast at Snobs, and got John Kelly in because people always seemed to like dancing to him. With our all-night licence we were convinced on the opening night that we were going to smash it. Then a couple of days before we launched we opened MixMag and saw that Renaissance was opening on the same night with Sasha, "new residency", etc, plastered all over it.

Most of our mates suddenly said, "sorry boys, we're not coming to your night now, Sasha's got a new residency in Mansfield". It wasn't "we're going to Renaissance", it was "Sasha...we're going to see Sasha".

We did OK that night, though, and over the following weeks we started to build things up. However, if it wasn't for Renaissance I might be in the Bahamas now with a speedboat, because from that point on we were always up against Sasha and Renaissance and they even did big, one-off parties on our patch in Birmingham, at The Que Club, later on too.

The spring of 1992 was, indeed, a busy time for UK club launches, but Wobble began to build steadily and soon Gifford and Long were looking to expand.

The capacity of The Attic, as it had been officially named, was legally around 150 when we first started, but we used to get about 300 people each week. There was another club downstairs, which was like a karaoke/car salesman-type place and which actually had a separate entrance in another street. As we got busier over the weeks, when downstairs shut at 2am they'd clear it out and then open that for us and we'd get a total of about 700 in through the night.

Then after 18 months, during the summer of 1993, the owner offered to do the whole club out for us. And we actually managed to trick some people into thinking it was a different club altogether because when we reopened we used the entrance round the corner in Branston Street. The whole place was smartened up, made a bit more snazzy, the toilets done up, etc. Now the capacity was legally 700, but during the whole night, from 10pm to 7am, we'd get anything up to 1,500 passing through.

So Wobble went from a modest 150 capacity to 10 times that amount in under two years, with the "new" club - when it relaunched on Saturday, August 28, 1993 - now named The Venue. Regular guests over the next few years would include Jeremy Healy, Chris & James, Allister Whitehead, Luvdup and Kevin Hurry and Kevin Swain from D.O.P.

And as accidental as it may sound, the ease with which an initially vague 150 capacity at The Attic was later dwarfed by the regular weekly four figure turn-outs should not be underestimated, particularly during an era of intense Birmingham clubbing. However, Gifford and his partner Silong, as his DJ name had become, were far from in tune musically. Although singing from the same hymn sheet, they were not always on the same page.

At the start me and Si had completely different ideas about music. He was into American and deep house and I was just into anything that made you throw your hands in the air, having come from a bit of a rave background. Si's history was more of a deeper club background, so when we started, for the first hour, you might hear Bizarre Inc and some classic rave tunes and then Si would come on and you would hear dark, dirty, deep stuff, and because we were on all night, from 10pm – 7am, it kinda worked.

Then, when we expanded on to two floors we tried all sorts of things upstairs; rare groove and hip-hop. The Chemical Brothers came up regularly when they were still the Dust Brothers and played hip-hop and that sort of thing, but that "alternative" music policy upstairs never really worked.

Finally it came down to the top floor being deep house and techno, with Si always doing the first few hours, and the ground floor being more vocal, arms-in-the-air house, which gradually, over a period of time, went a little bit more up its arse with the Chicago house sound, and then into the French filtered house stuff, with deep and tougher techno upstairs.

We later realised that DJs actually pulled in numbers so we got some of the bigger Americans in - Robert Owens, Kevin Saunderson, people like that - because if you were prepared to pay the extra money you could book them. It was a while before we could get the really big UK players then, like Jeremy Healy who was massive at the time, but he came eventually, loved it, and then played every month for us. Carl Cox... we'd wanted him for quite a while and we eventually got him too. Laurent Garnier, he was on our wish list for a while too, and obviously once people like that came down and played and loved it, they wanted to come back and then it all fed back to the agents, who would help you get the other DJs you wanted - Derrick Carter, Josh Wink, those sort of people. But it did take a few years to spread the word, so to speak.

By now the British clubbing revolution was well under way and with success came the sort of fame most promoters with busy clubs could expect at that time. That meant previews, reviews and various articles in respected magazines.

And with the Wobble brand out there, not only were Gifford and Long being booked to play at other clubs - with Wobble in brackets by their names - but Wobble tour nights around the UK and one-offs in Ibiza, at the likes of Es Paradis, would also further promote the reputation of the club and help boost the Wobble coffers even more.

We realised the club was a success when we saw all our faces in magazines, and I thought "fame at last". We had a full page spread in The Face, which was our style bible. We had a few pictures in I.D, and DJ Magazine came down to do a review of the night too. It took MixMag a bit longer, but they eventually came down as well, and I guess success equals column inches at the end of the day, and we were happy with that.

The extra curricular DJ bookings for Gifford, Long and The Lovely Helen, another Wobble resident, all helped spread the club's name further, even if Long was less than happy dumbing down at the various

*(clockwise) * Those trademark Wobble boobs*
* Phil Gifford being interviewed for One More, 2010
* A Wobble Si Long/Lovely Helen mix cassette cover
* (main picture) Si Long (bottom) and Gifford (left)

Volum

1996

Si Long
The Lovely Hele

guest spots on offer. Gifford, however, admits he was not averse to "selling his soul".

We did joint nights at Wobble with people like Hard Times from Leeds and Club For Life from London, but we were also doing the circuit as guest DJs, playing in London at clubs like Club UK, the Leisure Lounge and Ministry Of Sound, as well as all over the place at clubs like Back To Basics and Cream.

Initially it was Phil Gifford and/or Silong with Wobble in brackets next to our names. Then when we started advertising ourselves in MixMag, people started asking about Wobble nights, so it was a case of Phil Gifford for £500, me and Si for £800, and a grand for me, Si, Helen and the use of our logo.

I saw this as a really good way to a) promote Wobble, b) DJ in other clubs and c) earn more cash. But Si didn't want to play the game. He'd rather play deep house and techno back at Wobble in the upstairs room than earn extra money selling his soul to the various handbag house clubs around the country. I, on the other hand, was more than happy to sell my soul, and pick up loads of birds at the various handbag house clubs around the country.

So a lot of Saturdays I was doing exactly that, but with our 7.30am finish I could pretty much make it back from most places to do the last set at Wobble. And that included, on occasions, travelling back from the likes of Middlesbrough or Brighton.

Wobble, like many clubs in the Midlands and the surrounding areas, benefited from the positive words of mouth between the various clubbers and DJs passing through.

DJs talk among themselves, and Justin Robertson might tell Dave Clarke Wobble was really great and so on. Most of the top British jocks at that time played at Wobble and they all talked to each other. Dimitri from Deee-Lite came over from New York, and he was great, but our favourite had to be Josh Wink. It took us a while to get him and then, bosh, he came back three times.

When Josh first played, his anthem Higher State Of Consciousness was going mad in the national charts. He was only meant to do an hour and a half, but he played for five hours. He went from Higher

State…and some rave tunes, through to stuff like James Brown's Sex Machine, and that was a big thing for us, because our music policy was all over the place too. We liked to drop a few Balearic things and Josh Wink coming and doing that too was brilliant for us. We used to particularly like Dave Clarke as well, because he used to play electro and house, as well as techno, and on the house floor Chris & James were always good, as was Jeremy Healy, of course.

These days, as well as the odd reunion party, the now industry standard Facebook revival page is a place where 'Wobblers' can go and reminisce.

As for the club's legacy? Well, you look on Facebook and there is a group of a thousand people talking about Wobble still, and the great times they had, so I'll leave the legacy for other people to discuss.

My favourite memories? I suppose it was like the '60s, if you can remember it you weren't really there. We were wide-eyed and bushy-tailed until seven in the morning every week and it's all good memories, not many bad. I was carried out of there a few times after drinking too much, which is probably not a good look if you're DJing.

One memory that sticks out was a time when DJ Dimitri played a record out at the time by Moby called Thousand. Dimitri had played at Venus beforehand and said, "I've got this record, man, you gotta hear it, it's got a thousand BPMs". And this record just builds into this one 1,000 BPM machine gun rattle, and if you can imagine, with the strobes going off, and the whole place going absolutely mental, that was a great memory. You won't get that these days, you won't hear that at Gatecrasher.

Meanwhile, Gifford is quick to rattle off the names of anthems that became synonymous at Wobble.

Higher State Of Consciousness by Josh Wink and I Am Ready by Size Nine were pretty big in making Wobble; Dave Clarke's Red 2 as well, because that got played on both floors. Someone downstairs would play Red 2 into Dan Hartman's Relight My Fire, while upstairs Red Two would be mixed in and out of, for instance, Richie Hawtin's Plastikman.

Then there was all the really great Chicago stuff from the likes of Derrick Carter. Then all that DJ Sneak stuff... the Polyester EP, that was on repeat, it seemed. And anything by Daft Punk or Thomas Bangalter. I had Daft Punk's Homewerk double album on white label, and pretty much, every week, for three or four years, every track on that album got played.

Downstairs was always more for the girls, and the bread and butter, more commercial stuff that people wanted with guests like Jeremy Healy and Jon (Pleased Wimmin). While Si was playing deeper stuff and techno upstairs with clever guests like Gene Farris, Nick Holder, Harvey, Bob Sinclar, before he blew up, and also DJ Deep.

In fact, I would be playing anthems like Outrage's Tall and Handsome downstairs, and then would nip upstairs and play some more underground bits - stuff by then, I liked more - as and when I could. Then at some point we stopped booking Jeremy Healy and co and put the deep house and the good house on downstairs and techno and weird stuff upstairs, and completely forgot what people actually wanted.

The Wobble story came to an abrupt end in 2000 as the dreaded curse of the club fire struck. However, Gifford now wishes he had gone out on a high, long before that.

Unfortunately we didn't really know the end of Wobble was coming. Me and Si had split our partnership and he'd gone on to open a club in Leamington Spa. Wobble was really on its last legs anyway. I'd carried on, but attendances were down from a thousand to about 250 and we were just open on one floor. You know, clutching at straws, hoping people would come after the other clubs to make it busier. So really at some point during the last 18 months we should probably have had a big party and said goodbye, but, you know, flogging a dead horse, we kept it going.

Then one day I got a phone call from The Lovely Helen, saying, "I've just spoken to someone and the club has burned down". I said, "don't be stupid", but I made a few calls and it had indeed burned down. That was it, we never opened again.

For the last two years of Wobble's existence, like Jon Hill at Golden, Gifford was involved in a mini-transfer of his own when the

Ministry Of Sound opened a bar in Birmingham city centre and asked the Wobble boss to be their promotion manager and DJ booker.

To be honest, I was happy to take a wage for that and when the Ministry bar finished at 2am, try and leave with as many people as possible, and head to Wobble for the rest of the night. And because I was doing the Ministry bar's Millennium Eve night for them, which was a sell-out at £15 a head, I didn't do Wobble and instead rented out the club to some local promoters who thought they could have it off. Let's just say, instead of losing loads of money on that night, I charged those guys enough rent to clear a couple of grand, plus a holiday in Thailand that January. Personally, I could see that night was going to go tits up.

The Ministry Of Sound bar closed its doors after two years, and by then Wobble was no more either. As you may expect from this happy-go-lucky promoter there are no regrets from the Gifford camp.

We never really had a last "we're going to close the club forever" record, because of the fire and the club not opening the next week. But there were many classic end of night tracks, which were a bit off-kilter or a bit silly. In particular, there was the DMC remix of local lads Duran Duran's Save A Prayer. For the first few years, people would shout out at the end of the night "play that Duran Duran record", which was a bit embarrassing. And I even played that at midnight on New Year's Eve at a Wobble reunion night a couple of years ago at the Rainbow Warehouse. But there was also the obvious camp disco, like Sister Sledge, that sort of stuff, nothing too serious...send people home smiling.

You know, we had a good time, and I got to DJ. In fact, I got to travel the world DJing and we rinsed it for a while. I'm not driving a Porsche around, but we did OK. I wouldn't say we changed anyone's lives, but if you read some of those comments on Facebook, I'd say we possibly did without realising it at the time. Unless that was the drugs.

These days I'm concentrating on my career before I was a club promoter and DJ, which is hairdressing and I've just opened my own salon in Birmingham City Centre. We do a monthly word of mouth night in various random places in Birmingham, called Enid Blyton, which is going really well, attracting a mixture of shop workers in their 20s with funny haircuts and old Wobble regulars who should know better. Other than that I look after my dogs and go for walks in the country. Time to keep my nose clean, simple as.

PROGRESS

Derby is the last place you would associate with "Mafia Dons", but when it comes to the British superclubs of the '90s, Progress head honcho Russell Davison's analogy of so-called 'Godfathers' protecting their turf is a fitting one.

And with Derby nestling nicely next to neighbouring Nottingham - and only half an hour's drive from Birmingham - Davison's patch was prime real estate where 'superclubbing' in the early '90s was concerned.

Once Progress was established, another club had become an integral cog in this new clubbing machine, its influence surprisingly far reaching.

For Davison, it all started with punk rock and reggae, but he was also a regular at The Garage in Nottingham and a huge fan of a certain Graeme Park. He argues that without The Garage there would have been no Venus, let alone Progress.

My brother and sisters were always into music and I started DJing at local parties when I was at school. At an early age I was a punk rocker and then I really got into reggae, putting on blues parties in the inner city of Derby.

Then I started promoting funk and soul events for predominantly black crowds. This was in the mid-'80s. Then when house music came into the country I started putting on warehouse parties, and the whole thing evolved that way. If truth be told, I was not really into acid house, I was more of a soul boy. I did like it when Todd Terry brought out his first few mixes but I didn't like that whole harder-edged thing.

I didn't get into the hard rave scene, and I didn't like walking around fields with mud up to my knees. That didn't really turn me on. I was more of a cool clubber and a soul boy, so for a time I was continuing to promote club nights when the whole club scene had died, when the whole rave scene effectively killed clubs.

Davison wasn't totally convinced he and any of his ambitious club nights would ever succeed in the face of a growing commercialisation of the rave scene.

I remember saying that nobody will ever go to a club again, because Pepsi were sponsoring raves. When you had companies like that involved there was a rave going off somewhere in the country every weekend. I was trying to book people like Mike Pickering in a small club in Derby, at a night called G Spot, and, you know, we did OK, but it was a struggle, a real struggle, because everyone was going to the raves.

That stopped almost overnight, as if there was a mass consciousness. People got fed up with getting ripped off, paying £5 for a bottle of water, and also got sick of wearing trainers and baseball caps in fields. All of a sudden people wanted to do something cooler, and that was really up my street.

So another of our club bosses was in the perfect place to seize on the cultural shift happening, and a spin on the initial shift at that. And Davison had certainly done his time in the '80s.

Before Progress, where the whole cool thing happened outside of Derby was at The Garage in Nottingham, in the Lace Market. I started going there when I was 18 in 1985. This was a club on three different levels, and the top floor was where Graeme Park was resident and he was smashing out records that I'd never heard before.

Overwhelmingly, the music was black music, but the crowd was mixed.

At the time I was an 18-year-old funk and soul DJ, playing to a mainly black inner city crowd, but I would also run coaches up to The Garage in Nottingham. Graeme Park was our hero, and that was the first time I saw a mixed crowd dancing to this amazing selection of music. The basement of the club was full-on indie whatever night of the week, including Saturdays when Graeme played the top floor all night, while the middle floor was a bar. Along with the amazing music that Graeme put together, the door policy was something else too. You had to look different to get in there. I'll always remember that.

The Garage became a really cool club. Graeme was playing stuff like Grace Jones and Talking Heads mixed in with hip-hop like Schooly D, and then introducing bits of house as well. From that starting point, Venus became a great club in Nottingham, and I don't think Venus would have happened if it wasn't for The Garage, and those clubs in turn both acted as massive inspirations for me.

Davison is not averse to saying exactly what he thinks, with the words "cat", "among" and "pigeons" probably quite apt. He will certainly ruffle a few feathers with his claims that house music in the UK started in Nottingham, and that he was behind the first ever "exclusive house night" in the UK.

I don't know what was going on in Manchester and London at the time, because I wasn't there, but as far as I'm concerned house music started in the UK at The Garage in Nottingham in 1985 and it was started by Graeme Park. That's when JM Silk's Music Is The Key, the first house track, came out, and that's when Graeme started playing house music.

Graeme will be the first to admit that he got lucky. He worked in a great record shop, and the owner, Brian Selby, opened a club. Graeme really had no choice, he was the resident DJ by default. But he really did create something magical there, and he inspired me to do something myself in Derby. When Graeme left The Garage, that really was an impossible act to follow, but Allister Whitehead, to his credit, did actually manage to pull that off.

As Park made his first appearance at the Hacienda, Davison was establishing his own innovative house night in Derby.

In 1987 I started a new night called House Nation at a brilliant club which had just opened, called 20th Century. It was because of Graeme's influence and because I had seen house work so well up the road.

I came up with the name House Nation because of the 1987 track by The Housemaster Boyz And The Rude Boys Of House. The club held 800 people and we ran for more than six months weekly on a Saturday. I believe, and have been told, it was the country's first pure house night on a weekly basis.

I booked Graeme for £50, paid Marshall Jefferson £200 to come and play, and also booked Farley Jackmaster Funk. We charged £2 or £3 on the door and I was making good money for a few months, until the owners got rid of us because they thought our door deal was too good.

That old chestnut, huh? Now Davison was back on civvy street, albeit he was only just out of school.

Supposedly on his way to university, when he was 19, he instead landed the manager's job at a venue in Derby called The Blue Note, much to the dismay of his middle class family. Later he also juggled a job as a social worker at a children's home with promoting warehouse parties in the area.

At House Nation the crowd was at least 50% black and, drug-wise, there wasn't much ecstasy about. Then when acid house hit, in my opinion, my black crowd didn't like the music or the drug involved. And then all the raves took over. It became big business, but a lot of the promoters just weren't into the music. The raves became more about money, and more and more chavvy football hooligans in baseball caps started to go to them. I actually found the whole thing very unpleasant and believed the club scene was dead, because thousands and thousands of people were going to these raves.

But there was some light at the end of the tunnel for Davison because Venus in Nottingham was flying, and flying in the face of adversity caused by the rave scene.

By now Venus was going extremely well. James was very intense, it was like he was doing something new in Nottingham every few months and there were some remarkable things he put on there. They were all cool, but they weren't what depicted Progress. We would go on to be cooler than the rave scene, but you wouldn't say Progress was as cool as Venus.

Around 1990, I was trying to put on a serious house night called Catalonia in a club called Holy Trinity. It only held around 200 people and I had the likes of Sasha, Laurent Garnier and Carl Cox as headline guests, but I couldn't fill the place because suddenly a rave would pop up at Donnington or somewhere and literally everybody in the area would be off there.

I was still chasing the music and door policy of The Garage, and getting more and more despondent. Even Shelley's, which was amazing, attracted a lot of what you would now call chavs. Then slowly, one by one, there were more chinks of light, rays of hope. Venus continued to thrive, then Renaissance opened, Golden opened and Cream opened, all in 1992. Suddenly it seemed to be coming back to clubs.

At the same time I had been talking to a live music promoter called Paul Needham, who was running a venue in Derby called The Wherehouse, and had been the first promoter to bring the likes of Gil Scott Heron and Roy Ayres to the area. There was a space above the venue, which he was turning into a club, and he let me design everything upstairs. In December 1992, I launched Progress.

By the time Progress had opened, Davison had belatedly enrolled at university, to study for a degree in social work and - never a dull moment - had fathered a baby boy!

My son Benjamin had just been born and I was struggling financially, but I didn't start Progress because of money, it was never about money back then. However, on the first night it just exploded. I knew it was going to be massive, everything was right for it, but I was at university and I needed a business partner and that's when I said to Pete Wye, "if you do most of the work, I'll give you 50% of the profit each week". And Pete still had that deal nine years later. I had no idea how long it would last, I thought it would last longer than six months, but if it lasted a year, I would have been surprised. It was like being in a successful rock band - you expected to stop selling records at some point.

Pete Tong was great for us, and if there is one person I'd like to thank, it's his manager Eddie Gordon, who got Pete up there for us. Pete was blown away, and on his Radio One show the next week he said we were the best club in Britain. Pete came from a jazz funk background, I came from a funk and soul background and we just clicked. Pete Tong was saying we were the best club in Britain, and someone from DJ Magazine had been down, and we were No 1 in the Top 10 clubs in the UK for months at the same time too.

Progress was never about building the music, it was straight up, hands- in-the-air from the start, and Pete at that time fitted in really well. Pete Wye was a much better DJ technically than me, but together we made a good team, and, as Pete & Russell, we went on to DJ all over the country and the world.

We hadn't promoted Progress outside Derby and hadn't even thought about it at that point, or even needed to. Suddenly Derby had a club of notoriety, bigger than what was going on in Nottingham, Leicester and Stoke and that was amazing as far as I was concerned.

Like any aspiring "Mafia Don", at first, Davison knew his place and exactly where he stood in the pecking order.

Within months of each other Golden started in Stoke, Back 2 Basics started in Leeds and Cream started in Liverpool. And all these nights began because the guys behind it loved it, way before money was really part of it. I mean, James and Darren in Liverpool, they just wanted to put a night on, one of them was a hairdresser or something, they just loved it. As did Jon Hill, as did Dave Beer. And then Geoff Oakes from Stoke went over to Mansfield and started Renaissance at Venue 44, which was amazing. You know, everyone at that time was putting on great nights in the Midlands.

With all due respect to Derby, it's a great place, but it's not a big city and it couldn't compare to Liverpool and Leeds or Birmingham or other places so we got a little bit in their slip stream and we were like, "if it can work in these places, why can't it work in Derby?"

We were looking at the DJs, some of which I'd heard of, some of which I hadn't. Some of the London DJs getting booked were big in London, but not outside London, but I put this night together and I was pretty confident about it.

Progress ran at The Wherehouse until the end of 1994. In terms of advertising I wanted to move completely away from what was around at that time, which was all sold on sex or sci-fi or Salvador Dali-style imagery, none of which was me at all. I came from an angle of "let's do it child-like" and the device was a hand-drawn thing that I

(clockwise) * Judge Jules' trumpet phase at Progress
* Russell Davison outside site of The Wherehouse
* Judge Jules and the famous Progress logo
* Russell Davison with Lisa Loud

sketched. I didn't do it as an end project, more like a sketch for the graphics guy to work off, but when they tried to work on it, they couldn't recreate it so they used the original.

Progress was built on a lot of experience from me running smaller nights, little cool ones here, some failures there, and I think, as with any business, you can sometimes learn more from the failures than you can out of the successes. When Progress started I was really set right, so was Derby and so was the country, for something that simply became huge.

And like many of the best nights featured in One More, Progress was primarily launched to please the social and demographic needs of the promoter in question.

Progress was always, up until the last few years, essentially about me having a great time. It started because I wanted to have a great night to go to in my area. Of course, there was money involved and, of course, we made a lot of money out of it in the end. You'd be hard-pushed not to with a thousand people in your club every week paying £10 for that many years, but the original ethos was to have a great time and to connect with people.

Very early on we made sure we were building relationships with the people coming, making sure they felt part of it. And I believe we created something very special with Progress. Obviously there were lots of other great nights up and down the country, and we know a lot of those promoters and we have great respect for them, but with Progress it was a real family thing and people in Derby really got behind it.

A lot of people who came to it were from out of town, but our Derby core really did get it going. We had something to be really proud of because Derby had always played second fiddle to Nottingham in the region, and even Leicester and Stoke. We'd had the Blue Note, which was great, but it wasn't really that huge, whereas Nottingham had The Garage and Venus. Even Leicester had a small cooler scene. So when Derby got Progress it became one of THE big things in the area and became a Midlands superclub.

Mark Moore's path to this particular club night was, again, via Chuff Chuff.

Pete or Russell rang me up and said they had heard me play at Chuff Chuff, and they'd really like to book me, and that really was the first time I'd heard of Progress. I remember thinking, "Derby? OK, I'll give this a go". And the first booking was amazing. It was pretty much up there with Venus and Moneypenny's in terms of debauchery. I told all my mates, "you've got to come down to this club in Derby called Progress, it's brilliant", and they were like, "yeah, right, see you later".

I think people in London could get their heads around Nottingham and Birmingham or Manchester and Liverpool, but not the likes of Derby. I have to say, though, Progress was right up there with all of them at the time, a completely classic club. You could get away with a few of the early trance tracks, which I loved, but I would also mix it in with New York house and some progressive house too. At Progress, musicians would be playing bongos and saxophones on stage. It was complete chaos and at some points you couldn't tell what was being played live and what was on record.

Davison believes that a contrast of dance music persuasions with that of Pete Wye provided a healthy range for the Progress faithful to tap into.

Our music policy at Progress was born out of quite a distinctive taste between myself and Pete. I was a soul boy and Pete liked harder stuff, so when it came to booking the DJs it was often a case of pleasing both of us. We weren't afraid of putting a Tony De Vit on with a Graeme Park, so that also was quite a unique factor. I would always play the last hour and a half of the night, playing garage, which is what it was called then. Now people would say it was soulful house.

Earlier on in the night Pete would be playing something a bit more banging and the guests would play anything they liked, and they seemed to be able to throw anything at the Progress crowd. What we didn't do was, say, put on Roger Sanchez with Graeme Park. We always mixed it up, tried to put a soulful DJ with a harder one, and that just seemed to work. Certainly up until the last couple of years the music policy was really varied.

When we started, Progress was promoted through this childlike imagery, which I thought was innovative in that nobody else was doing it, and I liked the simplicity of it. The original flyer was this house in the middle of this traditional setting, with stick figures and a sun in the sky and we kept that theme going, and eventually we started cutting the house out, and as a cut-out flyer it stood out really well because then most flyers were still traditional A5 or A6 rectangular sizes.

It became a cut-out that people used to stick on their fridges and used to put everywhere. We used to get stickers made and put them all over the place so our logo and flyer was so distinctive that kids would collect them. I remember at our office, 12 and 13-year-old kids appearing just to get a flyer or a sticker. They would pass them around school and, from a marketing point of view, I knew they were our future customers.

So while we fell down on slick design - ie we weren't Cream and didn't have a massive marketing department - we did have an instant mass appeal. Our MixMag adverts looked a bit cowboy to be honest, but our logo carried us right the way through.

From that 1992/93 time, when there was a handful of things beginning, it seemed that in every city, in every town there was something starting up. And the rest, I suppose, is history, because later on in the scene nights started which weren't born out of, what I would call the realness that Progress came from. Nights like Godskitchen, great promoters, they did a great job, and even Gatecrasher, which I felt was always more about "this is a superclub, this is going to be a great business".

And you know, then people started talking about their club nights being brands, which was never a term we used at the start, that was very alien to us. At the start, the fact that the cash tills started to go 'kerching' pretty quickly had actually been a bonus, certainly for me anyway.

But when he was hit with the bombshell news that Renaissance were moving their operation to Derby, Davison was not sure how much "ker" was left in his "ching". However, when you ask him about the "Renaissance move", there's a big sigh first...followed by a few hearty chuckles.

There was a brand new club in town opening called The Conservatory, with a capacity of 900 as opposed to ours of 400, and loads of work being done on it.

Renaissance had been doing great things at Venue 44 at Mansfield and I had a reasonably good relationship with Geoff Oakes because I was also managing Allister Whitehead and Geoff had booked him at Mansfield. Geoff was a great innovator, and he saw business opportunities that other people couldn't. He had an eye for cool, more than most, I think.

However, in my opinion Renaissance had taken a bit of a dive, towards the end of its time at Mansfield, and it was only the last Saturday of the month that was really busy. That's why, in my view, they left Mansfield. At the same time, the owners of The Conservatory had managed to persuade Geoff to move to Derby.

For me, Renaissance got a bit geeky when Sasha and Digweed started taking the mixing really seriously, and the music got much more minimal. I like Sasha and Digweed, both great guys, but I thought they started getting away from the party element. I mean, when Sasha played for me in 1990 he was effectively playing handbag house.

But Geoff always had big ideas for Renaissance from the start, and had been written about loads in the press. It was very much "Geoff Oakes and Renaissance". We had our props, but not many people knew about us outside of Derby, so finding out that Renaissance were coming to Derby really was such a blow, and I really thought it would wipe us out.

I wouldn't be beaten, though, and I decided to fight fire with fire. We upped our game and played on our family vibe. We took out a monthly full-page advert in MixMag, which cost about £500 and was a big deal for us then. And we started doing silly little things like giving out sweets on the door as people came in and free shots of tequila at the end of the night. We also got various musicians in, like bongo players, saxophone players and guitarists, when people weren't really doing that sort of thing.

Then Renaissance came, and on their first night absolutely smashed it. There were queues round the block, but we were really busy that night too, maybe because of the overspill. Then the second week wasn't so good for them, and they only really lasted a few months in Derby after that.

Allister Whitehead is another fan of the Progress session band.

It was the first time I'd played with live musicians and the first time I'd seen that. But it did work because they were good musicians, they were all in key and you could play around with them a little bit. They had a percussionist and a guitarist, and every now and then I would drop things down and just leave a beat going, leave them a bed to work on, if you like. And it was a really good thing for the crowd there, because it gave them a bit of a different lift, when they maybe needed it, as well as giving me a bit of break. I was quite happy with that, while other DJs maybe thought it should be all about them still. I welcomed it and thought it was a chance to do something different, and it was good fun. It was then done by lots of other clubs too after that. With varying degrees of success, I would add.

The crowd in Progress were probably one of the most ecstatic I came across, though. It was hands in the air all the way. The hands in the air thing is often over-used today, but it is true in this case.

Davison now had a MixMag advert to justify, but had been talking to Venue 44 owner Dave Knowles about his cunning plan for the now vacant former working men's club.

I knew that for Renaissance the last Saturday of the month had still been working in Mansfield so I launched a brand new night called Hot To Trot, which lasted there for 24 months on that last Saturday. We did pre-tickets and each month for those two years we sold out before each party. We were still full at Progress on those nights too and the feeling when you're driving up to a sold-out 1,000-capacity club, and you've got another busy one down the road as well, is just amazing.

The icing on the cake for me was when we moved Progress to The Conservatory in 1994, and spent every Saturday there for another two years. We ended up in the new club that had been kitted out for Renaissance. However, I really didn't want to leave The Wherehouse, and it was with regret, because it left a hole for those guys. I had to wait for The Conservatory to be ready, though, because it was one big room, and I insisted that they create a second room before I moved over there.

We did really well at The Conservatory, until we got raided. I was outside at the time, Tony De Vit was playing, and I watched the police running in, all a hundred of them, jumping out of a seven-ton lorry, with sniffer dogs, with 20 more coppers inside the club in plain clothes. Loads of the clubbers inside threw their pills on the floor, and the police ended up with a bag of stuff, made 20 arrests, and charged two people, neither of which were convicted. The police had been on the mic, saying, "this is a raid, this club is closed...for good", and stuff like that. They'd had the club under surveillance for six months, and I was told the whole operation had cost almost a million pounds. The club's licence was revoked, but it stayed open on appeal, and I stuck with the owners to support them, as long as I could. As far as I know, neither the doormen, nor the management, and certainly not us, were making money out of drugs at the club. At the end of the day, I think the powers that be locally were looking for a nice headline.

Alex P was never quite sure which club in Derby he would end up at, but welcomed another Midlands pit-stop en route to more northern territories.

Russell and co put a lot of effort into giving the club a cabaret atmosphere, with the musicians and everything, but to me Progress always had a nomadic feel to it, because it was always moving. You'd go and play for them the next time and they would often be at another club. Clubs like Progress and Golden were good, though, because you could stop off at those places and then go and play in Manchester or Liverpool on the same night. People in the Midlands area and the north were a lot more easy-going, while the London clubbers generally, without tarring everyone with the same brush, seemed to be a bit more reserved.

In 1996, without a club with any long-term guarantee of a licence, and with a seemingly continual need to satisfy more demand, Davison reluctantly completed a move to a former Ritzy venue, owned by High Street chain Rank Leisure.

It didn't feel right but, financially, it was the best thing we could have done. We moved to The Eclipse and put 1,700 people in there every week for another two years. At the same time, Hot To Trot was fizzling out at Venue 44 and Simon Raine approached us to do a joint Gatecrasher/Hot To Trot party at The Arches in Sheffield. We did one with him, which was really busy, and then he did the second one on his own, and it was rammed. But I still maintain it was our crowd. Then Simon moved to The Republic and did amazingly well there with Gatecrasher

Bizarrely, Davison claims not to remember the names of too many records, due to being dyslexic.

I used to DJ on the basis of what the records looked like, the artwork on the cover or the record centre. I never used to know who the producer was or what the mix was, so I was never really a trainspotter like that.

But I can tell you that the big records for Progress were Lisa Lisa's Let The Beat Hit Em, and the Morales mixes of Mariah Carey's Dream Lover and Jamiroquai's Space Cowboy. And that the last record played at many Progress nights was Hey Mr DJ by Screen II, the Jon Da Silva mix - an absolutely stunning record, timeless, in fact. Whenever I hear that record now it still makes me want to go out. And it really was like a Progress record. I'm not sure how often it got played in other clubs, but it got played to death at Progress.

Davison cites 1998 as a particularly bad year for Progress, although they were boosted by a Top 10 hit for a crossover club track released on their Progress record label, and some other unusual revenue streams.

Our profile was helped at the end of 1998 when we had a No 7 national hit with Progress Presents Boy Wonder, which was produced by another of my residents, Rob Webster. Rob was the Boy Wonder, Pete worked on the music and I did some lyrics. We had a little studio set-up and released about 15 tracks in total, but this one sampled the strings at the start of Madonna's Papa Don't Preach, and we knew we wouldn't get sample clearance so we put it out on white label.

When Judge Jules came to play around that time, just before he was going on, I dropped the track and said, "watch the reaction to this". Jules signed it on the spot to his label Manifesto, and Madonna eventually agreed to the sample. She got 90% of publishing and we got the other 10%, but we kept all the royalties. We had people going out to PA it around the UK, so we made some money on that, and nearly got the Christmas No 1. I think we were beaten by Craig David, but we all got on Top of The Pops, so that was a good day out.

As the business side of things continued to get tougher, Davison wasn't going down without a fight, without a meeting of "Mafia" heads and without, as it would turn out, setting himself up comfortably for life. This included relieving Walls Ice Cream of a cool £100,000 to promote Calypso Shots, and £30,000 a piece from Grolsch and Malibu.

I took that money, yes, and then spent lots of time convincing various brand managers that their logos should be really small on our advertising and promo material because "less is more". Loads of promoters were taking sponsorship money like that. Moneypenny's had a big deal with Marlboro cigarettes. Then the scene in 1998 started to diminish really fast for us and pretty much, for most of us outside of London anyway, it was amazing how fast.

So I instigated some conversations with some of the other clubs and managed, after quite a lot of trials and tribulations, to get a very, very top secret meeting in a hotel in Birmingham with me, Darren Hughes from Cream, Simon Raine from Gatecrasher, the Ryans from Moneypenny's and Jon Hill from Golden all in attendance. The idea was that we had created a monster. Firstly, in the form of MixMag, which started off as an independent magazine, which was great, and quite cheap to advertise in - like £500 to have a full page advert in a national magazine. That was decent, but then, all of a sudden, MixMag doubled their price. Tony Prince was preparing to sell the magazine to EMAP Metro. Fair play to him, but we couldn't afford it anymore.

On top of this, the DJs who were playing for three or four hundred pounds, had doubled, tripled and quadrupled their fees, and it got to the stage where it would cost £2,000 to book Tall Paul. He's a great DJ and he's a great guy, and all that, but we just couldn't afford it. It got to the stage where, certainly I felt, this had to change. Our numbers were going down, but our advertising and DJ bills had gone through the roof. I just felt like a money collecting agent for the DJs, not a promoter. We weren't making anything like what the DJs were anymore and so I got this meeting together, and it was like a crime family meeting or something. In fact, I felt the whole club scene was run like a crime family, without - I have to say - the crime, because we were all nice guys who never got involved in anything nasty like that.

We had our own patches like Mafia Dons would, so we respected that, but we were also competing against each other. We met in this hotel and it was exciting actually. I really felt we had an opportunity to change things and rescue our fantastic scene from what looked like disaster. I was putting together proposals and saying, "look, let's go to MixMag, because we are MixMag - without us, what has MixMag got? We are that magazine, they write about us, but they take our money and they're trying to double their prices. We'll start our own magazine if they don't drop their prices and we can make our own new superstar DJs if we want, if the current ones don't play ball either."

You know, I am, and was, a competent negotiator, and I reckon if it just was me, the Ryans and Golden, we could have persuaded Simon Raine, because we were all from the Midlands. But Darren was from Liverpool, and I think he knew he held the power. He kept his cards a little bit closer to his chest. But I knew that the funding around that table was more than enough to start our own new magazine. If we had got Darren, we would have got Simon, I'm sure of it. At the end of day, none of us were tight with Darren, and I'm not blaming him, but I do strongly believe we could have changed what happened, and I don't think we would have all ended up with the kamikaze night that was Millennium Eve if we had been unified.

It was hugely disappointing, because at the end of the day we couldn't let the 'Francescas' and the 'Jennys' know that we were trying to undermine the 'Jeremys' and the 'Dannys', or MixMag clubs editor Dan Prince find out that we were trying to fuck over his dad. And it wasn't really that we were trying to fuck over anyone, it was just that, as far as I was concerned, in the end, it was greed that killed our scene.

Davison is certainly one who subscribes to the Millennium being instrumental in clubland's downfall.

I strongly believe that the end of it really was Millennium Eve, because these superclubs, even Progress, weren't promoting from the heart anymore, they were just promoting from the wallet. Towards the end I was putting on hard house DJs, whose music I didn't even like. Progress had become a cash cow that I wasn't really even interested in milking anymore, so for the Millennium many of the clubs were putting out ticket prices like £100. Some even wanted more. I was saying there was no way people will pay that sort of money and why would they? It's only a night out. My business partner was saying he wanted to charge X amount of money and I was saying, "let's just charge £25 like we always do on New Year's Eve".

In the end we charged £50 and we did OK, but not that well. Most clubs were empty. It was that night that really kicked everyone in the goolies because it exposed the club scene for what it was. The DJs were asking for £10,000/£20,000 that night, the promoters were wanting hundreds of pounds to get in on the door and the punters were thinking that the whole night out, with drinks, cabs and whatever, would cost them the best part of a month's salary. So they decided to stay at home and have their own parties and, you know what, they've done that ever since because before then NYE was THE biggest night out of the year. Not after that, though.

In the last two years, from 2000 to 2002, when we moved back to The Conservatory for Millennium Eve, for a few months, and then on to The Gatehouse, I was definitely promoting from the wallet, because I couldn't afford the big house DJs. I was booking hard house DJs like Lisa Lashes and The Tidy Boys because they were cheaper. I can't stand hard house, but it was all I could afford.

Eventually I'd had enough, and I wanted out. I gave my half of the shares to Pete who carried on for a bit, and by then I had opened my bar in the area, Susumi, which is Japanese for Progress. There was no leaving night for me at Progress, my bar had opened, I was doing well, and I was all consumed by that. I based it on The End's AKA bar in London and ran it for seven years. We won loads of awards and then I sold that on in 2008.

Maybe Davison can afford himself a rather more romantic look back at proceedings than some. A shrewd business head meant he got out at the right time, and got out good.

I feel so privileged to have experienced everything I did, all the clubs promoted and played at, DJing all over the UK, all the club tours we did, and DJing in places like Hong Kong, California, Russia, Dubai, Las Vegas, etc.

Over the years, fortunately, I've had the good sense to put my money in property so I've got quite a big portfolio now. I look after that, eat organic food, do yoga, keep myself fit and I'm in bed most nights before 10pm. I don't go clubbing at all, apart from with my son, who has taken over the family business and is a DJ and promoter in Nottingham called DJ Rudes. He's out there using my old sound system and, for me, it doesn't get much better than that.

GATECRASHER

Now the dust has settled somewhat, it's probably safe to say that the word superclub was banded about far too often in the '90s, but one club that surely deserves such an accolade is Gatecrasher.

Despite the huge cost of putting on the event, no other promoters can boast filling an athletics stadium on Millennium Eve, and with the rest of clubland crumbling around him, 'Crasher boss Simon Raine's achievement was even more significant.

With most clubbers snubbing overpriced tickets and labelling the UK's promoters greedy, Raine managed to shift an impressive 25,000 at a juicy £107.50 each. And while many promoters were sweating up until the last minute, spending the last seven days of the year fearing the worst, Gatecrasher had sold out before Christmas. Instead of having to sell his club or fold his night, as many did, Raine was able to kick on and buy more venues.

But, of course, Rome was not built in a day and Raine has given us an exclusive insight into just how he built his empire. It was certainly some journey.

Gatecrasher really started in my mind on a Monday night in 1988 on an impromptu visit to a nightclub in London called Heaven. Spectrum was being run there by Paul Oakenfold and Ian St Paul, and that's where it all began for me.

Gatecrasher actually started five years later in 1993 at Bakers nightclub in Birmingham, which is probably about 150 metres away from Gatecrasher's current flagship venue in Broad Street. Heaven was really my inspiration, because that night at Spectrum was my first taste of acid house.

I wasn't even in the business, I was just a guy out on a Monday night and I got sucked in like a bit of fluff. There was an explosion of colours and flashing lights and, for me, that was my sound, that was it, I was hooked. I was totally bitten by acid house and from that point onwards I spent a lot of time driving round and round the M25, jumping up and down in various fields with lots of other people, having battles with the authorities. I was just a customer then, but at that point I knew that's what I wanted to do, it was so dynamic and so exciting.

At that time I admired the Hacienda in Manchester, which was a huge influence, I think, on every club in the UK then, and it's obviously still an influence today. But the first club that got me and the club that is my clubbing spiritual home has to be Heaven, under those arches in Charing Cross, London.

They ran various nights there, including big gay nights, but Spectrum on a Monday was the one. It later became Land Of Oz, because of bad press with all the drugs. I think the owner at the time, Richard Branson, had said Spectrum needed to change their name, so the party carried on as Land Of Oz.

The other club night there was called Rage, and was run by a guy called Jeremy Millins, who also ran the Dance 89 and Dance 91 events.

Other inspirational clubs were in Ibiza, Pacha and also Ku, the name of Privilege back in the day, before they put a roof on there and the rules changed. There are a lot of other clubs - The Brain Club in London was fantastic in its time and Shelley's in Stoke back in the day was also amazing.

Before Gatecrasher started in earnest in '93 Raine had been putting in the hours on an impressive clubbing apprenticeship. But more importantly, he also put on a massive rave in Tamworth, just outside Birmingham in 1989, using the name Spectrum, which he had licensed from St Paul.

I met some guys in Birmingham and we decided to put on an event using the Spectrum name. A deal was done with Ian St Paul and our version of Spectrum took place on September 23, 1989, in a farmer's field just off the B5000 in Tamworth.

The Spectrum party was really the first acid house party, which we then called a "dance music festival", outside of the London area, other than the raves up in Manchester. And it was lucky that the B5000 straddles two police forces – Warwickshire and Staffordshire. The guys from Staffordshire landed in a helicopter in an adjoining field, but weren't that bothered because the party was technically on the other force's patch. We did, however, lose a total of £30,000 and got into a lot of trouble with people in the local area. But the party was absolutely fantastic, and for me, I was off and running. I was in the business.

Following that Spectrum event and the big loss - which we all thought was a result, because we were now involved in clubbing - we then moved on to create a brand name called Time and did various events in and around Birmingham, the most notable at the Rag Market, a big indoor town centre space. They were massively successful, but after that party, the Time organisation was disbanded.

Although he wanted to stay in the promotion business, Raine needed something more secure than the unpredictable world of one-off events in random spaces or buildings.

I thought, 'enough is enough, I need to get a proper job', and I went and approached Bakers nightclub in the town centre, and asked if I could put a night on at the club. The first night I did there was in conjunction with Ministry Of Sound. It was their first tour night outside of London actually, which I worked on with Lyn Cosgrave, who was then the club's booker, and ran Saturdays there.

We did a deal with Lyn, for Tony Humphries, the Ministry's resident at the time, to headline and to use the club's brand, logo, etc. It was a Sunday...May 4, 1993, and it was so successful that the owners of Bakers offered me a job because they reckoned I could put more people in the club than them.

My training was very simple. The owner Mark Jones, who had a partner called Keith Williams, threw me the keys and said, 'all you need to know, Rainey, is that you treat the club as if it's your home and you spend as much time there as possible'. And that was it, I was a nightclub manager. I had a regular income and nobody was chasing me around a field trying to get paid.

And it was at Bakers that Raine met two men who would inadvertently help inspire the clubbing brand that would go on to become his life.

After 12 months of being paid on time and living the good life, I teamed up with the two guys who were running the Wednesday night at

Bakers, a hairdresser called Dave Rowley and Carl Lester, who had a fashion outlet in the town centre. The three of us decided to put on a night and that's when we sat around a table and talked about possible names. Someone present, who wasn't even involved and never has been, came up with the name Gatecrasher, and we just looked at each other and said, 'what a great name'. And that was it, Gatecrasher was born.

So Gatecrasher had a home at Bakers and we started off doing some small bank holiday parties. DJ-wise, if you booked Jeremy Healy at that time you had a full house, loads of beautiful girls and loads of really cool guys. Other DJs of the day were the likes of Dave Dorrell, Terry Farley and Pete Heller.

However, we soon outgrew Bakers and decided to put on a summer event outside of the club. There was a venue called The Engine House, out in the sticks in a place called Tardebigge in Bromsgrove, and we had a line-up including Jeremy Healy, Boy George live, and Farley and Heller.

Gatecrasher would go on to become the kings of promotion and must have spent more than most on magazine advertising over the years, often employing leading advertising agencies to come up with ingenious marketing campaigns, and regularly taking out five or six pages at a time, back covers, inside covers, and double page spreads inside.

In the early days of Gatecrasher, however, Raine says that progress was much more organic.

To promote at the start it was very different. We didn't have a marketing plan and we didn't have the internet at that point. It wasn't a business so you didn't attack it as such. It was a scene and you were out in it, 24/7. You got your venue, you booked your DJs, and the DJs were people that you knew. You pulled it together and got something printed up. It was all about printed literature in those days and you also called as many mates as you could. If you were lucky, before you knew it, you had several hundred people and you had yourself a party.

In '93 and '94 in the Birmingham area, the biggest club brand was Miss Moneypenny's, which obviously went on to be a global club brand too. They had the best crowd, the best DJs, they were the biggest promoters with the best looking and most fashionable crowd. They also took the most money as well. You also had Fun, which was down the road at The Steering Wheel, and you had Wobble with Phil Gifford and Si Long.

But Raine would soon be on his own where Gatecrasher was concerned.

After a while, Dave and Carl came to me and said they didn't want to do this Gatecrasher thing anymore. And, you know, it had become rather intense and although it was still a lot of fun, it was a lot of hard work, too.

So Dave and Carl left and I was running Gatecrasher on my own, while still the manager of Bakers. Everything was looking good so I went on holiday for two weeks. When I came back there was a phone call and I'd lost my job... so it was a case of "fucking hell, what am I going to do?".

It had to be Gatecrasher. I had a call from a guy called Stuart Reid, who ran the The Eclipse in Coventry. He said there was a club in Sheffield that I should have a look at and he took me up there. It was called The Arches, at a place called The Wicker, which was these rundown old railway arches. However, this venue had a fantastic sound system so we struck a deal with the woman who owned it to do a monthly party there and that was Gatecrasher's first step to the north of England and Gatecrasher's first big regular monthly event.

Gatecrasher was building at a frightening pace, and the promotion had already set up base in another town, the fourth location so far for Raine, if you count the Tamworth rave. He soon worked out that getting some influential media partners on board would certainly help the cause further.

Gatecrasher Sheffield moved quite quickly for us. It started in 1994 as a monthly and the capacity at The Arches was around 900 people. We filled it on regular basis quite easily and the night soon went weekly. From a DJ perspective, initially we had everybody from Sasha, Keoki, Chris & James, Mark Moore, Jon of the Pleased, John Kelly and Judge Jules, and Jules became a fortnightly resident. He had a radio show on a small station called Radio 1...haha...which meant he was obviously very good at spreading the word for us and also speaking to other high profile people in the business.

We also teamed up with MixMag, which was pretty much the bible of the day. There were lots of other magazines which came and went and tried to challenge them, but MixMag was the biggest. Owned by Tony and Christine Prince, their son Dan Prince was the clubs editor for the magazine and we met and befriended him. Together we put on a monthly co-production, Gatecrasher & MixMag presents:-, and Dan was great at getting us good press and speaking to other DJs.

And then the club moved again...and again, but both times stayed within Sheffield, a town that was increasingly becoming Gatecrasher's spiritual home, and where a loyal fan base was building nicely.

We went over to The Adelphi, which was in the gay part of Sheffield. We befriended another Radio One DJ, Annie Nightingale, who also became a resident and who used to play more alternative stuff in a tent in the car park, which was massive and was needed to meet demand.

The club was going from strength to strength, and there was a venue down the road called The Republic, which had been set up by a local businessman and a local promoter, and which had gone into administration. I went to have a look at it, walked in and thought "we have to buy this nightclub". At that time Gatecrasher had moved from nightclub to nightclub. It was weekly, but we were also doing lots of one-off shows and events. At that point we were confident we knew more about clubs and clubbing than the people who owned the clubs, so we put in a bid.

The Republic was up for £750,000 and we managed to scrape together £100,000 and put that down as a deposit, only to find that when we were signing on the dotted line we only had a month to find the other £650,000. But we were fearless in those days so we put the deposit down and left the meeting.

We spent the next 29 or 30 days frantically trying to get together the rest of the money, which we did with the help of a brewery, a bank and some very good friends in Birmingham who put some money up. Thanks guys, you know who you are.

And that was Gatecrasher's final move in Sheffield. We'd gone from The Arches to The Adelpi, via some one-offs at The Leadmill, and we were now at The Republic, at what was Gatecrasher's final and spiritual home in Sheffield.

But how much did the DJs influence the music policy then? For instance, Judge Jules started off as a house DJ who ended up playing trance, a musical direction which mirrored that of Gatecrasher.

DJs had an influence to some degree, yes, but not totally. You know Tony De Vit was a really influential DJ then. He played it quite hard, but was also very trancey. Jules wasn't trancey at that stage and we also booked the likes of Chris & James and Mark Moore who weren't trance DJs, and even Sasha, who wasn't that trancey then either.

Gatecrasher's move from dance music or house music to trance music, I think, was just a natural progression of where the music was going at the time with the big room clubs and the music that was being made.

Sure, you had influential figures at the time, who helped it go in more of a trance direction. I remember Danny Rampling coming back from Goa in a pair of combats and he was suddenly playing trance, and he was the man from Shoom! Then you had, probably the biggest pioneer of dance music, Paul Oakenfold. When he started playing trance music he set the scene and tempo for a lot of people and from then on it was clear that for the next eight or so years trance music was going to rule.

By the time we'd moved to The Republic nightclub, which was a much bigger and more impressive building than we'd been in before, getting the DJs wasn't actually that difficult. However, because of our standing by this time there was now a goalkeeper involved...welcome the agent.

The agent made it much smoother in some ways, but more expensive in lots of other ways. From that point on, though, as long as you were paying good money and your club was where the DJ wanted to be in terms of reputation and musically, then you didn't have much problem getting who you wanted.

My favourite DJs? Well, that's probably an impossible question. There are house DJs, trance DJs, drum and bass DJs, lots of fabulous DJs, so I can't say...I'm still thinking.

Sonique's break at Gatecrasher was an important career move. It was reward for her regular work at clubs like The Hippo in Cardiff, and led to even bigger bookings, and there were not many bigger than Gatecrasher back then.

Word had been spreading about this DJ singer girl, but it ticked all the wrong boxes at that time, really. I was a girl, I was singing, and it wasn't even like many black girls even listened to dance music around that time. But Gatecrasher booked me and they were the first superclub to do so.

I used to do the late sets between six and eight, and they had this amazing soundsystem and I was like, "you know, I'm going to bust them speakers up", but you could never bust them up. I would try and try, and that, for me, was perfect, because I knew I was in the right place at the right time. And Gatecrasher just grew and grew - that was the thing. And then it got to a point when it got a bit 'glowsticky'...and I didn't mind it, but I started to move to Ibiza more around that time, around 1996/97, to do my Manumission residency. I was getting fed up with the glowsticks, it was like, "guys, guys, we're here for the music", but at the end of the day, anyone who stayed to the end was good enough for me, whether they had a glowstick in their hands or not.

The two Simons that ran Gatecrasher were cool - Simon Raine and Simon Oates - and I did complain to them at the time that they didn't give me a residency, but I got the residency at Manumission soon after so I couldn't complain really.

I really, really enjoyed DJing at Gatecrasher. It was big, and even though it got that bit bigger, it was still real, and the people were real, and just so into the music, and with that soundsystem, it was just the ultimate club in the country, for me. And playing at those clubs at that time, you knew the clubbers were loyal to the DJs, because I'd be DJing in Manumission in Ibiza, and they would all come up to me, and say "we saw you in Gatecrasher", or "we saw you in Godskitchen". They were loyal followers, all right.

This was all happening at a time when I really didn't have a memory. I was just so mashed, but real good mashed, basically like floating on clouds the whole time. A couple of years ago I realised I hadn't even stopped to look back at those times, and it knocked me back when I did, not that I can remember that much. My best memory was one New Year's Eve, when I was playing at Gatecrasher and all the MixMag readers had just voted me their favourite DJ. That I remember!!!

Sonique's schoolfriend Judge Jules soon became a vital cog in the hugely successful trance machine that Gatecrasher became, devoting his career to trance in the mid-to-late '90s.

Gatecrasher had gone through a couple of different venues, and grew in popularity, and really became an institution when it moved to The Republic, which the promoters bought outright. That was nice, because it was great to see promoters that you've worked for get some bricks and mortar behind them, rather than just being fly-by-night operations.

In my career there have been around three clubs I have felt most close to and have the fondest memories of. One would have been something I did in the acid house era, the second would be my Judgement Sundays residency in Ibiza, and thirdly, but equal first if you like, would be Gatecrasher, for so many reasons. Firstly, I guess, because it was the burgeoning moment that everybody discovered trance. You know, I'm a DJ who stuck a lot of his reputation and belief behind trance and Gatecrasher was Britain's first trance superclub... arguably, in fact, the world's first trance superclub. It just had this amazing sense of community. While there were different people in and out each week, there were an enormous amount of regulars who came week-in, week-out too, and they were the nucleus of what made the venue and club what it was.

With Gatecrasher, I spent a period where I was a weekly resident. At the very least I played fortnightly. It was a very late night venue, and at the beginning of the late-night licensing in Britain. It stayed open until six, and it stayed busy until six, so I was able to get there from virtually anywhere else in the country and play there most Saturdays, certainly if I was in the UK.

It was the ultimate litmus paper for me. When you're a DJ touring all the time, you don't get a chance to test your music very often in front of the same crowd, in the same scientific way. Whereas, if you go to your residency and look at the same dancefloor, the same smiley faces, you can test new tunes. It's the best way to work out what your sets are all about, and it was incredibly influential at the time for those reasons.

The venue and the crowd at Gatecrasher were just absolutely unbeatable. It had one of those large DJ booths, so you could bring all your friends in, and that created a family feel to it. You could see 75 per cent of the club from that booth, which was neither too far away that you felt aloof, or too close that you missed out on the panoramic view. Of course, you had the phenomenon of the Crasherkid too, which, along with clubs like Sundissential, developed that spiky haired day-glo look, and that definitely inspired a generation.

Two of my favourite Gatecrasher memories were, on two separate occasions, the 2,000-capacity crowd at The Republic, singing happy birthday to me. As I've got older I haven't really celebrated my birthdays, so I wasn't exactly shouting about it on each occasion, but the people knew, and they were definitely tear-jerking moments.

Gatecrasher was now entering superclub territory and when you're in that kind of league you're also entering the colourful world of the fanatical. Raine continues:-

There were three real superclubs in my opinion, and lots of tribute clubs: there was Ministry Of Sound, Cream and Gatecrasher. The superclub came first, then lots of clubs looked at that formula, what we were all doing and tried to book the same DJs and emulate us. Things got a little bit more difficult when the DJ fees went up, but trance was exploding by then.

The Crasherkid phenomenon was around 1997, 1998, when we were building a new reputation at The Republic. We would walk up

*(clockwise) * Mad-for-it 'Crasher Kids' doing what they do best*
* Simon Raine being interviewed for One More at GB, 2010
* The Republic fire
* SundaySonic duo Stuart Patterson and Leo Elstob
** Crowd and external shots of The Republic * A 'Crasher tattoo*

The Republic   S1 1DJ

Gatecrasher

Gatecrasher

and down the queue, picking, and anyone who was well-dressed would get walked straight in. Then we noticed that there were some people who were wearing make-up, slightly fetish in style really, so we used to walk those people straight in as well. The Crasherkid came from those people being escorted in, combined with the emerging trance scene. Then the fluro colours, which was going hand in hand with the trance sound, started to re-emerge and this cult began to take off as quickly as we had.

The Crasherkids became very popular, but they were almost the antichrist at one point. Judge Jules famously banned them and their glowsticks, but looking back you'd actually die for people who were that passionate about your business.

The whole Crasherkid thing became very shit very quickly, though. It became a monster. You'd get this guy who would drop out of a local bar in some shit trousers and some shit shoes and he'd put a T-shirt on, paint his hair blue, act like a bit of a prat and say he was a Crasherkid.

But when it first started it was actually quite cool and started by a group of people who actually had a hierarchical structure within our club. There was a staircase at the back, and the higher up the staircase they stood, the higher in the pecking order they were. These were people who were absolutely fanatical about everything we did so we have to say "respect" to the original faction of Crasherkids because they really did rock our world.

However, like everything, when everyone else cottons on it suddenly stops being cool. We then banned glowsticks and put posters up about it. Jules announced the ban on Radio One and then the whole thing got out of control. It ended up as not a very fashionable look.

By that point the club had cost us the £750,000, plus another £75,000 so £825,000 in total. So, it wasn't like we were just running a party anymore, and it was only about peace and love. It was still a party, but there was a balance sheet and a profit and loss column at the end of it too. All this negative press changed things and from that point on we had to say 'enough is enough'.

The Crasherkids were, and are, an integral part of Gatecrasher's success and history. They simply became too popular and were mimicked, and from that point on there was a downward spiral.

We are able to get inside the mind of a Crasherkid through the "crashkids/cyberkids - ashamed of your roots?" thread on MattHardwick.com, dated 27/03/06.

Smaul Paul, Skipton, north Yorkshire

I don't do it now but want to get back into it. I don't think I will ever be ashamed of my cyber roots.

Johnny Be Good, Manchester

I just loved going cyber. It was a part of clubbing at the time as much as throwing shapes, talking rubbish or getting trollied was.

Alli X, north Yorkshire

My fav outfit was a white hot pant set I bought. The top had drawer strings on the front so you could make it shape like a bikini, and you could scrunch up the sides of the the hot pants. I used to start getting ready at four on Saturday afternoon to make sure I looked pristine. I remember my friend Alex and I, if we could not afford the tickets he used to nick the money from the ice cream counter where we worked in the week. Around £10- 20 a day so he raised £80 before Saturday night. LOL.

Gazra

Deffo not ashamed of it. I just see it as part of my clubbing roots, and had some great times all dressed up, like. Wasn't it expensive. though? I've till got some Cyberdog bottoms in the house somewhere - think they were £65!

Leon B, Manchester

I completely agree with Gazra. No regrets whatsoever, it was all part and parcel of going out, getting ready with your mates, etc. It gave us a unique identity. I love looking back at the photos and seeing myself and everyone in cyber. Such a mission, though, doing cyber spikes and red Dax Wax was evil stuff!

Ash Prendergast

I don't regret cybering up, and I don't think there's owt wrong with it. Acupuncture trainers were the cyber shoes - comfy, warm and the little trench in the sole kinda locked onto the railings perfectly in Crasher, so you didn't fall off.

Jay K

I never wore Acupuncture trainers, always used to have an extra comfy pair of Air Max on! It was hard to try and be different. I modified a Cyberdog top so it had the pulse rate light on the front and a Gatecrasher lion on the back. Wore it for the first time, some lad walks up to me, asks how I made it, then turns up with the same top a week later! After that I turned into a jeans and trainers type!

It is true that the Crasherkid became a source of amusement for many in the club scene, and even the DJs who played there. Brandon Block, booked to play at various Gatecrasher events over the years, remembers:-

The Crasherkids were funny...with their Kermit The Frog backpacks and Teletubby outfits. But it was a bridge too far for even my silliness. We used to giggle in the DJ booth when we were playing, but at the end of the day we recognised that they were paying our wages, and big ones at that.

But it wasn't just DJs who were playing at Gatecrasher, who were poking fun at the trance revolution.

Such was the club's notoriety, that later in 2003, west London Soulsonic duo Stuart Patterson and Leo Elstob doffed their deep house caps to the Crasherkid, with a Christmas instalment of their Sunday Sonic session at The Notting Hill Arts Club, aptly called Notting Hill Gatecrasher, which hilariously featured the duo pictured on the flyer, dressed as Crasherkids, wearing rave antlers, and complete with alphabet fridge magnets on their foreheads.

Alex P, like many early Gatecrasher DJs, had been playing for Raine at his popular midweek Decadence night at Bakers.

I first heard about Gatecrasher from Simon, and when Gatecrasher started it was the likes of me, Blocko and Julesy, and other DJs on rotation at Decadence, who got booked. Gatecrasher was great, and like the rebirth of the whole lightstick, rave thing, but eventually the music got too harder-edged for me, and after a while I was out on my elbow.

I'd play some of the techno-edged stuff, but not the hard house. That was the time for me to move on. I think the harder-edged music kind of imposed the Crasherkid thing on the people who went there. I mean, I've dressed up and gone to clubs wearing various silly outfits, on numerous occasions, but not every week. The Crasherkid thing was like a cult, and I think, Passion in Coalville was actually equally responsible for the mad scene that developed up there. It certainly wasn't a massive thing down in London, where the clubbers always seemed to prefer more traditional clothes, you know, whatever was fashionable at the time. The Crasherkid madness definitely started in the Midlands and spread up through the north.

Mark Moore wasn't averse to a bit of trance back then, just not all night or for the whole of his set.

Gatecrasher was an incredible, incredible club, which I particularly liked, before it became all about trance music. When it started, it was in this mad warehouse-type place, really dark and dingy, in the middle of nowhere and it felt really underground and it was as if everyone there was on a mission to discover new music. They moved it around to different venues, and it always had a grand scale to it. Even when they bought the nightclub the music was still mixed.
I got fed up with it all when you turned up and were expected to play just one type of music, but at Gatecrasher they used to say to me, "Mark, we want you to come in and shake things up a bit, and not play trance all night", and I tried to do that, but after a while I could see all the people there thinking "what's does he think he's doing, playing all this vocally stuff?". Yeah, I kind of stopped doing Gatecrasher after a while.

Back in the late '90s, Raine never ceased to be amazed at the tattoo culture that was engulfing Gatecrasher.

The Crasherkids started upping the ante with tattoos. One guy had the Gatecrasher lion outlined across the whole of his back and when it got to that point it was past impressive. The general policy was that if you had a tattoo you were walked in without paying, but we weren't encouraging them to have the tattoos. If they had got them done, then respect.

At that point the club wasn't just a club, it had definitely become a brand. We were doing tours all over the world. I remember we landed in Australia once and when we went into the hotel lobby there was a group of kids from Sydney waiting in reception, dressed as Crasherkids. I wasn't exactly into that side of it then, but let's just say, we travelled well.

It's things like the tattoos that, at the time, made you stand back and realise how successful and how big the whole club had become. That and things like people stealing your posters and branding from shops and street corners on a regular basis. When that's happening, then you know you're in business.

It was time for Raine to turn his attention to compilation CDs and a serious stab at Ibiza.

To move from running a club night to the CDs, the merchandise, the tours, it wasn't set out as a business plan, but it is the natural progression of having a hugely successful club night, so that's what we did. We struck a deal with Lyn Cosgrave, who was now a vice president at Sony Music, and we released a series of fantastic albums, which all did really well.

In 1998, we also did a deal with Pacha nightclub in Ibiza, with Roger Sanchez as resident, at the height of the Crasherkid and trance music phenomenon. But we got to the island to find that our club logo had been registered by another club in Ibiza, and it pretty much ended it for us that season.

We had a brand that was infamous with trance music, but we'd always been into house music, so it was pushing the boundaries for us and Pacha was arguably the best club in the world at that time. However, as soon as we landed, we were served a warrant by the police saying that we couldn't use the Gatecrasher name or logo in Ibiza.

We tried to take the people and club in question to court, but if you've ever tried to pursue anyone legally at the peak of the Ibiza season then you'll find that there are no judges or anyone available until the end of September.

We did subsequently take those responsible to court. They had done it deliberately and we did get the name back, but it cost us in the region of £200,000 in legal fees, so that was a very expensive season in Ibiza.

And if it was easy to put a price on the Ibiza fiasco then it was impossible to measure the loss of three lives – young Gatecrasher clubbers who died in a car crash as they approached Sheffield City Centre in May, 2002. You don't get as far as Simon Raine has in the business without being hard-nosed and ruthless, but the club boss broke down when talking about the deaths of Katie Emmott, 18 and Lauren Charteris and Sam Furness, both 19.

The people that were killed on the Parkway were regulars at Gatecrasher, and were a very popular group of clubbers. And they were apparently on the way to our club that night. We had a plaque made and we held a night in their memory.

The club burnt down on June 18, 2007, and we didn't have permission to get back into the building because it was unstable, but we did get back in with the help of South Yorkshire Fire Service, to recover the fire book from the safe, so we could prove everything was in place so the insurance would pay out. We managed to get some cash from the safe as well, thanks guys. And the only other thing we took out of the building was that plaque.

With The Republic such an important club for Judge Jules, it's no surprise he remembers exactly where he was when the dreaded curse of the 'club fire' struck Gatecrasher.

I know I was in Ibiza in the office at Eden, where I do my residency, when I heard the news that The Republic had burned down. That's how significant it was.

For me it was like a "where were you when Diana died" moment, it was that traumatic.

My dad lives in Yorkshire, and as soon as I got back, I went up and saw him, and actually visited the boarded up site to pay my respects. It was a sad end of an era, because Gatecrasher had enjoyed such a golden era. It had stopped being a weekly night, it was on a more irregular basis, but those events were getting bigger and bigger and building up a head of steam again, so it wasn't when Gatecrasher had lost it. Cream wasn't weekly anymore, neither was Progress. But I think Gatecrasher was at the point where it may have gone weekly again, and then suddenly the fire happened. It was devastating for me personally because so many memories literally went up in smoke.

Those tragic deaths and the subsequent fire poignantly aside, happier Gatecrasher memories are naturally easier for Raine to talk about and none comes bigger and better than Millennium Eve, possibly Gatecrasher's finest hour, even if for Raine, the most important moment of the night was somewhat tainted.

My favourite memories of Gatecrasher are Lotherton Hall, which was the setting for joint events between Gatecrasher and Ministry Of Sound, and, of course, Don Valley Stadium on Millennium Eve night, which was called 2000GC and which we put together in the world's largest portable structure. This massive Millennium party was actually launched at Lotherton Hall in June, '99 - that's when we started marketing the event.

The idea was that we wanted to put on the biggest event in the UK, and we started talking to a company called Gearhouse, which had this structure Tensile 1. It was actually built in the UK, but at that point was in Dubai. Some rich guy had wanted a tent for a party that would hold 20 -30,000 people, we got to hear about it, we did a deal and on December 1, 1999, around 25 40ft trucks rolled into the Don Valley stadium in Sheffield to erect the tent. A chap called Peter Hayward, who went on to do lots of work for Godskitchen and put on their Global Gathering events, project-managed this one brilliantly for us.

The DJs for Gatecrasher 2000GC were The Chemical Brothers, Sasha, Paul Oakenfold, Judge Jules, Tall Paul, Sonique, Paul Van Dyk, John Kelly, Carl Cox (live via ISDN, because that's what you did in those days, as he was doing two shows Down Under), Scott Bond and Matt Hardwick. We sold out about 25,000 tickets by December 23 or 24, and I remember in the run-up to it, we put a strapline together, a mission statement for one night, which Saatchi and Saatchi were commissioned to come up with, and that was 'it will always be with you'. That it was ultimately all about one second. The key numbers, which were on the promo material, were 31121999235959.

We had approached Sheffield Council and persuaded them to give us the stadium, which at the time had hosted the Commonwealth

Games so it was very high profile. We had got the DJ line-up from heaven, everyone we wanted on there, and we had commissioned The Designers Republic, run by Ian Anderson…respect…to put together the artwork, and, in my opinion, he put together probably THE best marketing campaign for a club event ever.

Radio One were all over it and I remember doing an interview for them on the Pete Tong Essential Selection show and the tickets were flying out. I think the interview went out a couple of weeks before the event and Pete asked how the ticket sales were going. They were priced at £107.50, including booking fee, I may add, and I gave him the ticket count live on air, which at the time was 18,000. That wasn't bullshit. And I swear to God, in the seconds after the interview the tickets went mental and we sold out within a couple of days.

The build started a month before the event and the breakdown itself afterwards took seven days. Everything we'd ever learned about clubbing we put into this one event and ultimately it was all about one second.

So it was ten to twelve, 31121999235000 in fact, and Paul Van Dyk was on the decks and he was preparing to drop his anthem For An Angel, which is seminal now, but at the time was absolutely massive too. Suddenly we all noticed that this one guy had started climbing up a king pole in Tensile 1. He was hanging off the scaff, above 25,000 people. We had to stop the music and, because he was the only one qualified, we had to send a rigger called Spider up to get him down. Well done Spider!

However, it ruined midnight really because suddenly the big countdown wasn't about 31121999235959, it was about this real prick who was 80ft up in the air. The guy was eventually brought down and welcomed on stage by security and a certain DJ, who probably hit him with the best right hander I've ever seen. Putting the event together was fantastic. The whole show was amazing, but that one second got ruined.

And while Raine still finds it hard to put into words the angst of that momentous midnight moment, when we spoke to clubland boffin Judge Jules he swallowed a dictionary especially to describe his take on it all. Not many DJs will use the words "quasi" and "anachronism" when describing a moment in clubbing history.

There has been a long legacy of big outdoor events in the UK, but doing quasi open air events in the middle of the winter was certainly a one-off, and I think one needs to remember the dawning of the new Millennium behind the backdrop of what everybody thought was going to happen. The phrase 'Millennium Bug' turned out to be a complete anachronism, which everybody laughed at in retrospect.

People did think that planes were going to fall out of the sky. They thought the clocks would stop working, and computers would simply pack up, and it reached such levels of lunacy, where in order to get a licence for Millennium Eve some promoters were forced to have a 30 or 40 person morgue, in situ, underneath the venue. And, I guess that definitely added to the whole mystique of it all.

The other backdrop was that just about all the other venues were overpriced and didn't work. It was a big disaster for a lot of promoters, with the exception of Gatecrasher, who sold out their event. It was an amazing event, it was a little bit cold, but it was one of those memories for life for everyone that was there.

I had just finished my set and as we approached midnight, with Paul Van Dyk on the decks, someone climbed up the huge stanchion pole in this vast marquee. I was actually at the other side of the tent, in a lighting pit, and was asked to get on the mic, to try and get this guy down. I was a little bit tipsy, and I was saying things like, "get down, you're ruining it for everybody". The next thing I heard on another mic was "this is Sergeant so and so of the north Yorkshire police, Judge Jules, can you please be quiet". I guess I wasn't exactly saying what was required to get a potentially very out of it, and deranged person, who was about 100 feet up, to come down again. So that was a lesson for me in crowd control and public order.

Jules may have been brought down a peg or two by the local constabulary, but his old mate Sonique was not impressed with his hogging of the mic either.

There had been a massive build-up to what Gatecrasher were doing on Millennium Eve. I'd been all over the advertising, and it was the first time the country had seen such a massive event. It was gigantic, and they were bigging it up like you can't imagine. I was meant to be playing at a smaller event, but that had problems with its licence, so I ended up in that big tent at the stadium. But, boy, there were so many egos in there, and I was a woman. You know, even at Homelands or Creamfields I was always the only woman.

I was in that tent fighting for the microphone and trying to get on, but I didn't get to play, and I was devastated. I was on the phone to my mum, crying like a baby, blubbing "they won't let me play". And she was saying, "you know it's going to be OK, because they don't know you've got a record out in America, do they?". And I was saying "no, but I don't care about that, I need to play, they're my people". I was devastated, it was like someone had stabbed me, and I was just lying there, screaming "they're killing me". You had people like Jules running off with the microphone, and not letting anyone get near it, and I was like "OK..."...and then after that life changed for me. Feels So Good came out, and then it was just like, whoooosh. My life just sky-rocketed into space.

Another great memory for Raine is building Gatecrasher One in Sheffield, which he did in 2003, when he refurbed and rebranded The Republic. While winding up German DJ Paul Van Dyk at a Summer Soundsystem event is right up there too.

Gatecrasher One was great for us as individuals, because there was a real sense of achievement, taking a building from one point to another. That was good for us.

Then there was one of the Summer Soundsystem events at the Turweston aerodrome in Northampton, when England had been playing Germany at football. It was a red hot day, we had sold 25,000 tickets and everyone in the world was performing there. Radio One were there and we had these massive screens behind Paul Van Dyk in the arena that he was playing in. The match had just finished and the visual guys, typed up 'Germany 1' and then added 'England', but left the cursor flashing for about 10 seconds, before eventually adding the number '2'. England had won 2-1 and that was possibly the biggest cheer that Paul Van Dyk ever got while DJing.

There are a million other memories from all the clubbers who came to the club so a massive thanks to them all. As for the music and specific tracks, well, a lot of my favourites are going to be huge trance anthems because we were the pioneers of that sound. We were the club that pushed that forward nationally and internationally. We were once described as the "club who changed the nation" by Pete Tong.

Ministry was focused on house, Cream crossed all the boundaries, but we were known for trance. It's virtually impossible for me to choose any favourite tracks, as such.

The last record at The Engine House, Bromsgrove? I wouldn't have a clue. At the end, me and Dave Rowley were in the booth, playing with the lights, jumping up and down, because it was the best night we'd had at that point. Jeremy Healy had been on way too long and the owner was looking for me and Dave. The crowd were hanging off the ceiling in a very, very sweaty marquee, there was someone letting fireworks off next to a farmer's field and then the plug got pulled. That's why there was never another Gatecrasher at the Engine House, Bromsgrove.

The last record played at Gatecrasher One, Sheffield, was Seven Cities by Soular Stone, and the night was June 15, 2007.

But the Gatecrasher success story shows no signs of waning and you suspect, with Raine at the controls, there is plenty of life in it yet.

The modern-day Gatecrasher? Well, we have moved on massively. We opened the GB (Gatecrasher Birmingham) club in 2008 with a 2,408 capacity. It's got three rooms, we play everything from R&B, to house, trance and drum and bass and have a massive student night too. Musically as a brand we've moved on, but so has the rest of the nation. We've got a club in Nottingham called Ultra Gatecrasher, and we've got a club in Leeds, called Gatecrasher7. We'd liked to open more Gatecrasher clubs in the UK, but it would have to be the right city, the right economic climate and the right building. The building we're in is what Gatecrasher is about today.

For me personally, and for the brand, it was really important to come back to Birmingham. We moved from Birmingham in 1994 and came out of Sheffield in 2007, but only because the club was destroyed. Then we opened GB in Birmingham in September 2008, and it's now our flagship club. We've had everyone here from Deadmau5 to David Guetta, Paul Oakenfold, Paul Van Dyk and Sasha, and a thousand other DJs, who have all been fantastic, as have all the clubbers who have come.

Gatecrasher has survived because we've moved with the times, sometimes ahead of the times. We invested money in clubs as opposed to just promoting events. That has its pros and its cons, because essentially Gatecrasher is buildings not just nights. By opening clubs we've delivered more depth to the brand and we have appealed to all sorts of styles of music and different people. So as long as music is still being played and we're still building great clubs, there will always be a Gatecrasher.

THE HIPPO CLUB

South Wales dance music fans had been hungry for a Hippo Club style of venue for some years, frustrated that they often had to travel far and wide to hear anything vaguely resembling decent music.

Then fairy godfather Peter Loughlin came along and in 1994 opened his two-floored venue - a sweaty rave pit of epic proportions. For many Welsh clubbers, it was simply the best club in the world.

Original resident DJ Ollie Jaye had the unique honour of playing both the first and last record at the Hippo, and was instrumental in the success of the seven years of memorable Cardiff clubbing in between.

Peter realised there was a massive niche market in South Wales, let alone Cardiff. There was no underground dance scene at all so he brought guys in who were on the fringes, round and about the area. He decided to have one big party and The Hippo Club was born.

At the start it was just "let's have a party" really. There was no "right, we must get this many through the door", or "we must make this much money". It was never about that.

It was about putting on a good night for the Cardiff people, but eventually for clubbers from all over the country too. It just became synonymous with having a great time. Luckily, from its humble beginnings it went on to become a much bigger institution. Initially, though, it was just a bunch of friends getting together and having a good time.

The Hippo Club started life as a one-off event at a club in Cardiff called Silhouettes, but would soon have a more permanent base. And the Hippo may seem a weird name, but Jaye claims Loughlin wanted one with the initials THC, in tribute to Tetra-Hydro-Cannabinol, the bit in cannabis that makes you high...perfect for this late-night joint.

And, given that he ended up with H for Hippo, it would be fair to assume that some 'THC' may have been consumed during the final stages of the name-choosing process. Jaye could not care less what the club was called, he had his big break, and he was going to seize this opportunity with everything he had.

I never really knew what Peter did. He was a local boy done good, a big Cardiff City fan, like Craig Bartlett from Lamerica. He gave me an opportunity and I'll never forget that. He made everything I went on to achieve possible, really. At the start I barely earned £100 a weekend, for both nights, but I got to DJ every weekend, make music, and then DJd all over the UK and the world. And, I also got to enjoy Peter's famous hospitality every weekend as well.

For Jaye it was a step up from his first 'residency' at a nightclub, just down the road in Penarth. His family had moved to Wales at the age of 16 when his barrister father needed to be closer to his chambers in Cardiff, and a career path as a lawyer had already been mapped out by his parents. However, the closest Jaye would get to joining the legal profession would be DJing alongside Judge Jules at the Hippo.

I was brought up in Chelmsford in Essex and also went to school in Kent, so when we moved to Cardiff in 1987, I had this Essex-come-Kent-come-east London accent, which I've thankfully retained throughout my time in Wales. In my teens I had been going to see big hip-hop shows that Tim Westwood was hosting at a leisure centre in Tonbridge in Kent. I saw Ice T and LL Cool J on the same bill, and also Big Daddy Kane and the Beastie Boys there at other Westwood shows. I was properly into my hip-hop then, rappers like KRS1. Then there was the transition from new jack swing to house, and that took over. Pump Up The Volume was the first house record that I bought on 12" vinyl, and I remember thinking that track was amazing.

When we got to south Wales, there was this club called Shabees in Penarth, which was in the back waters of Wales and I bowled in there, at the age of 16, and said that I was a well-known DJ from London. The club was being run by a couple of local likely lads, and they said, "OK, come back tomorrow night, and let's see what you can do". I turned up the next night with no records, no headphones and used the residents' stuff instead...totally blagged it. He didn't mind because it meant he could have a break and go and snog his girlfriend in the corner of the dancefloor.

I had to play all sorts of music, and I ended up playing there a couple of nights a week - pop, rock, all sorts of shit. I tried to chuck a bit of house in, here and there, early bits of Marshall Jefferson, but nobody there had a clue what it was. I had also started going to a record shop in Cardiff called Spillers Records, which is literally the oldest record shop in the world. It famously opened in 1894, selling phonograph cylinders, and is still open to this day.

I was doing mixes on cassette, and it wasn't like doing one on a computer now - C90 tapes, so 45 minutes each side, and I always seemed to fuck up a mix around the 34 minute mark, and have to start all over again. I would hang around Spillers in the early '90s, and they were getting sent all these free dance and house promos and would sell them to me at ridiculously cheap prices. I'd give my mixtapes to Jane at Spillers, who passed them on to Pete Loughlin. I was then asked to be resident at The Hippo Club by Pete, and here we are today.

It wasn't long before Jaye was joined in the DJ booth at the Hippo by some illustrious guests, but he and Loughlin never followed a set music policy. A variety of headline DJs set an unpredictable tone - one week Tony De Vit, Derrick May the next, then Sasha the week after, a resident's night the next week, Kelvin Andrews the following week... and so on.

Musically, it was completely across the board, and as residents, we just went with what was big at the time. We weren't there to impress the head-nodding society or for people to be staring at their feet all night. It was unashamed anthems all the way.

Having said that, the mid-'90s to the early 2000s was the best period for that. We went through all the handbag anthems and all the big trance tracks, all the big house tunes, and it worked because it really brought everyone together. There was nothing better than being on that DJ stand and seeing a thousand hands and arms go up in the air when you dropped a big breakdown. So, yeah, no music policy whatsoever, it was just "let's have it".

And if The Hippo Club's music policy had not come from any great musical beliefs, then the promotion wasn't exactly groundbreaking either.

We promoted the club primarily the same way everybody did in those days.

There was obviously no internet so it was a case of sending all the flyer teams out to the local record shops, like Catapult, and Spillers, and Whoosh, all those guys. But eventually it didn't really need that much promotion and the flyers would go out regardless. The Hippo became such an event in itself that people came even if they had never heard of the DJs playing because it was a learning experience for them as well. The promotion worked on its own most of the time.

The Hippo Club was the first underground club of its kind in south Wales. Sure, there were other nights that came through. The Escape came to Cardiff for a while and then you had Time Flies, which put on massive quarterly events, and later the US house stuff Craig Bartlett was putting on with Lamerica, but there wasn't a regular weekly thing like the Hippo.

Other than that there were your bog-standard commercial clubs, affectionately known as 'meat markets'. Various drum and bass and hardcore nights would be going on, but the Hippo was the most regular thing on the underground dance scene here.

There was never any animosity between ourselves and Craig at Lamerica. In fact, Craig was always in the office at the end of the night, even if the music at the Hippo wasn't really his thing. The main rivalry was between us and Time Flies, and that was because we had so many big DJs locked down with us that Time Flies struggled to get the big names they needed.

One by one, clubland's heavyweights ventured down to Cardiff to see what all the fuss was about and it wasn't just the DJs' agents who were encouraging their clients to take the Hippo gig.

We managed to attract pretty much all of the big DJs at that time, everybody we wanted, at least, and that's because every DJ who came to play for us was looked after very well indeed. They all wanted to come back and play for us. There was a fridge in the office, there was a little party going on in there all the time.

I heard that the DJs' various drivers would be fighting with each other to get the Hippo gig, because it wasn't just the DJ who was looked after, but the whole entourage as well. We had no problems getting anyone in and it was no problem getting people back again, because most of them had made sure they'd got their next booking sorted before they'd left the building.

Hippo Club regular guest DJ Miss Jo Lively remembers that hospitality well.

The Hippo was one of those clubs that DJs wanted to play and if anyone can tell you what was played at the end of the night then they're fibbing because we were normally all in the office with Peter getting absolutely twatted. It was just one of those clubs.

I used to play a banging set because it was such a banging club, but it was a real favourite with the DJs because of Peter's hospitality, which was pretty legendary. He put us all in five star hotels and he treated the punters really well too. It was this dark, cavernous club, a great place.

My One More track during this period was often True Faith by New Order. It just worked really well.

Meanwhile, Ollie Jaye has no doubts about the impact a certain Sasha had on the proceedings at the Hippo.

Personally, my favourite DJ, the one that brought the party to the club, well, it has to be Sasha. His parties were an event in themselves. It didn't matter whether some had heard of him or not, people would come because they knew everybody else was coming out. It was rammed every time.

We also had DJs from all over the world and I'm lucky enough to have warmed up for pretty much all of the big DJs at that time. The only big one who never came down was Pete Tong.

Other favourites included an American guy called DJ Duke, who had a track out called Blow Your Whistle, he was superb. Masters At Work too and Kelvin Andrews - lovely bloke, Kelvin. Sonique was great too. She sang over one of my tunes when she played. In fact, that was one of the highlights of my career, when she dropped my tune at the time and sang over it, that was amazing.

There was Judge Jules, who came down with his trumpet, although fortunately that didn't last long. And there are so many other DJs I could mention - anyone who just entertained the crowd, I guess, which was most of them.

Ollie Jaye certainly had an impact on Sonique, with her claiming she used his style of hosting as a blueprint for an important residency of her own.

As a resident Ollie was just so caring. There was no chance of any DJs messing up there because Ollie was always hanging about the booth, really appreciating what the guests were doing, and making sure everybody was looked after. Through that he actually taught me how to be the resident at Manumission in Ibiza, I took all that with me to Ibiza for the two years I was at Privilege. Yeah, Ollie was one of my favourite DJs at the time, and had a style that I really admired. He had a couple of tracks out then which worked really well at the time and I'm surprised he wasn't bigger than he was.

Peter the owner and and the security were all absolutely amazing guys too. The people who went to the Hippo were great as well, and the crowd is really important at any club, but if the team who are running the place are cool then everything's going to work anyway. Those Hippo security guys were these big huge blokes, but they were just the sweetest guys, and they just used to crack me up. I used to stay back late after the club and talk rubbish to all of them, it was the best fun.

When the Hippo got going, Judge Jules and I were big mates, hanging out, like a fresh out of school vibe, and he told me all about it. And when I did get to play there it was the first time I had been block-booked a few times for the same club so I was super, super excited.

It's hard to describe the Hippo. It was so dark, but not seedy. Dark, but happy. Fresh, but still underground. I'd play very trancey there, but you could also sling in some deep, minimal records too. The atmosphere there was very intense and very happy, and I'm not sure the words "intense" and "happy" go together, but they did at the Hippo.

*(clockwise) * Hippo Club bouncers Meady (left) and Paul Bowen*
* Ollie Jaye outside the site of The Hippo Club
* Ollie Jaye being interviewed in his radio studio, 2010
* Sonique being interviewed for One More, 2011

R GRAPHICS Ltd 01222 318791

THE HIPPO CLUB

DOORS 9-4/6AM ADMISSION £10

3	NICK WARREN GRAHAM GOLD OLLIE JAYE & SHANE
10	ALEX P STEVE THOMAS STEVE LAWLER (CREAM)
17	CRAIG RICHARDS (TYRANT) OLLIE JAYE & SHANE
24	JOHN KELLY OLLIE JAYE & SHANE
	EVERY SATURDAY RESIDENTS OLLIE JAYE & SHANE

THE HIPPO CLUB 3 -7 PENARTH RD CARDIFF CF10 5DH
TEL 01222 341463

THE HIPPO

JULY 1999

DESIGNED BY
MIKE J.
01971272978

It was also one of the first places where I started singing over records, but not in a "oh, look at me, I can sing" way. More to add a little flavour to the night.

Judge Jules' experimental brass section phase was, thankfully, a short one, but Ollie Jaye and everyone involved with the Hippo were quickly able to blow their own proverbial trumpets.

We realised the club was a success after we had more than 10 people through the door, after the first couple of weeks, and when we could remove the heater from the top of the stairs, which we'd put there because it was freezing!

Seriously, though, the fact that people were coming back again and again, sometimes from the Friday, coming back again the next night on the Saturday - that was a massive thing for us. And when you had big nights and they were queuing half a mile down the road, or when you had big queues for bog-standard residents' nights, and when the big DJs kept asking to come back. They were all real highlights.

The legal capacity was actually about 230 people, but we managed to get about 1,500 people in there on the big nights over two floors and an average attendance of around 800 or 900 people when it was just the top floor.

Downstairs, believe it or not, was a rock club, but every now and then we'd kick all the rockers out for a big night when Sasha or someone was on. The rock club was called Bogiez, and so most weeks there was a load of pissed-up rockers downstairs and pilled-up clubbers upstairs. Everyone would meet on the stairs on the way out and would be hugging each other. Bogiez had all the big Welsh acts play there - the Super Furrys, Catatonia..., Rhys Ifans was down there loads too. It was run by this guy we called Dungeon Master Mike, with long blond hair and black finger nails - he used to live in the rock club, literally kip down there in his sleeping bag.

Time Flies did great big halls and filled those places out, but on average I think we managed to put the most people in on a regular basis. I think it's fair to say that Health & Safety would have had a field day with us if we'd done that today, but they didn't seem to be around much in those days. So, relative to capacity, we did very, very well.

And Health & Safety, had they ventured to the Hippo, might well have had something to say about the rock promoter living in the basement. Meanwhile, it's clear that Jaye, above all, remembers the DJs he got to play alongside and the Hippo regulars with most affection.

Considering we had seven good years in the place, there are so many favourite Hippo memories. Every night was an event in itself and the birthdays were obviously very special. There was a little garden at the back that we could use and we'd set up decks and have BBQs going. Funnily enough, though, the food didn't get eaten that much. I used to love playing in the garden, doing little party hip-hop tricks, mixing with my chin and stuff like that… all good fun.

One of my personal favourite memories, however, was playing back to back with Sister Bliss in the main room. To be working with someone who was part of Faithless and who had created one of the best house records of all time in Insomnia, standing next to her playing tunes, for me, as a DJ, that was a great personal moment.

Simply watching people on the dance floor, hugging each other, is up there too. And there was never any trouble. People would make their own mad clothes to wear there. There was one girl, I swear to God, who made her outfit out of Kit Kat wrappers, which she covered in cellophane; little things like that still stick in the memory.

We brought people in and let them do what they wanted to do and they were comfortable there. There was no attitude, no hassles, no problems with blokes bothering women. It was a family vibe and that's probably one of my favourite memories, the family vibe, and the fact that 'family' still remains, even after the place has gone.

As for the music that typified The Hippo Club, Jaye didn't just play the first and last record, he played a lot of his own tracks in between as well. And I think we can let him off for playing his biggest release as that poignant final track.

For the weekly end of night tracks, well, I'd usually be finishing off at the end of the night, and I'd stop the record, the crowd would go mad, shouting "one more, one more". There are a couple of tracks that come to mind, that sum up the Hippo, and for two different reasons.

One, by probably my favourite remixers/producers at the time, Tin Tin Out, was a cover of Dusty Springfield's Always Something There To Remind Me. That was our last tune for about a year, and people would go home singing it. If I play it today the hairs still go up on the back of my neck. That track to this day is still synonymous with the club and everybody who went there will tell you that.

The other one, which is a bit big-headed I suppose, is Jon The Dentist vs Ollie Jaye and our track Imagination. If it hadn't been for the Hippo I wouldn't have met Jon and wouldn't have been able to send my music over to him or gone into his studio and made that track. It went on to sell thousands all over the world, which is something I'm very proud of and the track also became synonymous with the Hippo. I still get asked to play it now, and everyone who went to the club regularly knows the lyrics to it. So they were the two tunes that really sum up the Hippo, and hopefully most regulars would say the same.

Jaye still bemoans missing out on every DJ/producer's guilty pleasure dream of appearing on Top Of The Pops with his and Jon The Dentist's follow-up single, Feels So Good.

We were tipped for the Top 10 with that, and had been promised a spot on Top Of The Pops if we made a decent video. Radio 1 were saying we'd get on the A playlist, so we realistically needed to spend £25,000 on a video, which was the norm then. Me and Jon had ideas of us screeching around in a Ferrari, loads of girls and then DJing in a club, but we were signed to TidyTrax, Andy and Amo's label, and our video cost £3,000 and was filmed in Amo's sister's council house in Rotherham. For some reason I spend most of the time sitting on the bog. The BBC subsequently banned the video, we got knocked off the playlist, and ended up at No 74. Gutted.

However, I can't really grumble. I was lucky enough to play the very first record at the Hippo, which was Way Out West's Shoot. And that last record I played? Well, because it was the Hippo anthem, and the place I love, it had to be mine and Jon's track, Imagination.

The last night was amazing. There were people crying. It was certainly a touching moment, to say the least. I did give it some thought because I knew it was the last record and in the end it was a great way to go out. It was a banging anthem and I made the decision to go out with that about an hour before the end.

Meanwhile, another insight into the "family" feel at the Hippo comes from two of the club's bouncers. Head of security, Meady, remembers:-

The one bad moment was the infamous raid at the Hippo when the police turned up with 147 officers, four or five vans, a SWAT team, police on horseback and a helicopter. They even brought the electricity board with them because they thought the bouncers were going to cut the electric off when they saw the police, which was obviously nonsense. They arrived fairly early, around 11.30pm and didn't find anything.

My favourite DJ, and there goes a few... I suppose, was Sasha. He became a friend actually and I used to sort his dad out with rugby tickets. John Kelly became a personal friend too, and we also got to know Boy George, Jon of the Pleased and Judge Jules, who we knew before he went on to Radio One. The last night left a lot of sad faces, people crying, and it left a hole in the market in Cardiff.

As the building was getting knocked down, people came and took bricks as souvenirs. Clubbers, who were 18 and 19 back then, but are now mothers and fathers - they stop me in the street and say "do you remember me?", which is quite amazing.

Paul Bowen, who worked alongside Meady, adds:-

We only had about seven toe-to-toe fights in seven years and there was always a happy ending to those. We'll always remember the amazing atmosphere in the club, and we always looked forward to working at the Hippo. John Kelly was my favourite DJ. Other than the residents, when he played we had the least complaints from the punters about the music.

Alex P says that the Hippo became so notorious that some henpecked DJs had to give the club a wide berth.

All the other DJs used to talk about the Hippo, it was certainly the talk of the town for a while. It was literally like a black hole down there. You'd go and play, end up in the office with Peter and then you wouldn't be heard of for about three days. From the outside of the club there was just this little door, but inside was this amazing den of iniquity, and it got to the stage where a few DJs I know, well, their girlfriends wouldn't let them play there.

Newport clubber JJ met her husband at The Hippo Club on a Friday night in June 1998, and all these years later is still able to paint a detailed picture of the dancefloor.

We were both out on our own because it was that kind of place. It was friendly, people would talk to you and once you were on the dancefloor, being on your own just wasn't a problem.

The main room was fairly small with a wooden dancefloor, black walls and no seating. There was a platform around one side of the room that was used mainly for dancing and when full it added to the atmosphere because people covered every part of the club, no wall or floor space was visible, just a sea of happy faces. There was a small stage area at the front where the DJ box was situated, usually four deep with people dancing.

The lighting was incredible. In fact, at no time have I ever been in a club that was able to create the same level of atmosphere as the Hippo. There was a lighting guy and the result was better than any so-called "intelligent system" that I have ever subsequently experienced. The strobe was deadly, the smoke could disorientate and create a tiny bit of panic when the effect was momentarily isolating and then you couldn't see your hand in front of your face. It was certainly an intense experience. The sound was excellent - a loud, thumping bass and consistent clarity wherever you stood in the room.

And the crowd was always up for it. The Hippo had a reputation for being an underground dance club and people came for that reason. It was a relatively small venue and there were a core of regulars from Cardiff and the Valley areas but people would also travel miles for the Hippo experience. The Welsh crowd lived up to their welcoming reputation and in the chill-out room you couldn't help but strike up several conversations sitting on one of the leather sofas.

There were only two cubicles in the ladies' toilets and they were invariably flooded. The queue was often very long, spilling over into the chill-out area. And you could exchange life stories standing in that line.

Ecstasy was predictably easy to find and was the creator of loved-up, happy people who needed to dance to Hippo favourites like John Kelly, Boy George, Sonique, Jon (Pleased Wimmin), Judge Jules, Tall Paul, Trannies With Attitude, Brandon Block, DIY, Jeremy Healy, Nick Warren, Tony De Vit and Jon The Dentist.

The Hippo is legendary in Cardiff and I'm just glad to have been part of it. The relatively small capacity certainly contributed to the feeling of exclusivity and no superclub could ever live up to the experience there. I think the lack of attention to cleanliness and sophisticated decor was forgiven because the clientele knew that the money had clearly been spent on the important things. The sound and lighting has never been surpassed and the people who were part of it will never forget it. Ask anyone who was there and they'll tell you the same. But like everything in life, you never know what you've got, until it's gone.

Judge Jules has high praise for the Hippo crowd and all they stood for, but wasn't surprised when the venue eventually succumbed to commercial forces.

The Hippo Club was another late night venue which I felt was doomed to not be there forever because it was in such a central area. It was right next to Cardiff Central station and I always thought a developer or someone would see its potential. It felt like it was on borrowed time, and that actually gave it an extra edge. It had this really late licence, and the odd problem with the police, which also gave it an edgy vibe. The Hippo was one of the first truly late-night Welsh things that worked Fridays and Saturdays every week and that why it's the stuff of legends.

It was stripped down to basics clubbing, but always an amazing atmosphere. There hadn't been a great deal of money spent on decor or fancy stuff. It was always about the crowd, the atmosphere, and the DJs booked. And a Welsh crowd is always amazing. It doesn't matter what sphere of the arts you're from, every performer will tell you the same thing.

Jules' then Radio One colleague Danny Rampling is yet another DJ who cannot speak more highly about the Hippo and its inimitable landlord.

I always had a great time in Cardiff, but when I went into the Hippo it was a completely different world. It was a dark sweatbox, but there was a wonderful crowd at the Hippo, a wonderful energy, and I was playing a lot harder at that time, so they loved that.

I was going through a period when I was playing a lot of hard house and trance. I had been influenced by what the DJs were playing inside at Space in Ibiza, where it was dark, and where the music was harder and faster, and that's how they liked it at the Hippo, more 135 to 140 BPM banging stuff.

I would generally play on a Friday, and it would be a long drive down there, but it would be an even longer drive back, because I would finish at five in the morning, and would always be encouraged to stay, and the night would just continue really, there would be this big after party. Then we'd look at the watch and it would be nine in the morning, and we'd have this long drive back to London. We would get back at midday and then I'd have a radio show to do at six that evening. But it was a lot of fun, it was a great club, it was on its own there.

All great clubs are about great hosts, and Peter really looked after his guests in a big way. He was a larger than life, flamboyant character, who was always great fun to be around, and, for me, going to the Hippo was all about the host. The venue itself was nothing special, but it was the vibe of the place that drew people in there. It was always a giggle there, and when I left I always had a knot in my stomach where I'd been laughing so much because the host was just a natural born comedian. A great spirit there, and one of the most rocking clubs at the time.

Gone but clearly not forgotten, Ollie Jaye is content with the Hippo's legacy and proud of the part he played.

The Hippo basically finished because the lease ran out on the building in 2001. It wasn't renewed and same old story - no building, no club. It wasn't because of dwindling numbers and nowadays it's a British Gas building. It probably isn't as banging in there as it used to be.

The club's legacy is that it was Wales' first underground club. It's still remembered by people all around the world. There are countless Facebook groups devoted to it. People still reminisce about the Hippo and we've had a couple of large reunion parties, which have been massive, and the all the old guard came out for those - despite the fact they're all married with kids now - to see all the friends and all the old faces.

These days I spend two hours every Saturday night doing my radio show, called Club TX, on Radio Cardiff 98.7FM, which also goes out all over the world online and I'm quite happy with that, playing the music I love to people who I know love it. And after the radio show I get to go home with a nice clear head and don't wake up with a hangover.

When I was younger I wanted to be a DJ, make a tune, make a video and make an album, and appear on Top Of the Pops. I managed to achieve all that, apart from one, and all because of The Hippo Club. I had a hit with Imagination, and went on to make an album.

I'm now a manager at a call centre in Cardiff, but my radio show is streamed worldwide. And it's mad, I'm getting around 10,000 downloads a week, from people in Japan, Australia, Brazil, and all over Europe, and even islands that I've never heard of.

I still DJ every now and then and we will be doing new Hippo nights in dark and dingy places in Cardiff, because that was the original appeal of the place. It was dark and dingy and the toilets stank. So much sweat would be dripping from the ceiling, you'd stick to the floor, but nobody cared.

LAMERICA

Fellow Cardiff clubbing institution Lamerica was in some ways the complete antithesis of The Hippo Club, but that doesn't stop Craig Bartlett having the utmost respect for what Peter Loughlin and Ollie Jaye managed to achieve.

Yes, it was a dive, but it was a brilliant dive. At the end of the day we were all from Cardiff and we all wanted to make our mark, and I think we managed that.

And Bartlett is equally frank as to exactly why he started Lamerica.

I'd been playing second rooms all my life and I'd got fed up travelling up and down the country to see the DJs I wanted to listen to, as well as spin with. So in 1998 I decided I needed to get something off the ground.

After hearing an impassioned US soulful house pitch, the owner of The Emporium nightclub in Cardiff suggested American Independence Day, July 4, was as good a date as any to start. And so Bartlett's own south Wales clubbing legacy was born.

Four years earlier, the Cardiff clubbing fraternity had taken to The Hippo Club relatively easily, lapping up a new weekly dose of banging house. And although the Hippo had touched on soulful house, with Masters At Work duo Kenny Dope Gonzales and Little Louie Vega among early guests, Lamerica would be the town's first such dedicated session.

After our launch at The Emporium, which had a capacity of around 400 and where CJ MacIntosh and Paul Trouble Anderson guested alongside myself, Dave Jones and Gareth Hopkins, we ran there monthly for the next six months, putting on guests like Dimitri From Paris, Danny Krivit, Jazzy M, Rocky & Diesel, Farley & Heller and Bobby & Steve. We found our feet, while putting on exactly the DJs we wanted to put on in Cardiff, which was the first time that happened. Lamerica quickly became the spiritual home for American house music

269

in Cardiff. After six months we went fortnightly and continued at The Emporium every two weeks for the next five and a half years with more guests like Ricky Morrison, DJ Spen, Smokin' Jo and Danny Rampling.

Easy, huh? Well, not quite, because this was hardly an overnight success story. Bartlett had been plying his trade in Cardiff and the south Wales area since the late '80s, when a promising career as an architect gave way to...you guessed it...that serial seducer, acid house. And by 1990 Bartlett was behind the decks, feeling his way at the early underground dance nights the area had thrown up.

I knew Dave Jones from the football, following Cardiff City. And we used to meet in the local record shops and enthuse over tracks like Taste The Bass by Safire. The pair of us DJing together was a natural progression because we loved the same music. Dave was resident at a place called Ecuador on Fridays, where I would play occasionally, but my main thing at that time was my residency on a Saturday at Silhouettes. By that time, I'd given up on being an architect, I wanted to be a DJ and a promoter and own a record shop.

And Bartlett pretty much managed to do that, the duo cementing their DJ reputation and promotion credentials further in 1993 when they were approached by Cardiff University to get involved in a new student-orientated promotion called Spice Of Life. While the record shop ambitions were fulfilled when Bartlett opened his own town centre store in 1994, called Whoosh Records.

The idea of the university campus event was a weekly party strictly for students, from 7pm to 1am, and it ran successfully for 18 months, with guests like Sasha, John Digweed, Judge Jules, Jeremy Healy, Chris & James, Mr C and, early on, Paul Oakenfold, playing alongside myself and Dave, and it went off. Before long tickets and fake student passes were exchanging hands outside the university gates for £50.

At the same time I put on my first stand-alone American house promotion in conjunction with my record shop Whoosh, which was sponsored by Pepsi, with Todd Terry and CJ Mackintosh as guests. Other record shop parties we did had Noel Watson, Roy The Roach,

270

Linden C and Judge Jules, playing his first gig in Cardiff, on the line-ups.

The Spice Of Life parties came to an end because of licensing issues with too many non-students attending, and evolved in the mid-to-late '90s into the huge Time Flies parties, which for some unknown reason, given what was going on at the university, were allowed to take place on a one-off basis in the Cardiff City Council civic centre offices, with up to 1,500 in there each time off their heads.

So between 1996 and 1998 I was playing main room warm-ups, dropping decent dubs and stuff like that, for the predictable main room big guests who would come on after me. Myself and Dave also did the second room at those parties towards the end, playing soul, funk and hip-hop - stuff we liked.

There was definitely a rivalry between everyone in south Wales at that time, but it was a friendly one. There was a unity, because we were providing south Wales with an underground scene, but there was this big difference, because while the other promoters were trying their best to secure the services of Sasha and Judge Jules, I wanted to book people like Kerri Chandler, Burt Bevans from Studio 54 and Mood II Swing. And after going down to London loads in the early '90s, spending many weekends buying records, and going to Full Circle, Boys Own and Cowboy Records parties, I was now hooking up with people like the Faith boys, Stuart Patterson, Leo Elstob, Dave Jarvis and Terry Farley, and also Rocky & Diesel, and booking them for Lamerica too.

The connection with this so-called banging house scene, the harder-edged trance sound that was becoming more prevalent, was eating away at Bartlett. It was one thing hanging out in the office at The Hippo Club while it was being played in the next room, but another thing altogether having his name plastered all over flyers at similar parties down the road, where big beat and trance were against everything he believed in.

Then one afternoon, an innocuous sofa day watching the classic fight scene in West Side Story left Bartlett humming "la-la-la-la-la America" and the name of his new night was born.

Within a couple of years of launching Lamerica at The Emporium, and having to stick to a rigid pricing structure on the door there of between £5 and £8, we realised we couldn't afford the really big names that we wanted to bring to Cardiff, the Frankie Knuckles, David Morales and Tony Humphries of the world. So on May Bank Holiday 2001 we held our first big one-off at Liquid, a much larger Ritzy type venue in Cardiff town centre, where we would be the first outside promoters at a venue which was filled every other regular night with cheesy in-house promotions. Our first party was Roger Sanchez, then Erick Morillo for the August Bank Holiday and a Studio 54 special with original residents Bert Bevans and Kenny Carpenter as guests on Boxing Day.

And we put 2,000 people in there every Boxing Day and all the Bank Holiday Sundays each year until Easter 2010. The capacity there was only legally 1,180, but we regularly squeezed in 2,500. Highlights include celebrating Lamerica's 5th birthday at Liquid with Frankie Knuckles in 2003. After that we had anyone from Morales and Masters At Work to Moodyman and later the Germans, Dixon and Ame.

Our ethos was easy really, real music for real people. It was all about spiritual soulful house music and my love of American house music and soul, funk and disco and putting DJs on who had never even heard of Wales. I had a torrid time at the beginning, though, trying to entice people like Danny Krivit, Louie Vega and Dimitri From Paris to south Wales, or more importantly, convincing their agents. "Where's the club?" "It's in Cardiff", "Where's that?", "It's about two hours west of London", "OK, right, where's the nearest airport?", "well, you'll have to fly into Heathrow", etc, etc... but I stuck to my guns because it was simple, I just wanted to bring those international DJs and superstars to my home city.

My favourite DJs that we managed to get to Lamerica are Louie Vega and Kenny Dope, DJ Sneak, Danny Krivit, Tony Humphries, Knuckles and Morales. Every single one of them, and because they'd been booked for a reason. They weren't just booked because they were in vogue. I booked every single DJ who played at Lamerica because I wanted them to play at Lamerica. And I was happy that I had, what I would call, a monopoly on proper house music in the south Wales area and, if you like, the cooler people

(clockwise) * Craig Bartlett in action at Lamerica
* DJ Sneak headlines a Lamerica party
* Craig Bartlett being interview for One More, 2010
* Kenny 'Dope' Gonzales 'At Work' at Lamerica

Bartlett even started another night in nearby Bristol called Internationale, just so it could share some of the flight costs of his desired American heavyweights, who would then jet in for a Friday night slot there, followed by a Saturday night set at Lamerica.

But although Bartlett had created his own niche market in Cardiff, that didn't mean the lure of big names down the road at the Hippo, and other big local one-off nights, wouldn't prove too much of a pull, even for his specific crowd.

There were still difficult times because one weekend the Hippo would have Tony De Vit and Judge Jules on a Friday and Sasha and John Kelly on a Saturday, and Time Flies had hooked up with someone like Wobble, so had Phil Gifford and Si Long playing as well. And we were trying to put on a fairly underground house night just down the road. There were the usual poster wars and the vying for prime flyer spots in the local shops, but I think the rivalry created a healthy competition which helped make each of our nights better.

And we always got on very, very well with Ollie Jaye and Peter down at the Hippo. I played there infrequently - basically because the music they played at the Hippo was less and less about the American house music that I wanted to play - but I always used to hang out there, because they had a 6am licence, and our parties would finish around 3am or 4am. So most Fridays and Saturdays, and don't forget it was open both Friday and Saturday, I would roll out of the Hippo at around 8am and 9am, after very much enjoying Peter's hospitality.

And dealing with American DJs and their notoriously demanding egos would often throw up rather more interesting riders than that of your average British DJ done good.

There were different demands on all of us. I remember one night explaining to Peter Loughlin that Jazzy Jeff had asked for a certain flavour of Hubba Bubba bubble gum to be provided and he couldn't believe it. He said most of his headline guests were happy with a big bag of this and large bottle of that.

To be honest, we used to call the house they played down at the Hippo as "gypo house". You didn't have to dress up. It was blood, sweat and tears down there, you just cracked on with it. Whereas we had guys and girls who would dress up, with the women usually in designer gear and stilettos, the girls down at the Hippo would wear tracksuit bottoms, and if you wore white trainers they'd end up black by the end of the night.

Bartlett soon got attention from outside of Cardiff too, as he joined the UK guest DJ circuit and, inadvertently, with other like-minded suburban "proper house music" fans, created a modern day DJ network of his own.

Around 1998/'99, with the Lamerica name out there, I started to get booked by Gareth Cooke to play at the Ministry Of Sound in London, in The Bar, the second room there. There were also DJs there like Andy Ward and Patrick Smooth from Birmingham, Bob Povey and Jon Coomer from Bump & Hustle in Bournemouth, and Si Gracia and Seth Sanchez, the Bournemouth and Portsmouth boys, from To The Manor Born...guys like that. We all started getting booked by Gareth, and meeting up at the Ministry, and bringing loads of people with us from out of town, and then we started doing swaps, playing at each other's clubs.

Then in 1999 the Ministry were doing Pacha in Ibiza on a Friday, and I was asked to play in the second room there, and I was just amazed. I got my flights paid for, and although I was only earning £150, I was also given loads of drinks tokens and with drinks in Pacha between £10 and £15, they were actually worth more than the DJ fee. Whatever way you looked at it, it amounted to a free night out in Ibiza, which you can never complain about. Then I was asked to play at Space terrace on the Saturday morning, at the Ministry's after-party, and I was delighted. That season I ended up playing around six times on the terrace, and that's when I became very good friends with Brandon Block and Alex P

George Lamb, who has now gone on to enjoy a big television-presenting career, was Gareth's right hand man at The Ministry in London. He used to sort us out all our drink tokens and then he ran things for Gareth in Ibiza as well and we became great friends with George. Around that time Russell Brand was starting his presenting career, famously off his head, and filmed an episode of his DPM TV at a Lamerica party in a right old state. Russell was a great laugh, though, and has obviously gone on to have a massive career.

Like many involved in the dance music business for so long, Craig's memory is not what it could be and he cites unavoidable "recreational activities" as the main culprit.

With the long history of dance music culture and what goes along with it, your memories tend to be clouded, really. It started as a hobby for us, and then suddenly we had offices, phone lines and fax machines, and it quickly became a life choice. We were spending eight hours a day working to promote a night that happened once every two weeks. But they were great times, and you'd be hard pushed to find better times than I've had, DJing all over the UK, and the world, in Ibiza, Dubai, Argentina, Colombia and Spain. And for many years, that meant DJing most nights of the week from Wednesday to Sunday.

When Lamerica finished at its longest-running home, Liquid, in 2010, Bartlett was at pains as to what the last record would be, and with himself at the controls, he decided one vocal house anthem in particular was about as poignant as it could get.

After us being the first outside promoters in the club, it was quite apt that we played the last night there and the record I played at the end was Finally, the big Sandy Rivera track, aka Kings Of Tomorrow. You listened to the words, everybody in the club was singing, and they didn't know the club was closing, like I did. Sandy Rivera had played for us so many times and that track was so big at the club that the words just said it all. There was no other way of me doing it, unless I went on the microphone. I just let the words just say it all really. I just let the song do it and at half past six in the morning everybody was singing along and then the door closed. It happens.

As do huge losses in the promotion business, especially when the stakes are high, and the stakes are huge DJ fees. As the noughties wore on, and with DJ demands increasing, but public demand waning, Bartlett could make £10,000 in one night, but also lose as much in others. However, he never threw all his eggs in one basket and, like Golden founder Jon Hill and Hacienda resident Graeme Park, has since become an asset to the education system.

Lamerica is obviously no longer fortnightly or even monthly. We realise that our crowd have responsibilities now. It's about getting the timings right to get people out who are having to pay their mortgages and feed their kids, the same as me. These days I put on a Lamerica night every quarter at a club in Cardiff called Glam, which holds around a thousand people. But I also put on a couple of nights for the kids on a regular basis there too - a Hed Kandi night, and also a night called Disco Pup, with guests like Todd Terje and The Revenge. In July 2011 we celebrated Lamerica's 13th birthday, with myself and Grant Nelson playing the whole night.

But it's not all about promoting and DJing for me now. I'm also involved full-time with underprivileged and disaffected kids. Initially, I was approached by Cardiff County Council and the Community Education Officer there and asked to teach them DJ mixing and production. Then I was asked to talk to them about marketing, promotion and the music business itself. But at the same time I was encouraged to get some qualifications, so I went off to university and did just that between 2004 and 2008. I'm so glad I did because at the time, when the clubs are going well, it's so easy to think that it will go on forever. Then all of a sudden everyone wants to be a DJ, there is far more choice for the punters, more bars with DJs, then the economy suffers and so on.

With the kids I work with, I try to build up their confidence, take them go-karting or paintballing, whatever. I've also been working with a group of lads from Cardiff Prison. And I tell them that I've had some great times in my life, and done all sorts of things you're not meant to do, but the trick is to do it at the weekend, on a Saturday, when you have time to recover, and not on a Tuesday, when you've got something to do on a Wednesday.

Bartlett says that his family keep him on the straight and narrow. By the sounds of things, Mrs Bartlett helps put things in perspective, but then so did a night with Carl Cox towards the end of Lamerica's reign at Liquid.

I'm 43 now and my daughter is 16. I think I've matured at the right time in my life through her. She definitely came along at the right time for me and my wife. And fortunately, if I do get a bit carried away, I've got the missus at the other end of the phone calling me up, telling me

I'm not 19 anymore, and that I should get myself home as soon as I can.

I think maturity makes you allow for tomorrow. I was playing at the Southport Weekender recently, drinking all day and all night, etc, but I had a management meeting on Monday, and I knew I had to get home on the Sunday night so I was all right for that. But when we were younger we didn't care about tomorrow, we were missing flights, missing all sorts of things. Because we thought we could get away with it and because we didn't have a mortgage to pay. I think you know you're getting older when you'd rather go out on a Friday night than a Saturday because then you've got Saturday and Sunday to recover.

I knew things would never be the same again when I had Carl Cox headlining one night and I'd got 2,000 payers, but only made £17 profit. I still needed another couple of hundred through the door to make my money.

And when a promoter has put that many people in one nightclub, but has barely made enough money for his cab fare, then it's probably time for us all to go home.

NO MORE?

It's not all doom and gloom out there, though. There is still a club scene...of sorts.

Try telling the 6,000 people who make the annual pilgrimage to the Southport Weekender (albeit, it's in Minehead these days) that there is no club scene.

Try telling all the dubstep fans across the UK there is no club scene. Or the modern day clubbers who flock in their thousands to see David Guetta, Tiesto and the Norwegian Trance Gangsters...or whatever they're called.

In fact, try telling me (or anyone else) on the terrace at Stuart Patterson's excellent Canal Party in north west London over the summers of 2009/10/11 that there isn't a great party, tucked away somewhere you wouldn't expect to find it.

There are certainly still enough "secret locations" in Shoreditch and beyond to spring the odd surprise and keep everyone on their toes.

Not in doubt, though, is that you'll find fewer and fewer of the old big names on flyers these days. Fewer and fewer DJs, particularly from the house and trance scene, who can really pull a crowd.

Social networking has changed so much. In terms of promotion, the lead-up time to events has been halved at the most. DJs used to be booked months in advance, now it's a matter of weeks.

And, of course, it's no coincidence that this comes at a time when the way the music is played in clubs is constantly being reinvented.

A 20-year-old asked me recently about the late '80s, early '90s halcyon days of clubbing, and in a matter of seconds I explained that we didn't have mobile phones or the internet back then and DJs only played on vinyl. I must have sounded ancient.

However, vinyl is indeed all but an ancient relic where our clubbing heritage is concerned. A timely reminder, all the same, of when clubs were big, bold, ungainly and raw.

Here, some of the members of our One More panel tell us why they think clubland, as they knew it, is scratched beyond repair and spinning no more.

ALEX P

The decline came about with the Millennium, and its pricing. You could blame the DJs for that, but I don't think it was us ramping the prices up, it was the promoters offering us silly money to get to their clubs ahead of others, and then ramping the prices up to pay for us. I also think the licensing laws played a big part. Whereas people used to leave a pub at 10 or 11pm and go to a club that opened until 4am to carry on drinking, suddenly with the 24hr licensing in 2005 you could stay in a bar all night - glorified wine bars with DJs, if you like.

ALLISTER WHITEHEAD

When clubs like Golden or Progress shut it was definitely the end of an era, and it was a firm indication that we were on a decline, that things were receding a bit, and that places like Stoke and Derby could no longer justify a club like that on such a large scale.

After all this time there are only good memories. It couldn't go on forever, everything has to end. It was always sad when another club closed, but I was just glad I'd had played there.

There was a period of time in 1997 when things in dance music had stagnated a little bit, people were going to clubs en masse, and more or less each nightclub in the UK was playing the same ten records every night. With the music, we were always looking for that new high

- it started with rave, then accessible New York house, like Alison Limerick, then the progressive house, and then towards the end of the '90s came trance, this phenomenon, this huge tidal wave.

Then there was just so much trance you could have, and it just got to the point where that couldn't get any bigger. I think dance music reached its peak with hard house and trance and then there was nowhere left for it to go. It came to a natural end. Clubbing had burnt itself out, and on top of that, the bars could open later.

Things moved on and the new kids coming through weren't really aware of what had gone on, the concept behind it and they wanted to do their own thing and that's only natural. Realistically, you couldn't have three decades of clubbing like the '70s, '80s, '90s and expect the noughties to be the same.

I've not got any gripes, it went on for much longer than anyone had anticipated, and we all created a massive industry out of it. We took over the UK charts and to do that for 15 years is pretty good going. It was a unique part in our history and just great to be involved.

DAVE PEARCE

I've been lucky to have been involved in lots of different progressions of the scene - from deeper house at the start to rave, and then through to trance. But something certainly happened around 2002, 2003.

I think there were probably groups of promoters all of a certain age who got out because they didn't want to do it anymore. They were all brought up on these very exciting times of entrepreneurship. There wasn't a bank manager sitting there giving you loans, and someone telling you what to do, it was all about individuals getting off their arse and creating it. A lot of those people moved on.

Another aspect was that a lot of provincial promoters used High Street clubs, but one company gradually bought up all those clubs. Before that the local manager had quite a lot of power, in Northampton or wherever, and promoters could put nights on in their local clubs and have their own little bit of magic. We were still left with a lot of the big superclubs, but that other level of clubs was taken away.

Then there was the record shop situation. My whole life as a DJ and my childhood was spent hanging around record shops. Where I was filmed for the One More documentary in central London, near Soho, there were about five or six record shops, all slightly different, but you'd actually go to all of them. And in each record shop, the guy behind the counter would always have five or six special things that nobody else had, so if you went to each shop on the right day and got the relationships right, you would end up with stuff nobody else had. That gave you an exclusivity, but as soon as CDs came along, you could burn a copy for your mate, and your one record, of which there were only five copies, well, suddenly there were hundreds out there. Nowadays everyone has got it the next day on their phone.

People would come to a club to hear you play a certain track. Record companies would cut acetate, special one-off pieces of vinyl, so there were a few of us who would be the only people who had those tracks. Back then, as well, people were much more interested in looking at the vinyl being played, seeing the DJs touch the records, and mix them in, and for me personally, the technology has slightly killed it. You see some DJs playing on their laptop, and it looks like they're emailing their friends or booking their holiday, and I'm sure they are working hard really, but it doesn't have the same connection.

GRAEME PARK

I'm fortunate I've still got a busy diary and as well as the clubs, I do a lot of 40th birthdays, even 50ths. Big private events, in marquees and stuff like that. And they're great bookings because you get looked after and you don't get 20-year-olds who have absolutely no concept of why we have ended up where we are, asking for a shit electro record.

JEREMY HEALY

What was great about the whole thing at the start was that although all the promoters were rivals, they were friendly rivals and would help each other. However, once everybody started bitching against each other it kind of destroyed it. At the early point when it exploded everyone was getting on and helping each other and that was really nice.

JON HILL

*I think it was a number of factors and I think the whole thing had started to run its course. Dance music and British club culture had gone like that (*raises arm*) and I always knew there was a danger that when something goes like that, it would then go like that (*brings arm down sharply*). And that's exactly what it did, a firework industry, you could call it. Also moods changed, house music, became old hat. It*

became the music of mums and dads, and their kids didn't necessarily want to listen to the music their parents liked. Guitar music...The Strokes, The Libertines, that sort of thing, became more prevalent.

JON MANCINI

The scene in Ibiza, in the UK, and up here in Scotland, died somewhat at the Millennium. The Millennium was blown all out of proportion.

Dance music was already huge, it was enormous and I don't think it could get any bigger.

The corporates started to get involved, and it got dirty. They were throwing obscene amounts of money at clubs and records. The Millennium was over-hyped, over-priced and never delivered.

We ran a thing at Shots in Strathclyde, we did a massive event there, and we had DJs who were quoting telephone numbers instead of fees, and it started getting disgusting. Everybody wanted a piece of it, and that left a big sour taste in everyone's mouth. The Millennium was a disgusting thing, really.

I actually had the privilege of bringing in the Millennium live on Radio One with Dave Pearce in Glasgow. We also had Moby up at Edinburgh Castle, as well as the party at Shots. However, as far as I'm concerned, the Millennium is a swear word, because we lost a fortune. A lot of people bottled out of it, and I wish we had now, but we did do that night. The scene after that went (moves arm downwards) *from the Millennium onwards.*

JON (PLEASED WIMMIN)

With hindsight, it's very easy to say everyone was on ecstasy, and that's why the scene was a success. Not everybody was on ecstasy, but a lot of people were, and when they were, the barriers did come down. People just forgot about the normal crap. There was also a genuine atmosphere of people being open to new things. People weren't bothered about being deemed cool.

I've since read people who were big at the time saying they can't believe they played certain records, that it's embarrassing now, but that's the very reason they were successful in the first place.

So the moment people started trying to be cool, it just fell apart. I think that was what was so great about the early years, people thought

"fuck it, if it sounds great, let's just play it, who cares about being cool, we might be all dead tomorrow".

These days it's just not as spontaneous. I think once that spontaneity had gone the whole thing fell a bit flat. Looking back, the whole thing is like a surreal dream. When you talk to young people now about the '90s, they just don't get it. How often do you get a club these days with people not wanting to go home, and asking for more records? I didn't realise how big it had got at the time. I was just a young guy, dressing up, having fun and getting paid for it. In hindsight, I should have stepped back and looked at it as a career, but I was too busy kicking my legs up and getting wrecked.

I decided to stop dressing up in drag after about five years of DJing because it was so full on, it was murder. I used to have to shave my chest and arms three times a week. I'd drive up to Liverpool, and have to shave again by the time I'd got to the hotel. If you're doing it three times a week, living out of a suitcase, it becomes exhausting, especially getting on and off planes. You can't still be doing drag when you're 70.

I found a flyer in my scrapbook the other day, a really cheap flyer, saying the launch party of Nation in Liverpool, and it was the first night of Cream, which I didn't even realised I'd played at. It was really weird to see this cheap flyer with Letraset lettering and to think what that club became.

JUDGE JULES

There are a lot of reasons why clubbing has moved on. My diary is fortunately still busy, but a significant factor was definitely the bars getting later licences. That meant a lot of the UK's cities, with a long history of clubbing culture, like Leeds, Birmingham, Liverpool, Manchester, had these strips of bars playing 'dance music', with no admission or door fees.

I can say for sure that the decline in the so-called superclubs wasn't down to a diminishing popularity of dance music, it was more because it became more readily available. Radio 1 had more dance shows, the internet appeared so people could access dance music from different sources. Dance music never really waned or died, people were just able to access it in many more different ways.

MARK MOORE

People have been going out for decades, living for the weekend, getting slaughtered on a Friday and coming back on a Sunday. It was nothing new really in that respect, but what these clubs did, was to take it from an underground level and make it mainstream.

Soon it wasn't just a mad bunch of people on drugs, it was everyone in the club who was doing it. The whole attitude to taking drugs changed. I remember being at college and people finding out I took speed and everyone thinking I was mad. Yeah, people took drugs, but it wasn't the norm.

Suddenly you found out that normal people took drugs, and there was less of a stigma about it.

There were obviously people who went over the top, and a few casualties along the way, but soon the weird people were those in clubs who didn't take drugs.

RUSSELL DAVISON

It's no surprise to me that you never saw the club scene like it was after the Millennium. Remember, this was a scene that was born out of a genuine love for having a great time. The promoters were good time boys turned businessmen, and those businessmen got greedy. The DJs, who were also good time boys, got greedy too and the clubs evolved into brands. Those businesses became too big for their boots and distasteful to the love which had been generated by all those clubbers in the first place. I think it was a natural end, and I think it ended right and it had to come to an end somehow...and it was Millennium Eve.

SONIQUE

I could never guess why the scene ended. Maybe they don't like people being too happy or too close to happiness, because I can't see what was wrong with it. And the scene now? Well, there isn't one. Before it was a religion, and now it's not. You know...going out, partying, music...it was a religion. Now it's more about getting laid or how many bottles of champagne you can be seen with... booty in your face, etc. I

used to wear dungarees and I never had a shortage of offers, so I think people are a bit blind these days. Their insides are dead, because their everything is about the outside, and that scene is the complete opposite of what our scene was.

ACKNOWLEDGEMENTS – Matt Trollope

Massive thanks to older kids like Tim Barlow for the jaunts to Hitman Records in Soho to snap up the solitary twelve inch import I could afford by B.B. & Q. Band, Change, Loose Ends or whoever.

My original club crew - Andy C, Nicky Holt, Mem Mousa, Trev Ev, Sneds, Bentley, Spong, John Wiley, Phil Thornton, Alan Jones and Steve Holt.

All the clubbers/promoters who welcomed us north of Watford with open arms, especially Geoff and Mark at Renaissance.

Ash Kahn for all those Chuff Chuff parties...and a special mention to Simon Oates for his hospitality in Brum.

Brandon Block for the connect. Thanks bro!

To Steve 'Froggy' Howlett - the funniest man in the world, and not a bad DJ either. A true pioneer, your spirit lives on and on. RIP mate!

THANKS - One More founder Chris Good

Heartfelt thanks to Andrew Wallace, who ignited the One More idea and took me to most of these clubs in the first place.

One More wouldn't exist if my dear old mum, brothers Sean and Paul, Simon Wallace and beloved Monnie hadn't kept me going when it was all such a struggle!

A massive thanks also to Francis Maloney for all the hours of editing, and to Liam Ayres for his stirling work behind the camera.

ABOUT THE AUTHOR

Matt Trollope completed his NCTJ journalism degree at Harlow College in 1991 and blagged a job on his local paper, The Romford Recorder. His dance music journey began a decade earlier on a family trip to New York when, at the age of ten, his spends secured a seven inch copy of I'm In Love by Evelyn Champagne King. He had the beat in his young Essex bones as his East London background helped school him in jazz funk, before acid house exploded in the late '80s during his late teens. As Matthew James, Matt freelanced for DJ Magazine and M8 throughout the '90s and flirted with the national tabloids too. Dance music-related projects have included record shop Izit Dance ('94 - '96), a spin-off DJ agency ('96 - '03) and co-ownership of lovable rave den The Lodge in London, NW10 ('04 - '08). Matt lives in Ladbroke Grove with partner Jax. For full biography go to www.matttrollope.com.

* Matt is also the author of The Life & Lines Of Brandon Block - The Official Biography

QUOTE...UNQUOTE...

London had changed - all fuelled by this new drug called ecstasy.
Dave Pearce

We were happy getting pissed, then 1988 came along...it was the birth of a new era and suddenly everything changed.
Brandon Block

I knew something was happening when I bought my mum an oven from the takings of my Wednesday night acid house party.
Kelvin Andrews

We basically nicked what Alfredo was doing and did it better.
Nicky Holloway

There were kids outside licking cones, and kids inside licking their eyebrows.
Jon Mancini, Colours

The band were saying "we can't be associated with dance music", so I left. When I got back to Brighton ecstasy had been invented and "finally it was happening to me".
Norman Cook

This was clubbing of the highest order. As DJs we had the dancefloor in the palm of our hands and with the records around then we were like kids in a sweet shop.
Allister Whitehead

It was the '90s, 'Excess All Areas'. With the clubscene, Brit Pop and the festivals...the UK was party central for ten years.
Danny Rampling

We had our own patches like Mafia dons. Our clubs were so busy every week for years so it was hard not to make money, but it was greed that killed our scene.
Russell Davison, Progress

The decline in the so-called superclubs wasn't down to a diminishing popularity of dance music, it was because it became more readily available.
Judge Jules

It's wonderful that people are interviewing us now, in the cold light of day, not off our heads, not all egotistical
Graeme Park

ALSO AVAILABLE...

One More - the DVD

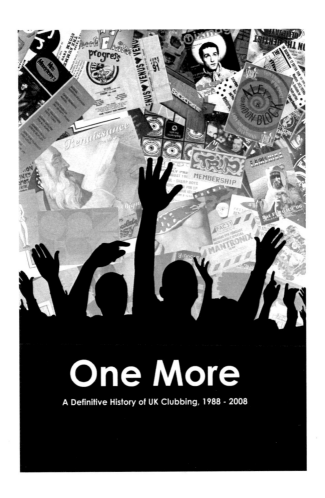

Available from amazon.co.uk, iTunes and HMV